Britain's
Best**Pubs**

This product includes mapping data licensed from Ordnance Survey® with the permission of the Controller of Her Majesty's Stationery Office. © Crown copyright 2009. All rights reserved. Licence number 100021153.

Maps prepared by the Mapping Services Department of The Automobile Association.

Maps © AA Media Limited 2009.

Advertising Sales:
advertisementsales@theAA.com

Editorial:
lifestyleguides@theAA.com

Assessments of AA inspected establishments are based on the experience of the hotel and restaurant inspectors on the occasion of their visit(s) and therefore descriptions given in this guide necessarily dictate an element of subjective opinion which may not reflect or dictate a reader's own opinion on another occasion. We have tried to ensure accuracy in this guide but things do change and we would be grateful if readers would advise us of any inaccuracies they may encounter.

Typeset by AA Lifestyle Guides

Printed and bound by Graficas Estella, Spain

Editorial contributors: Philip Bryant, Alison Moore and Penny Phenix

Cover credits
Front cover: The Bush Inn
Spine: Photodisc
Back cover: (t) The Stephen Langton; (c) The Duck on the Pond; (b) Butchers Arms

A CIP catalogue record for this book is available from the British Library

ISBN: 978-0-7495-6104-8

Published by AA Publishing, which is a trading name of AA Media Limited, whose registered office is:
Fanum House, Basing View, Basingstoke, Hampshire RG21 4EA
Registered number 06112600

www.theAA.com/bookshop

A03913

Britain's
Best**Pubs**

Contents

Welcome	4	**AA Ratings and Awards**	8
Using the Guide	5	**Useful Information**	11

Welcome

Britain's Best Pubs is for anyone who enjoys eating and drinking well in formal or informal surroundings. Where stars have been awarded, you can relax in the knowledge that the rooms have been inspected and rated by the AA.

Britain's Best

In this fully updated and revised guide to Britain's Best Pubs you'll find a selection of pubs and hostelries from cosy inns on old coach routes to smart gastro-pubs in towns and cities. Though very different in conception and setting, they all share a commitment to providing refreshment and serving good food based on fresh (and local where possible) produce cooked to order. Hospitality is warm and welcoming, and real ales and well-known brands are offered alongside decent wines. The index and map sections at the back of this guide will help you to find a wide range of towns and villages to visit in search of an authentic pub experience. To help you make the most of your visit we've included recommended places to see in the area of your choice.

A Place to Stay

Room prices for single and double occupation are shown where the accommodation has been inspected and rated by the AA under our Hotel and Guest Accommodation Schemes. Many places will also offer variable rates and special offer breaks so it's worth asking when you book.

Accommodation varies from pubs with two or three rooms, to much grander inns and hotels with all the extras (although most of the places included in this guide have fewer than 20 rooms). Whatever their size or style, all the places selected for inclusion in Britain's Best Pubs have the same best qualities in common: good food, beer served in relaxed and inviting surroundings and great value for money.

Using the Guide

Britain's Best Pubs has been designed to enable you to find both establishments and locations quickly and efficiently. Each entry provides clear information about the opening hours, food, facilities, and nearby recommended places to visit.

See page 3 to browse the main gazetteer section by county. If you want to find a pub in a specific location use the Location Index (page 323). Alternatively, use the Pub Index (page 330) to find an establishment by name.

Finding your way

The main section of the guide is divided into three main parts covering England, Scotland and Wales. The counties within each of these sections are ordered alphabetically as are the town or village locations (shown in capital letters as part of the address) within each county. Finally, the establishments are listed alphabetically under each location name. Towns names featured in the guide are shown in the map section at the back of the guide.

① ② ③ ④ ⑤ ⑥ ⑦ ⑧ ⑨ ⑩ ⑪

The Old Inn

★★★ ◉ INN

Address: Ash Lane, WHITCHURCH, Salisbury, SA38 2PP
Tel: 01963 300123
Email: oldinn@pubgroup.co.uk
Website: www.pubgroup.co.uk/oldrectory
Map ref: 3, TQ32
Directions: Next to church at S end of Whitchurch
Open: 11.30–3 5.30–11 (Sun 12-3) ▶ L 11–2 D 7–9
⦿ L 12–2 D 6–9 Rooms: 8 S £35–40 D £75–100 Facilities: Gardens Parking: 22
Notes: ⌁ ⊕ Free House ♟ 7

Tucked away down a leafy lane, The Old Inn is the perfect place for a relaxing drink and a good meal. This old inn has been beautifully restored and extended, with its character carefully preserved. The perfect place for walkers hiking the nearby Ridgeway, the garden offers a shady retreat for lunch and in colder weather log fires and leather sofas provide a warm and welcome resting place. There are two bars, where meals can also be enjoyed, as well as a comfortable and spacious oak-beamed restaurant providing a more formal environment. The menu makes good use of local organic produce with well-cooked dishes that will satisfy the heartiest appetite. The en suite bedrooms are simply furnished and decorated with many of the thoughtful extras usually associated with superior hotels.

Recommended in the area

Salisbury Cathedral; New Forest National Park; Stonehenge and Salisbury Plain

---

① Stars and Symbols

A star rating denotes where an entry has been inspected under one of two separate schemes; either the AA Guest Accommodation Scheme or the AA Hotel Scheme.

Pubs rated under the Guest Accommodation Scheme have been given a descriptive category designator: B&B, Guest House,

Farmhouse, Inn, Restaurant with Rooms or Guest Accommodation.

Pubs in the Hotel Scheme also have their own descriptive designator: Town House Hotel, Country House Hotel, Small Hotel. See pages 8–10 for more information on the AA ratings and awards scheme.

continued

Egg cups 🥚 and Pies 🥧 – These symbols denote where the breakfast or dinner are really special, and have an emphasis on freshly prepared ingredients.

Rosette awards ◉ – This is the AA's food award (see page 9 for further details).

❷ Contact Details

The pub address includes a locator or place name in capitals (e.g. NORWICH). Within each county, entries are ordered alphabetically first by this place name and then by the name of the establishment.

Telephone and fax numbers, and e-mail and website addresses are given where available and are believed correct at the time of going to press but changes may occur. The latest establishment details can be found at www.theAA.com.

Website addresses have been supplied by the establishments and lead you to websites that are not under the control of AA Media Limited (AAML). AAML has no control over and accepts no responsibility or liability in respect of the material on any such websites. By including the addresses of third-party websites AAML does not intend to solicit business.

❸ Map Reference

Each establishment in this guide is given a map reference for a location which can be found in the atlas section at the back of the guide. It is composed of the map page number (1–13) and two-figure map reference based on the National Grid.

For example: **Map 05 SU48**

05 refers to the page number of the map section at the back of the guide

SU is the National Grid lettered square (representing 100,000sq metres) in which the location will be found

4 is the figure reading across the top and bottom of the map page

8 is the figure reading down each side of the map page

❹ Directions

Where possible, directions have been given from the nearest motorway or A road.

❺ Open

Indicates the opening hours of the establishment and, if appropriate, any dates when it may be closed for business.

🍴 Bar Meals

Indicates the times and days when the proprietors have told us that bar food can be ordered.

🍽 Restaurant

Indicates the times and days when proprietors have told us that food can be ordered from the restaurant. Please be aware that last orders could vary by up to 30 minutes.

❻ Room Information

Room information is only shown where accommodation has been inspected by the AA. The number of letting bedrooms with a bath or shower en suite are indicated. Bedrooms that have a private bathroom adjacent may be included as en suite. Further details on private bathroom and en suite provision may also be included in the description text (see ❿).

Always phone in advance to ensure that the establishment has the room facilities that you require.

Prices: Charges shown are per night except where specified. S denotes bed and breakfast per person (single). D denotes bed and breakfast for two people sharing a room (double).

In some cases prices are also given for family rooms, also on a per night basis. Prices are indications only, so check what is included before booking.

❼ Facilities

This section lists a selection of facilities offered by the pub such as garden details or children's play area. If you have young children it may be worth checking what facilities are available.

Additional facilities, such as access for the disabled, or notes about other services (e.g. if credit card details are not accepted) may be listed here.

❽ Parking

The number of parking spaces available. Other types of parking (on road or Park and Ride) may also be possible; check the descriptions for further information. Phone the establishment in advance of your arrival if unsure.

❾ Notes

This section provides specific details relating to:

Smoking policy: Smoking in public areas is now banned in England, Scotland and Wales.

The proprietor can designate one or more bedrooms with ventilation systems where the occupants can smoke, but communal areas must be smoke-free.

Dogs: Establishments that state 'no dogs' should accept assist/guide dogs. (Under the Discrimination Disability Act 1995 access should be allowed for guide dogs and assistance dogs). Some places that do accept dogs may restrict the size and breed and the rooms into which they can be taken. Please check the policy when booking.

⊞ This symbol is followed by text that indicates the name of the brewery to which the pub is tied or the company which owns it, or where the pub is a free house and independently owned and run.

♟ Indicates the number of wines available by the glass.

❿ Description

The description of the pub includes amongst other things, a background to the establishment, the type of eating options available and, where relevant, information about the accommodation.

⓫ Recommended in the area

This indicates local places of interest, and potential day trips and activities.

Key to symbols	
★	Black stars (see page 8)
☆	Yellow Stars (see page 8)
★	Red Stars (see page 8)
U	Unconfirmed rating
◉	AA Rosette (see page 9)
⌂	Breakfast Award in Guest Accommodation scheme
⌐	Dinner Award in Guest Accommodation scheme
3, TQ28	Map reference
S	Single room
D	Double room
⁆⁆	Children allowed
⁆⁆	No children under age specified
⊗	No dogs allowed in area indicated
⁆	Dogs allowed in area indicated
Wi-fi	Wireless network connection
⊟	Bar meals
⁆⊙⁆	Restaurant meals
L	Lunch
D	Dinner
⊞	Pub status (Chain or Free House)
♟ 30	Number of wines available by the glass

7

AA Ratings and Awards

Star ratings shown in Britain's Best Pub guide indicate where the accommodation available has been inspected by the AA under either its Guest Accommodation or Hotel Schemes.

Guest Accommodation and Hotel Schemes

The AA inspects and rates establishments under two different accommodation schemes. Guest houses, B&Bs, farmhouses, inns and Restaurants with Rooms are rated under the Guest Accommodation Scheme and hotels are rated under the Hotel Scheme. Establishments recognised by the AA pay an annual fee according to the rating and the number of bedrooms. This rating is not transferable if an establishment changes hands.

Common Standards

A few years ago, the accommodation inspection organisations (The AA, VisitBritain, VisitScotland and VisitWales) undertook extensive consultation with consumers and the hospitality industry which resulted in new quality standards for rating establishments. Guests can now be confident that a star-rated B&B or a hotel anywhere in the UK and Ireland will offer consistent quality and facilities.

The system of ratings also uses descriptive designators to classify the establishment – see pages 9 and 10 for a fuller explanation.

★ Stars

AA Stars classify guest accommodation at five levels of quality, from one at the simplest, to five at the highest level of quality in the scheme.

★ Yellow stars indicate that the accommodation is in the top ten per cent of its star rating. Yellow stars only apply to 3, 4 and 5 star establishments.

★ Red stars highlight the best hotels in each star rating category within the AA Hotel Scheme.

Check www.theAA.com for up-to-date information and current ratings.

The Inspection Process

Establishments applying for AA recognition are visited by a qualified AA accommodation inspectors as a mystery guest. Inspectors stay overnight to make a thorough test of the accommodation, food and hospitality. After paying the bill the following morning, they identify themselves and ask to be shown around the premises. The inspector completes a full report, resulting in a recommendation for the appropriate star rating. After this first visit, the establishment will receive an annual visit to check that standards are maintained. If it changes hands, the new owners must re-apply for a rating.

Guests can expect to find the following minimum standards at all levels:
- Pleasant and helpful welcome and service, and sound standards of housekeeping and maintenance
- Comfortable accommodation equipped to modern standards
- Bedding and towels changed for each new guest, and at least weekly if the room is taken for a long stay
- Adequate storage, heating, lighting and comfortable seating
- A sufficient hot water supply at reasonable times
- A full cooked breakfast. (If this is not provided, the fact must be advertised and a substantial continental breakfast must be offered.)

Designators (Guest Accommodation)
All AA rated guest accommodation is given one of six descriptive designators to help potential guests understand the different types of accommodation available in Britain. The following are included in this guide.

B&B: Accommodation is provided in a private house run by the owner and with no more than six guests. There may be restricted access to the establishment particularly in the late morning and the afternoon.

GUEST HOUSE: Provides for more than six paying guests and usually offers more services than a B&B, for example dinner, which may be served by staff as well as the owner. London prices tend to be higher than outside the capital, and normally only bed and breakfast is provided, although some establishments do provide a full meal service. Check on the service and facilities offered before booked as details may change during the currency of this guide.

FARMHOUSE: A farmhouse usually provides good value B&B or guesthouse accommodation and excellent home cooking on a working farm or smallholding. Sometimes the land has been sold and only the house remains, but many are working farms and some farmers are happy to allow visitors to look around, or even to help feed the animals. However, you should always exercise care and never leave children unsupervised. The farmhouses are listed under towns or villages, but do ask for directions when booking.

continued

AA Rosette Awards

Out of the many thousands of restaurants in the UK, the AA identifies some 2,000 as the best. The following is an outline of what to expect from restaurants with AA Rosette Awards. For a more detailed explanation of Rosette criteria please see www.theAA.com

◉ Excellent local restaurants serving food prepared with care, understanding and skill, using good quality ingredients.

◉◉ The best local restaurants, which aim for and achieve higher standards, better consistency and where a greater precision is apparent in the cooking. There will be obvious attention to the selection of quality ingredients.

◉◉◉ Outstanding restaurants that demand recognition well beyond their local area.

◉◉◉◉ Amongst the very best restaurants in the British Isles, where the cooking demands national recognition.

◉◉◉◉◉ The finest restaurants in the British Isles, where the cooking stands comparison with the best in the world.

INN: Traditional inns often have a cosy bar, convivial atmosphere, good beer and pub food. Those listed in the guide will provide breakfast in a suitable room, and should also serve light meals during licensing hours. The character of the properties vary according to whether they are country inns or town establishments. Check arrival times as these may be restricted to opening hours.

RESTAURANT WITH ROOMS: These restaurants offer overnight accommodation with the restaurant being the main business and open to non-residents. The restaurant usually offers a high standard of food and service.

GUEST ACCOMMODATION: Establishments that meet the minimum entry requirements are eligible for this designator.

Designators (Hotels)

All AA rated hotels are given a descriptive designator to identify the different types of hotel available. Included in this guide are the following:

HOTEL: The majority of establishments in this guide come under the category of Hotel.

TOWN HOUSE HOTEL: A small, individual city or town centre property, which provides a high degree or personal service and privacy

COUNTRY HOUSE HOTEL: These may vary in size and are located in a rural area.

SMALL HOTEL: Has less than 20 bedrooms and is managed by its owner.

www.theAA.com

- Go to www.theAA.com to find more AA listed guest houses, hotels, pubs and restaurants – some 12,000 establishments.
- The link to Travel on the home page leads to a route planner. Simply enter your postcode and the establishment postcode given in this guide and click 'Get Route'. Check your details and then click 'Get Route' again and you will have a detailed route plan to take you door-to-door.
- Use the Travel section to search for Hotels & B&Bs or Restaurants & Pubs by location or establishment name. Scroll down the list of finds for the interactive map and local routes.
- Postcode searches can also be made on www.ordnancesurvey.co.uk and www.multimap.com which will also provide useful aerial views of your destination.

Useful Information

If you're unsure about any of the facilities offered, always check with the establishment before you visit or book accommodation. Up-to-date information on all pubs in this guide can be found at the travel section of the www.theAA.com

Fire Precautions and Safety

Many of the establishments listed in the guide are subject to the requirements of the Fire Precautions Act of 1971. All establishments should display details of how to summon assistance in the event of an emergency at night.

Dogs

Some establishments that accept dogs may restrict the size and breed of dogs permitted. Under the Discrimination Disability Act 1995 access should be allowed for guide dogs and assistance dogs.

Children

Restrictions for children are given at the end of entries. When booking a meal you would be advised to check that children are welcome.

Smoking Regulations

Please see page 7.

Facilities for Disabled Guests

The final stage (Part III) of the Disability Discrimination Act (access to Goods and Services) came into force in October 2004. This means that service providers may have to consider making permanent physical adjustments to their premises. For further information, see the government website www.disability.gov.uk. The establishments in this guide should all be aware of their responsibilities under the Act. We recommend that you always telephone in advance to ensure that the establishment you have chosen has appropriate facilities.

Complaints

Readers who have any cause to complain about accommodation, food and drink or service are urged to do so on the spot. This should provide an opportunity for the proprietor to correct matters. If a personal approach fails in connection with accommodation, readers can write to the editor of the guide at Lifestyle Guides, Fanum House, Basingstoke, Hants RG21 4EA.

The AA may at its sole discretion investigate any complaints received from guide users for the purpose of making any necessary amendments to the guide. The AA will not in any circumstances act as a representative or negotiator or undertake to obtain compensation or enter into any correspondence or deal with the matter in any other way whatsoever. The AA will not guarantee to take any specific action.

Bank and Public Holidays 2009

New Year's Day	1st January
New Year's Holiday	2nd January (Scotland)
Good Friday	10th April
Easter Monday	13th April
May Day Bank Holiday	4th May
Spring Bank Holiday	25th May
August Holiday	3rd August (Scotland)
Late Summer Holiday	25th August
St Andrew's Day	30th November (Scotland)
Christmas Day	25th December
Boxing Day	26th December

ENGLAND

East Dart River near Postbridge in Dartmoor National Park

Market Cross, Leighton Buzzard

The Rose Garden, Robert Adam Mansion

The Falcon

Address: Rushden Road, BLETSOE, MK44 1QN
Tel/Fax: 01234 781222
Email: thefalcona6@aol.com
Website: www.thefalconbletsoe.co.uk
Map ref: 3, TL05
Directions: 9m from M1 junct 13, 3m from Bedford
Open: 12–3 6–11 (Sat 12–11, Sun 12–10.30)
L 12–2.15 D 6–9.15 L 12–2.15 D 6.30–9.15
Facilities: Garden Parking
Notes: CHARLES WELLS 13

A beautiful centuries-old coaching inn, The Falcon is set in the rolling hills of north Bedfordshire. A dining terrace provides an attractive spot for summer meals, overlooking the large mature gardens, which sweep down to the Great River Ouse. Step inside and you'll be greeted by the relaxed ambience of a country inn, enhanced by the inglenook fireplace and an abundance of oak beams. At lunchtime there is a range of crusty sandwiches, farmhouse ploughman's and salad bowls in addition to a lengthy menu of steaks and traditional dishes, such as steak and kidney pie, and beer-battered cod and chips.

Recommended in the area

Glen Miller Museum; Santa Pod Raceway; Body Flight – Europe's largest indoor skydiving tunnel

BERKSHIRE

Woodland Trust's Bisham Woods in Cookham Dean

Hinds Head Hotel

Address: High Street, BRAY, Maidenhead,
SL6 2AB
Tel: 01628 626151
Fax: 01628 623394
Email: info@hindsheadhotel.co.uk
Website: www.hindsheadhotel.co.uk
Map ref: 3, SU97
Directions: M4 junct 8/9 take exit to Maidenhead
Central. Next rdbt take exit for Bray & Windsor.
After 0.5m take B3028 to Bray
Open: 11–11 (Sun 11–10) ᵇ L 12–2.30 D 6.30–9.30 (Sun 12–4) ⑆ L 12–2.30 D 6.30–9.30
(Sun 12–4) Closed: 25–26 Dec Facilities: Parking Notes: ⊞ Free House ⒤ ⚲ 15

This much-loved village tavern has been at the heart of life in Bray for over 400 years. More recently
it has been taken over by AA five Rosetted-chef Heston Blumenthal, who also owns the famous Fat
Duck across the road, and it is now a gastronomic destination as well as an inviting local pub. The
short, inviting seasonal menu offers British classics such as potted shrimps, oxtail and kidney pudding
and treacle tart alongside rediscovered historical dishes like ham cooked in hay and quaking pudding.
Sandwiches and bar snacks including devils on horseback and Scotch quail's eggs are available at
lunchtimes from Monday to Saturday. There is an interesting selection of real ales at the bar featuring
local breweries and seasonal guest beers. The interior has everything you'd expect from a traditional
English inn, from sturdy oak panelling and beams to leather chairs and crackling fires, and there
are two stunning rooms available for private hire (The Royal Room (50 guests) and the Vicar's Room
(22 guests)).

Recommended in the area

Dorney Court; Cliveden; Look Out Discovery Centre

The Horns

Address: CRAZIES HILL, Nr Wargrave,
RG10 8LY
Tel: 0118 940 1416
Fax: 0118 940 4849
Email: reservations@thehornspub.com
Website: www.thehornspub.com
Map ref: 3, SU78
Directions: Off A321 NE of Wargrave
Open: 11–11 ⓑ L 12–3 D 7–9.30 ⓘ L 12–3 D 7–9.30
Facilities: Garden Parking **Notes:** ⊕ BRAKSPEAR ⁛ ⋔ ⏲

If the meandering Crazies Hill is well named, so too is this
beautifully restored, traditional 16th-century pub. It started life
as a hunting lodge, to which a barn, now the dining area, was added some 300 years ago. Inside are
three interconnecting terracotta-coloured, oak-beamed rooms full of old pine tables, stripped wooden
floors, open fires and rugby memorabilia. Horns are everywhere, beginning with the huge pair of
antlers that watch over the entrance. Today's peaceful atmosphere is untroubled by music, electronic
games or anything else that would disturb a passing stag. The restaurant and bar have an informal,
relaxed atmosphere and offer a good selection of imaginative dishes, such as red snapper fillets with
spicy tomato and avocado salsa. More traditional are chef's pie of the day; liver and bacon with rich
onion gravy; sirloin steak with a choice of sauces; coq au vin with spring onion mash; pork tenderloin
with black pudding and light Dijon mustard gravy; and salmon and haddock fishcakes with prawn and
smoked salmon sauce. Freshly-filled baguettes and home-made desserts are also available. There is
an extensive and secluded garden with a children's play area, and ample parking. Regular jazz and
comedy nights are held.

Recommended in the area

Legoland; Wellington Country Park; Beale Park

The Crown & Garter

★★★★ INN

Address: Inkpen Common, HUNGERFORD, RG17 9QR

Tel: 01488 668325

Email: gill.hern@btopenworld.com

Website: www.crownandgarter.com

Map ref: 3, SU36

Directions: From A4 to Kintbury & Inkpen. At village store left into Inkpen Rd, follow signs for Inkpen Common (2m)

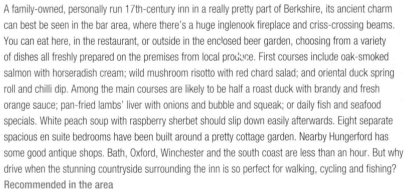

Open: 12–3 5.30–11 (Sun eve 7–10.30) **Closed** Mon–Tue lunch **L** 12–2 **D** 6.30–9.30 **L** 12–2 **D** 6.30–9.30 **Rooms:** 8 en suite (8 GF) **S** £69.50 **D** £99 **Facilities:** Garden Parking **Notes:** Free House 9

A family-owned, personally run 17th-century inn in a really pretty part of Berkshire, its ancient charm can best be seen in the bar area, where there's a huge inglenook fireplace and criss-crossing beams. You can eat here, in the restaurant, or outside in the enclosed beer garden, choosing from a variety of dishes all freshly prepared on the premises from local produce. First courses include oak-smoked salmon with horseradish cream; wild mushroom risotto with red chard salad; and oriental duck spring roll and chilli dip. Among the main courses are likely to be half a roast duck with brandy and fresh orange sauce; pan-fried lambs' liver with onions and bubble and squeak; or daily fish and seafood specials. White peach soup with raspberry sherbet should slip down easily afterwards. Eight separate spacious en suite bedrooms have been built around a pretty cottage garden. Nearby Hungerford has some good antique shops. Bath, Oxford, Winchester and the south coast are less than an hour. But why drive when the stunning countryside surrounding the inn is so perfect for walking, cycling and fishing?

Recommended in the area

Newbury Racecourse; Combe Gibbet; Highclere Castle

The Swan Inn

★★★★ ⊜ ⇔ INN

Address: Craven Road, Lower Green, Inkpen,
HUNGERFORD, RG17 9DX
Tel: 01488 668326
Fax: 01488 668306
Email: enquiries@theswaninn-organics.co.uk
Website: www.theswaninn-organics.co.uk
Map ref: 3, SU36
Directions: S down Hungerford High St (A338),
under rail bridge, left to the Common. Right to Inkpen

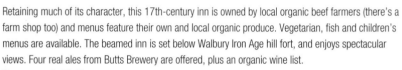

Open: 11–11 (Sun 12–10.30) ⊯ L 12–2 D 7–9.30 ⏍ L 12–2. D 7–9.30 **Closed:** 25–26 Dec
Rooms: 10 en suite **S** £60–£70 **D** £80–£95 **Facilities:** Garden Parking **Notes:** ⊕ Free House ⫶⫶

Retaining much of its character, this 17th-century inn is owned by local organic beef farmers (there's a
farm shop too) and menus feature their own and local organic produce. Vegetarian, fish and children's
menus are available. The beamed inn is set below Walbury Iron Age hill fort, and enjoys spectacular
views. Four real ales from Butts Brewery are offered, plus an organic wine list.
Recommended in the area
Kennet and Avon Canal; Newbury Racecourse; Avebury Stone Circle

The Dundas Arms

Address: 53 Station Road, KINTBURY, Hungerford,
RG17 9UT
Tel: 01488 658263
Fax: 01488 658568
Email: info@dundasarms.co.uk
Website: www.dundasarms.co.uk
Map ref: 3, SU36
Directions: M4 junct 13 take A34 to Newbury, then
A4 to Hungerford, left to Kintbury. Pub 1m by canal
Open: 11–2.30 6–11 ⊯ L 12–2 D 7–9 ⏍ D 7–9

Closed: 25 & 31 Dec (Sun Eve) **Facilities:** Parking **Notes:** ⊕ Free House

In an Area of Outstanding Natural Beauty, this inn has provided sustenance for travellers since the
late 18th century. It has been in the Dalzell-Piper family for over 30 years and proprietor David has
cooked here throughout that time. On a fine day, sit outside with a steak and kidney pie from the bar
and a locally brewed pint, watching the narrow boats chugging along The Kennet & Avon Canal. The
restaurant, which has something of a French auberge about it, offers modern British cuisine.
Recommended in the area
Newbury Racecourse; Highclere Castle; Watermill Theatre

Bird In Hand Country Inn

Address: Bath Road, KNOWL HILL, Twyford,
RG10 9UP
Tel: 01628 826622
Fax: 01628 826748
Email: sthebirdinhand@aol.com
Website: www.birdinhand.co.uk
Map ref: 3, SU87
Directions: On A4, 5m W of Maidenhead,
7m E of Reading
Open: 11–3 6–11 (Sun 12–10.30)
L 12–2.30 D 6.30–10 L 12–2.30 D 7–10
Facilities: Garden Parking Notes: Free House 12

Dating back to the 14th century, this charming country inn has been owned by the same family for three generations. Legend has it that George III granted it a royal charter in the 18th century for the hospitality he was shown, and a royal welcome is still the order of the day. Today the inn serves a host of real ales and a large selection of wines by the glass in the oak-panelled bar, which in winter boasts a huge open fire. In summer months, a pretty beer garden and fountain patio provide the backdrop for the brick-built barbecue and spit roast. Inside, an extensive menu is available from both the bar and the attractive restaurant, which overlooks the courtyard and fountain. Diners can choose from a range of traditional dishes, such as hearty steak and kidney pudding with Guinness, pork belly in Calvados or whole roast stuffed quail with apricot and thyme, through to European-based options such as tapas, mezze and paella. There are also a number of daily specials and a cold buffet is available at lunchtime. The inn's en suite bedrooms have all been newly refurbished and include many modern facilities such as Wi-fi and direct-dial telephones.

Recommended in the area

Legoland; Odds Park Farm; Wellington Country Park

The Yew Tree Inn

◎ ◎

Address: Hollington Cross, Andover Road, Highclere,
NEWBURY, RG20 9SE
Tel: 01635 253360
Fax: 01635 255035
Email: info@theyewtree.net
Website: www.theyewtree.net
Map ref: 3, SU56
Directions: A34 toward Southampton, 2nd exit
bypass Highclere, onto A343 at rdbt, through village,
pub on right
Open: 10–12 ⬥ L 12–3 D 6–10 ☺ L 12–3 D 6–10 **Facilities:** Garden Parking
Notes: ⊕ Free House ⌖ ♀ 8

This 16th-century inn belongs to the celebrated chef-turned-restaurateur Marco Pierre White. His famed perfectionism is evident everywhere, from the immaculate styling that blends original 17th-century features with the refinement of white tablecloths and sparkling glassware, to the menu, which performs a similar trick, offering both traditional British food and time-honoured classics from the French culinary canon. Your meal might open with a parfait of foie gras; calves' tongue with celeriac remoulade; or duck rillettes, followed by lobster thermidor; Dover sole meunière; or venison with sauce grand veneur. There is a relaxed, pick-and-choose feel to the menu, which includes lighter options such as eggs Benedict, Scotch woodcock, and various soups (game consommé en croûte; bisque of lobster Newburg). Tellingly, the desserts are described as 'puddings' and might include such familiar comforts as bread and butter pudding or rhubarb crumble. Good-value fixed-price menus are also a feature at lunchtime, early evening and on Sundays.

Recommended in the area

Highclere Castle; Hampshire Downs; Donnington Castle

BUCKINGHAMSHIRE

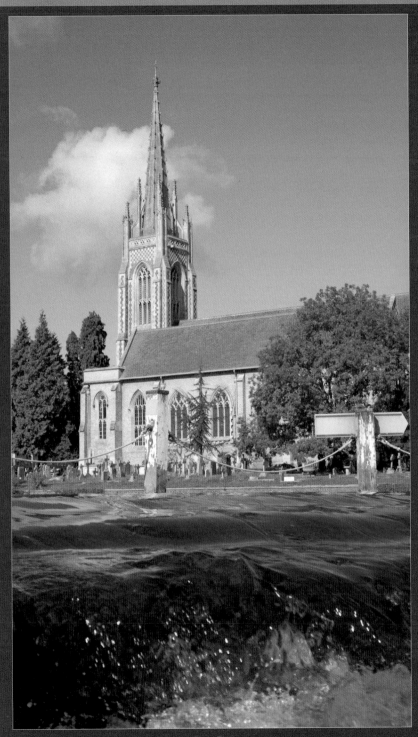

Weir and All Saints church at Marlow on the River Thames

The Royal Oak

Address: Frieth Road, BOVINGDON GREEN, Marlow, SL7 2JF
Tel: 01628 488611
Fax: 01628 478680
Email: info@royaloakmarlow.co.uk
Website: www.royaloakmarlow.co.uk
Map ref: 3, SU88
Directions: From Marlow, take A4155. In 300yds right signed
Bovingdon Green. In 0.75m pub on left
Open: 11–11 (Sun 12–10.30) **L** 12–2.30 (Sat 12–3,
Sun 12–4) **D** 6.30–9.30 (Sun–Thurs) (Fri-Sat 6.30–10)
Closed: 26 Dec **Facilities:** Garden Parking
Notes: ⊕ SALISBURY PUBS LTD ♦♦ ♣ ♟ 19

Drive up the hill out of Marlow and you'll soon come across this old whitewashed pub. Sprawling gardens, fragrant kitchen herbs and a sunny terrace suggest that it is well looked after. Red kites, which were re-introduced to the Chilterns in 1989, now frequently soar majestically overhead. The interior is both spacious and cosy, with a snug with wood-burning stove, a rose-red dining room and rich dark floorboards. Plush fabrics and heritage colours create a warm background for the early evening regulars gathered around a cryptic crossword, or playing a tense game of cards. The imaginative British food is a big draw, not least because it derives from fresh, seasonal and, as far as possible, local produce. Fish, of course, has to travel, since Marlow isn't exactly on the coast, but a belief in good food ethics means choosing new and interesting varieties from sustainable sources, such as that new fish on the block, gurnard. Other menu suggestions might include veal and rosemary sausage casserole with Boston baked beans; and crispy pork belly with pig's cheeks on sticky red cabbage and cider gravy. Real ales from Rebellion Brewery in Marlow Bottom keep beer miles to a minimum.

Recommended in the area

Cliveden; Burnham Beeches; Hughenden Manor

The Red Lion

Address: CHENIES, Chorleywood, Rickmansworth
WD3 6ED
Tel: 01923 282722
Fax: 01923 283797
Map ref: 3, TQ09
Directions: Between Rickmansworth & Amersham
on A404, follow signs for Chenies & Latimer
Open: 11–2.30 5.30–11 Sun 5.30–10.30
L 12–2 D 7–10 **Closed:** 25 Dec **Facilities:**
Garden Parking **Notes:** Free House 10

Michael Norris has been at this popular hostelry for around twenty years, and under his expert direction
the pub has achieved considerable renown. He is keen to stress that this is a pub that does food,
not a restaurant that does beer, but that's not to say that the quality and range of food on offer is in
any way an afterthought. Michael has put together a menu that has something for everyone, with a
wide range of snacks, starters and main meals. Among the listings you'll find the ever-popular jacket
potatoes; pasta carbonara; and a tasty beef, mustard and cheese pie, plus a number of more exotic
dishes that might include Moroccan chicken breast with couscous; pork fillet with prunes; oxtail with
root vegetables; and fresh tuna loin with roasted Mediterranean vegetables. Not so much exotic as
downright unusual, the hot bacon and Milky Bar in a bap has its fans, too. But even with all this choice,
it would be a shame not to try the famous Chenies lamb pie. Needless to say, the real ales on offer are
kept in perfect condition and there are some good wines to choose from too. The Red Lion is not far
outside the M25 at junction 18 and is well worth making a detour to enjoy its pleasant, country-pub
atmosphere – the way that pubs used to be before piped music and fruit machines were invented –
and the garden makes for enjoyable alfresco summer lunches.

Recommended in the area

Legoland; Bekonscot Model Village; Odds Farm Park Rare Breeds Centre

The Swan Inn

Address: Village Road, DENHAM, UB9 5BH
Tel: 01895 832085
Fax: 01895 835516
Email: info@swaninndenham.co.uk
Website: www.swaninndenham.co.uk
Map ref: 3, TQ08
Directions: From A40 take A412. In 200yds follow Denham Village sign on right. Through village, over bridge, last pub on left
Open: 11–11 (Sun 12–10.30) **L** 12–2.30 (Sat 12–3, Sun 12–4) **D** 6.30–9.30 (Sun–Thurs) (Fri-Sat 6.30–10) **Closed:** 26 Dec **Facilities:** Garden Parking
Notes: ⊞ SALISBURY PUBS LTD ⋔ ⋔ ⚲ 19

The Swan is probably everyone's idea of the traditional country inn – Georgian, double-fronted and covered in wisteria. The surprise, though, is that the secluded village of Denham is really no distance at all from the bright lights of both London and its premier airport at Heathrow. The interior is cosily welcoming, with a large log fire and pictures picked up at local auctions, while outside is a sunny terrace, and gardens large enough to lose the children in (only temporarily, of course). Though The Swan is still very much a pub, the quality of the food is a great attraction, with fresh, seasonal produce underpinning a menu that reinvigorates some old favourites and makes the most of market availability with daily specials. For a starter or light meal look to the 'small plates' section, where you'll find Marlow Rebellion (a local beer) steamed mussels with garlic herbs and onion rye bread; and pan-fried balsamic chicken livers on 'eggy bread' brioche with crispy pancetta. Among the main meals you'll find plenty of variety, from slow-cooked Chiltern lamb shoulder on smoked potato mash with cep roasting juices, to Indian-spiced Cornish mackerel with sautéed okra, saffron potatoes and courgette, lime ginger chutney.
Recommended in the area
Burnham Beeches; Cliveden; Dorney Court

The Nags Head

★★★★ ⊛ INN

Address: London Road, GREAT MISSENDEN,
HP16 0DG
Tel: 01494 862200
Fax: 01494 862685
Email: goodfood@nagsheadbucks.com
Website: www.nagsheadbucks.com
Map ref: 3, SP80
Directions: 1m from Great Missenden on London Rd
Open: 12–11.30 (Sun 12–6) ⦿I L 12–2.30
D 6.30–9.30 Facilities: Garden Parking Notes: ⊕ ⚹ ⚲ 14

The Nags Head, which was originally built in the late 15th century as three workers' cottages, has played host to many famous names over the centuries, including Harold Wilson and the children's author Roald Dahl. The pub has now been taken over by the Michaels family, and they have transformed it, as they did with the award-winning Bricklayers Arms in Flaunden, into a foodie venue serving English traditional and French fusion cooking. Newly refurbished, it combines stylish new furnishings with original features, including a large inglenook fireplace and low oak beams; this level of style and comfort carries through to the en suite bedrooms. Food is the passion here, and the menus are based on the freshest organic produce from local suppliers. Favourite dishes include home-smoked fish, mixed and wild mushroom feuilleté, aged fillet steaks, local game, and steak and kidney ale pie, as well as daily fish options and a range of mouthwatering desserts. There's a carefully selected wine list to choose from and, in the bar, a selection of local ales are on offer. Weather permitting, al fresco eating and drinking can be enjoyed in the garden, with fine views of the rolling Chiltern Hills.

Recommended in the area

Roald Dahl Museum; Beconscot Model Village; Whipsnade Zoo

The Rising Sun

Address: Little Hampden, GREAT MISSENDEN, HP16 9PS
Tel: 01494 488393
Fax: 01494 488788
Email: sunrising@rising-sun.demon.co.uk
Website: www.rising-sun.demon.co.uk
Map ref: 3, SP80
Directions: From A413, N of Gt Missenden, take Rignall Rd on left signed Princes Risborough 2.5m. Turn right signed 'Little Hampden only'

Open: 11.30–3 6.30–10 (Sun 12–3 only) Open BH lunch 🍺 L 12–2 D 7–9 🍽 L 12–2 D 7–9
Closed: Sun eve & Mon **Facilities:** Garden Parking **Notes:** 🛢 Free House 👫 🐕 🍷 10

Tucked away in The Chiltern Hills and just three miles from the Prime Minister's country retreat at Chequers, is the Rising Sun, a 250-year-old inn that was once frequented by previous PMs Harold Wilson and Ted Heath. It is close to the Ridgeway National Trail and reached down a single-track road, surrounded by beech woods and glorious scenery. A network of footpaths begins just outside the front door, making it the perfect base for country walks, and there are a number of cosy rooms to stay in. An attractive new feature is the landscaped garden area with comfortable armchair seating and tables for outside wining and dining. Rotisserie paprika-seasoned corn-fed chicken and chips is a speciality here. There's also a daily blackboard menu offering some good seafood, such as hot dressed crab with cheese and grain mustard sauce, and pan-fried skate wings with scallops, lemon and capers. Otherwise look out for the popular Sunday roasts, as well as dishes such as warm smoked chicken and bacon salad with peanut sauce, or roast shoulder of lamb with rosemary and honey. In winter, guests can enjoy hot mulled wine and warm spiced cider by the wood-burning stove and open fire.

Recommended in the area

Coombe Hill and Low Scrubs (NT); Waddesdon Manor (NT); Whipsnade Zoo

The Green Dragon

◎ ◎

Address: 8 Churchway, HADDENHAM,
HP17 8AA
Tel: 01844 291403
Email: enquiries@oaktreeinns.co.uk
Website: www.greendragonhaddenham.co.uk
Map ref: 3, SP70
Directions: From M40 J7, A329 to Thame, then
A418 to Haddenham, 1st right after entering
Haddenham
Open: 12–11 (Sun 12–10.30) ᕮ L 12–2.30 D 6.30–9.30 ⓘ L 12–2 (Sun 12–3) D 6.30–9.30
Closed: 26 Dec **Facilities:** Garden Parking
Notes: Family and dog friendly ⊕ ENTERPRISE INNS ♟ 17

The Green Dragon is situated in the peaceful village of Haddenham just a few metres away from the village green and the church of Saint Mary the Virgin, which have been the backdrop for many a TV production. This Grade II listed building dates back to the 1700s when it was a manorial courthouse. 2008 saw a change of ownership and a complete refurbishment; the bright interior, modern decor and new menus and wine list and a great selection of real ales has returned the Green Dragon to a classic country pub. The menus are based on locally sourced ingredients whilst the fish comes fresh from Cornwall. Dishes might include battered fish with twice cooked chips, warm pork and black pudding terrine and the Green Dragon's famous Shepherd's Pie, made from braised lamb shoulder. The dessert list is equally tempting and can include strawberries with basil ice cream or chocolate and sour cherry brownie with cherry sorbet. On Sundays there is the outstanding traditional roast. The garden has two lawned areas with seating; families are welcome as are well-behaved dogs on leads.

Recommended in the area

Buckinghamshire Railway Centre; Waddesdon Manor; Claydon House

The Old Queens Head

Address: Hammersley Lane, PENN, HP10 8EY
Tel: 01494 813371
Fax: 01494 816145
Email: info@oldqueensheadpenn.co.uk
Website: www.oldqueensheadpenn.co.uk
Map ref: 3, SU99
Directions: B474 (Penn Rd) through Beaconsfield
New Town towards Penn, in approx 3m left into
School Rd, left again in 500yds into Hammersley Ln.
Pub on corner opposite church

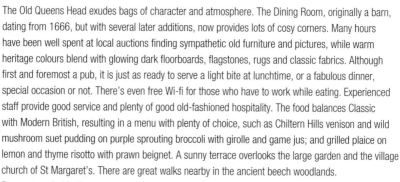

Open: 11–11 (Sun 12–10.30) **L** 12–2.30 (Sat 12–3, Sun 12–4) **D** 6.30–9.30 (Sun–Thurs) (Fri-Sat
6.30–10) **Closed:** 26 Dec **Facilities:** Garden Parking **Notes:** 🛢 👬 🐾 🍷 19

The Old Queens Head exudes bags of character and atmosphere. The Dining Room, originally a barn,
dating from 1666, but with several later additions, now provides lots of cosy corners. Many hours
have been well spent at local auctions finding sympathetic old furniture and pictures, while warm
heritage colours blend with glowing dark floorboards, flagstones, rugs and classic fabrics. Although
first and foremost a pub, it is just as ready to serve a light bite at lunchtime, or a fabulous dinner,
special occasion or not. There's even free Wi-fi for those who have to work while eating. Experienced
staff provide good service and plenty of good old-fashioned hospitality. The food balances Classic
with Modern British, resulting in a menu with plenty of choice, such as Chiltern Hills venison and wild
mushroom suet pudding on purple sprouting broccoli with girolle and game jus; and grilled plaice on
lemon and thyme risotto with prawn beignet. A sunny terrace overlooks the large garden and the village
church of St Margaret's. There are great walks nearby in the ancient beech woodlands.

Recommended in the area

Bekonscot Model Village; West Wycombe; Legoland

Knot Garden at Elton Hall

The Crown

Address: Bridge Road, BROUGHTON, Huntingdon, PE28 3AY
Tel: 01487 824428
Email: info@thecrowninnrestaurant.co.uk
Website: www.thecrowninnrestaurant.co.uk
Map ref: 3, TL27
Directions: Just off A141 between Huntingdon & Warboys, by church in village centre
Open: 11.30–3 6.30–11 ⓛ L 12–2.30 D 7–10
ⓘⓞⓛ L 12–2.30 D 7–10 **Closed:** 1–11 Jan (Mon–Tue)
Facilities: Garden Parking **Notes:** ⊕ Free House ♦♦ ⌐ ♟ 10

Picturesquely set beside the church in the beautiful village of Broughton, this idyllic pub dates back to the 18th century, when it incorporated a saddler's shop, thatched stables and piggeries. After closing down in 2000, 40 villagers banded together to buy and renovate their beloved local and it became a village-owned tenancy. Now a renowned gastro-pub, it is enthusiastically run by chef-patron David Anderson and his small team, which includes sous chef Dominic Hall and front of house manager Paul Littlewood. Together they have created a warm and friendly atmosphere in which to enjoy modern British cuisine with Italian influences. In the evening, an à la carte menu presents a seasonal choice of expertly prepared dishes at prices that, unlike all too many food-oriented pubs, have been steadfastly maintained to represent good value. The wine list may be small, but it has been carefully compiled to offer an interesting selection that caters for all tastes. At lunchtime, there's a set price menu, and throughout the afternoon you can get sandwiches and light meals, perhaps washed down with the current guest ale. At the back of the pub there's a good-sized garden in which summer events include jazz bands and hog roasts.

Recommended in the area

Hinchingbroke House; Huntingdon Racecourse; Flag Fen Bronze Age Centre

Kings College Chapel, Cambridge

The Anchor Inn

★★★★ ⊛ RESTAURANT WITH ROOMS

Address: Sutton Gault, ELY, CB6 2BD
Tel: 01353 778537
Fax: 01353 776180
Email: anchorinn@popmail.bta.com
Website: www.anchorsuttongault.co.uk
Map ref: 4, TL58
Directions: From A14, B1050 to Earith, take B1381 to Sutton. Sutton Gault on left
Open: 12–3 7–11 ⓑ L 12–2 D 7–9 ⓘⓞⓘ L 12–2
D 7–9 **Rooms:** 4 en suite **S** £59.50–£155 **D** £79.50–£155 **Facilities:** Garden Parking
Notes: ⊕ Free House ⅰⅰ Ⓨ 12

A family-run free house with a cosy atmosphere, scrubbed pine tables on gently undulating floors, evening candleglow and winter log fires. The inn has won wide recognition for its modern British cuisine using seasonal, local ingredients. Lighter lunches are available on weekdays and there are many wines by the glass. Some rooms overlook the river.

Recommended in the area

Cambridge; Wicken Fen NT; Newmarket Racecourse; Ely Cathedral

The Three Horseshoes

Address: High Street, MADINGLEY, CB3 8AB
Tel:. 01954 210221
Fax: 01954 212043
Email: thethreehorseshoes@huntsbridge.co.uk
Website: www.thethreehorseshoesmadingley.co.uk
Map ref: 3, TL36
Directions: M11 junct 13, 1.5m from A14
Open: 11.30–3 6–11 (Sun 6–8.30) 🍴 L 12–2 D 6.30–9.30 🍽
L 12–2 D 6.30–9.30 **Facilities:** Garden Parking **Notes:** 🍺 🍷 20

This is a picturesque thatched inn with a large garden that
stretches towards the local cricket pitch and open meadowland.
Its proximity to Cambridge makes for an eclectic clientele who lend a cosmopolitan air to the lively
atmosphere. The busy bar is stocked to please real ale enthusiasts with brews such as Adnams
Bitter, Hook Norton Old Hooky, Smile's Best and Cambridge Hobson's Choice, plus guest ales. The
food is even more enticing. Chef-patron Richard Stokes is a local, from the Fens, who has eaten
his way around the world, and his success can be gauged by the long queues for tables in the
conservatory restaurant. His menu features seasonal Italian cuisine, and there's a well-chosen wine
list to accompany the intense flavours of the imaginative dishes. A recent menu included pasta with
brown shrimps, trevise, parsley, dried chilli, Vermouth and olive oil; roast partridge stuffed with sage,
mascarpone and garlic with braised Casteluccio lentils, cavolo nero, carrots and Chianti; and pan-fried
sea bass with local pink fur apple potatoes, girolle and trompette mushrooms, Italian spinach and salsa
verde. Desserts feature such Italian favourites as pannacotta, zabaglione and chocolate truffle cake,
with a selection of Italian cheeses as a savoury alternative.

Recommended in the area

Cambridge; Wimpole Hall and Home Farm; Duxford Imperial War Museum (Aircraft)

The George Inn

Address: High Street, SPALDWICK, Huntingdon,
PE28 0TD
Tel: 01480 890293
Fax: 01480 896847
Map ref: 3, TL17
Directions: 6m W of Huntingdon on A14, junct 18
towards Spaldwick/Stow Longa
Open: 12–11 (Fri–Sat 12–12) 🍺 L 12–2.30
D 6–9.30 🍽 L 12–2.30 D 6–9.30 **Facilities:**
Garden Parking **Notes:** 🍺 PUNCH TAVERNS ♦♦ ♛ 25

Originally a private residence belonging to the Dartington family, The George's long history of providing hospitality to thirsty and hungry visitors dates back to 1679 when it opened as a coaching inn. It sits beside the manor house and overlooks the village green, and is currently run by The George Partnership of Mark and Louise Smith and Nick Thoday. The building retains a number of its historic features. Wall paintings, original beams and fireplaces all remain intact. The relaxing bar has comfortable leather sofas and Cask Marque ales, including Adnams Broadside and Green King IPA. There is also an extensive wine list. On fine days you can take your drinks outside to the beer garden. The lunchtime menu includes bar snacks such as Tuscan bean and tomato soup and The George's famous fish pie. There's also a separate award-winning restaurant, located in a beautifully converted barn, where traditional British and Mediterranean dishes are offered from a comprehensive menu. Typical among the starters is baked camembert with rosemary and onion foccacia, while mains might include home-smoked pork tenderloin with black pudding or crushed celeriac and mustard cream jus. Desserts might include a warm melting Valrhona chocolate mousse with pistachio ice-cream, Everything is home made (including the bread) and all produce is fresh, sourced locally and organic where possible.

Recommended in the area

Grafham Water; Hinchingbrooke Country Park; Hinchingbrooke House

CHESHIRE

Little Moreton Hall (National Trust)

The Bhurtpore Inn

Address: Wrenbury Road, ASTON, Nantwich,
CW5 8DQ
Tel: 01270 780917
Email: simonbhurtpore@yahoo.co.uk
Website: www.bhurtpore.co.uk
Map ref: 6, SJ64
Directions: Just off A530 between Nantwich &
Whitchurch. Turn towards Wrenbury at x-rds
Open: Mon-Thu 12–2.30 6.30–11.30 (Fri-Sat
12–12, Sun 12-11) 🍺 🍽 **L** 12–2 **D** 6.45–9.30
(Sat-Sun 12-9.30) **Closed:** 25–6 Dec, 1 Jan **Facilities:** Garden Parking **Notes:** ⊕ Free House 🐾 🍷 11

The George family has a bit of a thing about this traditional village pub. In 1849 James George leased it from the local Combermere estate, from which descendant Philip George bought it in 1895, only to sell it six years later to a Crewe brewery. Ninety years later, in 1991, Simon and Nicky George were looking to buy their first pub and came across the boarded-up, stripped-out Bhurtpore. It ticked just about every box. Although it has been a pub since at least 1778, it was the 1826 Siege of Bhurtpore in India, where Lord Combermere had distinguished himself, that inspired its current name. With eleven real ales always available, a large selection of bottled beers and seven continental beers on tap, it is truly a free house. The award-winning food is fresh, home made and reasonably priced, both in the bar and the restaurant. Starters include spicy lamb samosas with yogurt and mint dip; potato skins with grilled cheese and bacon topping; and pork and black pudding patties with coarse grain mustard and apple sauce. Finish with spiced raisin and ginger pudding with toffee sauce, or a local farmhouse ice cream. Behind the pub is a lawn with countryside views. At the centre of the local community, the pub is home to an enthusiastic cricket team, a group of cyclists known as the Wobbly Wheels and folk musicians.

Recommended in the area

Hack Green Secret Bunker; Cholmondeley Castle; Historic Nantwich; Stapeley Water Gardens

The Cholmondeley Arms

Address: CHOLMONDELEY, Malpas, SY14 8HN
Tel: 01829 720300
Fax: 01829 720123
Email: guy@cholmondeleyarms.co.uk
Website: www.cholmondeleyarms.co.uk
Map ref: 6, SJ55
Directions: On A49, between Whitchurch & Tarporley
Open: 11–3 6–11 ⎮ L 12–2.30 D 6.30–10
⎮ L 12–2.30 D 6.30–10 (Sat 12–10; Sun 12–9.30) Closed: 25 Dec Facilities: Garden Parking Notes: ⊕ Free House ⋔ ⌂ ⏆ 7

Guy Ross-Lowe was a solicitor until he, his wife Carolyn, and Lord and Lady Cholmondeley, the local landowners, converted this old school into a 'quintessential English pub', which has won many regional and national awards. All food is freshly prepared, using local produce wherever possible and the set menu offers sandwiches, steaks and lunchtime-only snacks. Specials include rack of lamb with flageolet beans; spinach, pine nut and pesto lasagne; and lobster tail with garlic butter.
Recommended in the area
Cholmondeley Castle Gardens; The Croccy Trail; Beeston Castle; The Sandstone Trail

---

The Davenport Arms

Address: Congleton Road, MARTON, SK11 9HF
Tel: 01260 224269
Fax: 01260 224565
Email: enquiries@thedavenportarms.co.uk
Website: www.thedavenportarms.co.uk
Map ref: 6, SJ86
Directions: 3m from Congleton off A34
Open: 12–3 6–close (Fri–Sun all day) ⎮ L 12–2.30 D 6–9 ⎮ L 12–2.30 D 6–9 Facilities: Garden Parking Notes: ⊕ Free House ⋔ ⏆ 9

The Davenport is an 18th-century former farmhouse standing opposite a half-timbered church, which was built in 1343. Over the last four years, the inn has been completely refurbished. The bar retains a traditional atmosphere with old settles and leather chesterfield armchairs. The flood-lit fresh water well is an unusual feature in the middle of the restaurant. Well kept real ales usually come from local brewers: Beartown Brewery, Weetwood Ales, Woodlands of Wrenbury and of course Macclesfield's Storm Brewing. Food is all freshly prepared on the premises using local suppliers.
Recommended in the area
Capesthorne Hall; Gawsworth Hall; Little Moreton Hall

The Goshawk

Address: Station Road, MOULDSWORTH, CH3 8AJ
Tel: 01928 740900
Fax: 01928 740965
Website: www.thegoshawk.com
Map ref: 6, SJ57
Directions: A51 from Chester onto A54. Left onto B5393 towards Frodsham. Enter Mouldsworth, pub on left opposite rail station
Open: 12–11 ⬛ D 12–9.30 ⬛ D 12–9.30
Closed: 25 Dec & 1 Jan **Facilities:** Garden Parking
Notes: ⬛ ⬛ 14

On the edge of the Delamere Forest, the Goshawk is just 15 minutes' drive from Chester. There is a good play area for children, and the decking outside overlooks a fine crown bowling green. The imaginative menu ranges from pub classics to more sophisticated fare. Everything is freshly prepared and you can eat in the bar, lounge or restaurant areas. A wide choice of wines from around the world is offered as well as real ales such as Timothy Taylors, Greene King and the changing casks of the week.

Recommended in the area

Go Ape at Delamere Forest; Mouldsworth Motor Museum; Sail Sports Windsurfing Centre

Blue Bell Inn

Address: TUSHINGHAM, nr Witchurch, SY13 4QS
Tel: 01948 662172
Fax: 01948 662172
Website: www.surftech.co.uk/bell
Map ref: 6, SJ54
Directions: A4, 4m N of Whitchurch, signed Bell O' the Hill
Open: 12–3 6–11 (Sun 12–3, 7–11) ⬛ L 12–2 D 6–9 ⬛ L 12–2 D 7–9 **Closed:** (Mon ex BHs)
Facilities: Garden Parking
Notes: ⬛ Free House ⬛ ⬛

Parts of this old black and white coaching inn date from the mid-16th century, although the main section was not completed until 1667. It is a character timber-framed building, including a bar with one of the largest chimneys in Cheshire, two low-ceilinged rooms with exposed beams that form the lounge, and a priests' hole. Artefacts discovered within the walls are on display. The menu is based on traditional English favourites, with daily specials. There is a garden, ideal for those real ales.

Recommended in the area

Bridgemere Garden World; Beeston Castle; Oulton Park

CORNWALL

Bedruthan Steps, near Newquay

The Halzephron Inn

Address: GUNWALLOE, Helston, TR12 7QB
Tel: 01326 240406
Fax: 01326 241442
Email: halzephroninn@gunwalloe1.fsnet.co.uk
Website: www.halzephron-inn.co.uk
Map ref: 1, SW62
Directions: 3m S of Helston on A3083, right to
Gunwalloe, through village. Inn on left
Open: 11–2.30 6.30–11 (Summer eve 6–11)
L 12–2 D 7–9 L 12–2 D 7–9 Closed: 25 Dec
Facilities: Garden Parking Family Room Notes: Free House 8

The name of this ancient inn derives from 'Als Yfferin', old Cornish for 'cliffs of hell', and this is an appropriate description of its situation on this hazardous but breathtaking stretch of coastline. Once a haunt of smugglers, the pub is located close to the fishing village of Gunwalloe and stands just 300 yards from the famous South Cornwall footpath. The only pub on the stretch between Mullion and Porthleven, today it offers visitors a warm welcome, a wide selection of ales and whiskies, and meals prepared from fresh local produce. These may be served outside, with views of the surrounding fields to the back or the ocean to the front, or inside, in a number of dining areas, from cosy nooks to a separate dining area or a family room (there's a thoughtful junior menu). Lunch and dinner bring a choice of fresh Cornish fare, accompanied by home-made granary or white rolls, plus daily-changing specials that might include roast monkfish tail wrapped in bacon on a seafood risotto, or seafood chowder. To follow there may be bread and butter pudding or hot chocolate fudge cake with Cornish cream. There's also a good wine list, with a choice of half-bottles.

Recommended in the area

Trevarno Gardens; Goonhilly Satellite Earth Station; RNAS Culdrose

The Crown Inn

★★★ INN
Address: LANLIVERY, Bodmin, PL30 5BT
Tel: 01208 872707
Fax: 01208 871208
Email: thecrown@wagtailinns.com
Website: www.wagtailinns.com
Map ref: 1, SX05
Directions: Signed off A390 via brown sign about
1.5m W of Lostwithiel
Open: 12–11 ⓫ L 12–2.30 D 6–9 ⓘ L 12–2.30
D 6.30–9 Rooms: 9 en suite (7 GF) S £39.95–£79.95 D £39.95–£79.95 Facilities: Garden Parking
Notes: ⊕ Free House ⓲ ⓴ ⓹ 7

This charming pub was built in the 12th century for the men constructing St Brevita's church next door. Such great age means everything about it oozes history – its thick stone walls, granite and slate floors, glass-covered well, low beams, open fireplaces and distinctive bread oven. The bar serves beers from Sharps of Rock and Skinners of Truro, and ten wines by the glass from a reasonably priced wine list. With Fowey harbour not far away, the menu will undoubtedly offer fresh crab, scallops, mackerel and more, while other local produce includes meats from a butcher in Par, fruit and veg from Bodmin and dairy products from Lostwithiel. At lunchtime, try chef's smoked mackerel pâté, or a proper Cornish pasty. Dinner might begin wth an appetiser of marinated olives and ciabatta bread, followed by a starter of locally smoked duck, Cornish charcuterie, or pan-seared scallops. Main courses include Greek-style salad; steaks with chips, onion rings and rocket and Parmesan salad; whole baked sea bass stuffed with lemon and fennel; and Laura's cheesy ratatouille. Some of the comfortable en suite rooms include children's beds, and in some dogs are welcome. The pretty front garden is lovely in warm weather.

Recommended in the area

Restormel Castle; Lanhydrock House; China Clay Country Park

Godolphin Arms

★★ 76% SMALL HOTEL
Address: MARAZION, nr Penzance, TR17 0EN
Tel: 01736 710202
Fax: 01736 710171
Email: enquiries@godolphinarms.co.uk
Website: www.godolphinarms.co.uk
Map ref: 1, SW53
Directions: Opposite St Michael's Mount
Open: 8–12 (8–11 Winter) 🍴 L 12–2.30 D 6–9
Rooms: 10 (2 GF) S £65–£110 D £85–£145
Facilities: Garden Parking Notes: ⊕ Free House ♦♦ ⊐

Locations don't come much more spectacular than this: the Godolphin Arms stands at the end of the causeway to St Michael's Mount, with steps leading directly onto the sandy beach. There are superb views from the bars, lounge areas and the terrace, and from many of the bedrooms, which all have en suite bathrooms. Family run, the pub is focused on a friendly welcome and good service. The varied menu includes fresh seafood, traditional pub favourites and the weekend carvery.

Recommended in the area
St Michael's Mount; Southwest Coast Path; St Ives

The Plume of Feathers

★★★★ INN
Address: MITCHELL, Truro, TR8 5AX
Tel: 01872 510387
Fax: 01872 511124
Email: enquiries@theplume.info
Website: www.theplume.info
Map ref: 1, SW85
Directions: Exit A30 to Mitchell/Newquay
Open: 9–11 🍴 L 12–5 D 6–10 🍽 L 12–5 D 6–10
Facilities: Garden Parking Notes: ⊕ Free House ♦♦

Since its establishment in the 16th century, the Plume of Feathers has played host to various historical figures, including the Methodist preacher John Wesley, and Sir Walter Raleigh. Today, thanks to its peaceful countryside location and loving restoration, it is the perfect place to relax over an award-winning real ale. The once-dilapidated stable barns now provide luxurious bedrooms, and the imaginative kitchen enjoys an excellent reputation for its food, which fuses modern European with classical British touches. The emphasis is on fresh fish and the best Cornish ingredients.

Recommended in the area
The Eden Project; Truro; Newquay's beaches

The Bush Inn

Address: MORWENSTOW, Bude, EX23 9SR
Tel: 01288 331242
Website: www.bushinn-morwenstow.co.uk
Map ref: 1, SS21
Directions: Exit A39, 3m N of Kilkhampton, 2nd right into village of Shop. 1.5m to Crosstown. Inn on village green
Open: 11–12 Food served all day
Facilities: Garden Parking
Notes: ⊕ Free House ♦♦ ♣♣ ♥ 8

Said to be one of Britain's oldest pubs, the Bush Inn was originally built as a chapel in AD 950 for pilgrims en route to Spain. It became a pub some 700 years later and has provided sustenance for visitors for hundreds of years. Smugglers and wreckers were among them, drawn by the inn's dramatic and isolated clifftop location on the north Cornish coast; nowadays the views over the Tidna Valley and the Atlantic Ocean are just as stunning as they must have been then. The unspoilt interior features stone-flagged floors, old stone fireplaces, a Celtic piscina carved from serpentine set into a wall behind the cosy bar, and a 'leper's squint' – a tiny window through which the needy could grab scraps of food. Today the meals are very different, with the emphasis on fresh local produce, including beef from the inn's own farm. Local shoots provide the game, and seafood comes from home waters. In winter, warming dishes include red wine and blue cheese risotto and venison stew, all served with Cornish real ales and a variety of fine wines. In summer, diners can enjoy a plate of mussels or beer-battered pollock and chips in the garden, which contains sturdy wooden play equipment. There are three bed and breakfast rooms and self-catering accommodation is also available.

Recommended in the area

Clovelly; Morwenstow Church and Hawker's Hut (NT); Boscastle

The Pandora Inn

Address: Restronguet Creek, MYLOR BRIDGE,
Falmouth, TR11 5ST
Tel: 01326 372678
Fax: 01326 378958
Website: www.pandorainn.com
Map ref: 1, SW83
Directions: From Truro/Falmouth follow A39, left at
Carclew, follow signs to pub
Open: 11–12 (Winter 11–11) ♿ L 12–3 D 6–9.30
(Winter 6.30–9) ▯◯▯ L 12–3 D 6–9.30 (Winter
6.30–9) **Facilities:** Garden Parking **Notes:** ⊞ ST AUSTELL BREWERY ⅰⅰ ⅿ ♉ 12

One of the best known inns in Cornwall, The Pandora is set by the water in the beautiful surroundings of Restronguet Creek. Parts of the thatched, cream-painted building date back to the 13th century, and its flagstone floors and low beamed ceilings suggest that little can have changed since. The atmosphere is splendidly traditional, with lots of snug corners, three log fires and a collection of maritime memorabilia. The inn is named after the good ship Pandora, sent to Tahiti to capture the Bounty mutineers. Unfortunately it was wrecked and the captain court-marshalled so, forced into early retirement, he bought the inn. A full range of drinks is served, including fine wines and beers from St Austell Brewery, HSD and Tribute. Meals are served in the bars or upstairs in the Sail Loft restaurant. When the sun shines, the tables and chairs set out on the new pontoon provide an experience akin to walking and eating on water. Food is taken seriously here, and the lunchtime and evening menus are supplemented by daily specials displayed on boards. Options range from sandwiches at lunchtime and afternoon teas to fine dining in the restaurant. Local seafood is a speciality of the house.

Recommended in the area

Trelissick Gardens (NT); National Maritime Museum; Pendennis Castle

Star Inn

Address: ST JUST-IN-PENWITH,
         TR19 7LL
Tel: 01736 788767
Map ref: 1, SW33
Directions: Telephone for directions
Open: 11–11 (Sat 11–12, Sun 12–11)
Facilities: Garden
Notes: ⊕ ST AUSTELL BREWERY 🚶 🐕 ♟ 5

A traditional granite-built Cornish pub in the village of St Just, near Land's End. Built in the 17th century, it still has a stone mounting block outside topped by an old ship's anchor, and a pavement seat that smokers no doubt find useful. Unspoilt inside, the walls around its horseshoe-shaped bar display lots of photographs and other items recalling the days when tin-mining sustained the local economy. John Wesley is believed to have been among its more illustrious guests over the years. These days, however, the well-known are likely to include actors, for the pub occasionally features in TV and film productions. St Austell Brewery beers and a comprehensive range of other drinks are served, but there is no food. You'll find a beer garden at the back of the pub and if the weather's a bit grim children's toys are available inside. Every Monday you can listen to live folk music; on Thursdays it's the turn of other entertainers, while most Fridays the Cape Cornwall singers perform. Formed in 1997, this all-male group resurrect a singing tradition that declined following closure of the tin mines. The Star has no car park, so use the one in Market Square nearby.

Recommended in the area

Minack Theatre; St Michael's Mount; Chysauster Iron Age Village

Padstow harbour

The Victory Inn

Address: Victory Hill, ST MAWES, TR2 5PQ
Tel: 01326 270324
Fax: 01326 270238
Email: contact@victory-inn.co.uk
Website: www.victory-inn.co.uk
Map ref: 1, SW83
Directions: Take A3078 to St Mawes. Pub up
Victory Steps adjacent to harbour
Open: 11–12 ₤ L 12–2.30 D 6–9.30
🍴 L 12–2.30 D 6.30–9
Notes: ⊕ PUNCH TAVERNS 👬 🐕 🍷 8

This friendly fishermen's local, with spectacular harbour views, is named after Nelson's flagship, HMS
Victory, and is now an award-winning dining pub, offering the freshest of local seafood. The blackboard
specials change according to the day's catch, with dishes such as fresh crab salad; lobster thermidor;
cod and chips; crab and mushroom omelette; and trio of fish with squid ink risotto. There's also pub
grub and lunchtime snacks. In addition to real ales, there's a decent selection of wines by the glass.

Recommended in the area

The Eden Project; Falmouth Maritime Museum; St Mawes Castle

The Mill House Inn

Address: TREBARWITH, Tintagel, PL34 0HD
Tel: 01840 770200
Fax: 01840 770647
Email: management@themillhouseinn.co.uk
Website: www.themillhouseinn.co.uk
Map ref: 1, SX06
Directions: From Tintagel take B3263 S, right after Trewarmett to Trebarwith Strand. Pub 0.5m on right
Open: 12–11 L 12–2.30 D 6.30–9
Closed: 25 Dec **Facilities:** Garden Parking
Notes: Free House

The Mill House dates back to 1760, and was a working mill until the 1930s. It is situated on the north Cornish coast in a beautiful woodland setting, just half a mile from the surfing beach at Trebarwith Strand, and a short distance from King Arthur's legendary castle. The Mill offers first class food and accommodation (eight elegant rooms, all with en suite facilities) in a charming stone building. The slate-floored bar with its wooden tables, chapel chairs and wood burning stove has a family friendly feel. You may also choose to eat on the partly-covered tiered terraces (with heaters) at the front. A new restaurant opened in July 2008 and is designed to blend in with the existing features of the Mill. Traditional bar lunches such as snakebite-battered local haddock or a Cornish smoked fish platter are followed by selections on the evening restaurant menu such as duo of Tintagel duck served with swede and carrot purée or grilled local halibut with spinach and prawn ragout. Sharps and Skinners local ales together with an imaginative wine list complement the regularly changing menus, which make use of the best locally sourced ingredients. The Mill House is licensed for wedding ceremonies and is a perfect location for receptions, parties and conferences.

Recommended in the area

Trebarwith Surfing Beach; Tintagel Castle; Delabole Wind Farm

Mousehole harbour

The Springer Spaniel

Address: TREBURLEY, Nr Launceston, PL15 9NS
Tel: 01579 370424
Email: enquiries@thespringerspaniel.org.uk
Website: www.thespringerspaniel.org.uk
Map ref: 1, SX37
Directions: On A388 halfway between Launceston & Callington
Open: 12–3 6–11 (Fri–Sat eve 6–12) L 12–1.45 D 6.30–8.45 L 12–1.45 D 6.30–8.45 **Facilities:** Garden Parking **Notes:** Free House 7

A friendly, traditional pub in the heart of the Cornish countryside offering delicious food, delectable ales, fine wines and great service. The old walls of The Springer Spaniel conceal a cosy bar with high-backed wooden settles, farmhouse-style chairs and a wood-burning stove to keep the chill out on colder days. There is a cosy candlelit restaurant, and for better weather a landscaped garden with outdoor seating. The menu features imaginative, contemporary dishes as well as traditional favourites and specialises in local, seasonal food including organic meat from the owners' farm.

Recommended in the area

Cotehele (National Trust); Mining Heritage Centre; Sterts Theatre, Upton Cross

The New Inn

★★ 78% ⑱ HOTEL

Address: New Grimsby, TRESCO, Isles of Scilly,
TR24 0QQ
Tel: 01720 422844
Fax: 01720 423200
Email: newinn@tresco.co.uk
Website: www.tresco.co.uk
Map ref: 1, SV81
Directions: By New Grimsby Quay
Open: 11–11 (Nov, Dec, Jan, Feb & Mar 11–2.30,
6–11) ⓑ **L** 12–2 **D** 6–9 ⑩ **D** 7–9 **Rooms:** 16 (2 GF) **S** £70–£157.50 **D** £140–£210 **Facilities:**
Garden **Notes:** ⊕ Free House ⥥ ♟ 12

The only pub on Tresco, The New Inn is on most visitors' itineraries, so it's a good idea to make a
reservation for a meal here. It stands perched above the harbour of New Grimsby, looking across the
narrow channel to Bryher and is the island's social centre, a natural interface between the islanders
– gardeners, fishermen, farmers, shopkeepers and estate workers – and visitors. The main bar is
panelled with exotic woods that were washed ashore from a passing ship, and here a range of real ales
is served, including the local Tresco Tipple. Outside there is a patio area with some of the sub-tropical
plants for which the island is famous. Wonderful, fresh locally caught seafood is the speciality of the
house, along with tender Tresco-reared beef, and the inn has an AA Rosette for its food. Special events
throughout the year include real ale festivals in May and September, and visiting musicians. Guests
visiting out of season might see the massing of migrant birds, witness whole fields of narcissi flowering
while the mainland shivers, or experience the full force of a winter storm from the sanctuary of the cosy
bar. Children's facilities are provided, and some bedrooms enjoy spectacular harbour views.

Recommended in the area

Tresco Abbey Garden; Valhalla Figurehead Collection; Sandy Beaches

CUMBRIA

Lake Grasmere, Lake District

Drunken Duck Inn

★★★★★ ◉◉ INN

Address: Barngates, AMBLESIDE, LA22 0NG
Tel: 015394 36347
Fax: 015394 36781
Email: info@drunkenduckinn.co.uk
Website: www.drunkenduckinn.co.uk
Map ref: 5, NY30
Directions: From Kendal on A591 to Ambleside, then
follow Hawkshead sign. In 2.5m inn sign on right,
1m up hill

Open: 11.30–11 ♨ L 12–2.30 D 6–9 ⓘ L 12–2.30 D 6–9 Rooms: 16 en suite (4 GF) S £90
D £120 Facilities: Garden Parking Notes: ⊕ Free House ♦♦ ♟ 20

This 17th-century inn is surrounded by 60 private acres of beautiful countryside. In spring, you can
barely move for flowers, and all year round there are striking views of fells and lakes. Under the same
family ownership since 1977, the Drunken Duck has been refurbished with a stylish mix of modern
luxury and old world charm. Expect plenty of sofas to lounge in, a pretty residents' garden, and
glamorous bedrooms. The bar, with its antique settles and log fires, serves beers from the inn's own
Barngate Brewery. These have been named after much loved dogs: Cracker, Tag Lag and Chester's
Strong and Ugly. The candlelit restaurant offers intelligent, modern British cuisine, with the same menu
offered at lunch and dinner, supplemented by specials. Start with smoked haddock and pea risotto, or
duck and spring onion confit with parmesan tuiles and chilli jam, followed by pan-fried Holker venison
fillet with wild mushroom and foie gras croûte, rump of Kendal rough fell lamb with minted pea purée,
Lyonnaise potatoes and rosemary jus, or hand-dived seared scallops. Desserts might include saffron
scented brûlée with sesame caramel and mango salsa, or you could try the gourmet cheese list.

Recommended in the area

Lake District Visitor Centre; Armitt Museum; Windmere Steamboat Centre

The Wheatsheaf at Beetham

Address: BEETHAM, nr Milnthorpe, LA7 7AL
Tel: 015395 62123
Fax: 015395 64840
Email: info@wheatsheafbeetham.com
Website: www.wheatsheafbeetham.com
Map ref: 6, SD43
Directions: On A6 5m N of junct 35
Open: 11.30–3 5.30–11 (Sun 12–3, 6.30–10.30)
L 12–2 D 6–9 ❍ L 12–2 D 6–9 Closed: 25 Dec
Facilities: Garden Parking
Notes: Free House 12

Discreetly tucked away in the picturesque village of Beetham, this family-owned free house dating back to 1609 is very much a dining pub, and is the perfect base for exploring the Lake District and Yorkshire Dales. The award-winning and seasonally-changing menu offers some of the finest home cooking the region has to offer. A menu of traditional English fayre is always supplemented by a selection of specials created daily by the Head Chef, who uses only the finest locally sourced ingredients. A typical dinner at the Wheatsheaf may include a pint of prawns, followed by Fell-bred fillet of beef, horseradish rösti and fresh greens with red wine sauce, and finished with Sandra's famous sticky toffee pudding. The cellar is always well-stocked with a range of traditional cask ales and a great choice of wines, 12 of which are available by the glass. All bedrooms have TV, tea and coffee making facilities, and a range of toiletries, and some enjoy stunning views across the many hills and features that surround the Wheatsheaf. There are also three rooms for conferences, training courses, receptions and private dining.

Recommended in the Area

Levens Hall; Lakeland Wildlife Oasis; Leighton Hall

Siney Tarn, Eskdale and Miterdale

The Boot Inn

Address: BOOT, Eskdale Valley, CA19 1TG
Tel: 019467 23224
Fax: 019467 23337
Email: enquiries@bootinn.co.uk
Website: www.bootinn.co.uk
Map ref: 5, NY10
Directions: From A595 follow signs for Eskdale then Boot
Open: 11–11 L 12–4 D 6–9 D 6–9
Closed: 25 Dec **Facilities:** Garden Parking
Notes: ⊕ HARTLEYS

Whether you are in the bar with its crackling log fire, in the light and airy conservatory, or in the dining room, which dates back to 1578, you can expect a warm welcome from Caroline, Sean and the friendly staff at The Boot Inn. Enjoy a drink in the bar or the snug and plan a day in some of the best scenery and walking areas in England. Traditional games, a pool table and a plasma screen TV are available in the bar. There is a good selection of real ales, a comprehensive wine list and some good malt whiskies.

Recommended in the area

Muncaster Castle; La'al Ratty Steam Train; Whitehaven Rum Story; Eskdale, Lake District National Park

Brook House Inn

★★★★ INN

Address: BOOT, Eskdale, CA19 1TG
Tel: 019467 23288
Fax: 019467 23160
Email: stay@brookhouseinn.co.uk
Website: www.brookhouseinn.co.uk
Map ref: 5, NY10
Directions: M6 junct 36, A590 follow Barrow signs.
A5092, then A595. Past Broughton-in-Furness then
right at lights to Ulpha. Cross river, next left signed
Eskdale, & on to Boot. (NB not all routes to Boot are suitable in bad weather conditions)
Open: 11–11(8–12 during high season) ⓑ L 12–5.30 D 5.30–8.30 ⓞ L 12–4.30 D 6–8.30
Closed: 25 Dec Rooms: 7 en suite Facilities: Garden Parking Notes: ⊕ Free House ⓲ ⓨ 10

A family-owned country inn and restaurant, and an ideal base for exploring Eskdale and the western
fells of the Lake District. The scenery is picturesque and dramatic, with rugged mountains, tumbling
waterfalls, lakes and tarns, and the river Esk winding its way through the woods. Delicious home-made
food is available all day in the restaurant, bar or snug, from a menu complemented by blackboard
specials. Main courses include duck breast with plum and orange sauce, and grilled sea bass with
roasted red pepper and tomato salsa. Daytime salads, and sandwiches made with home-made bread
are also available. There is an annual beer festival in June; and in the bar, well-kept real ales include
Timothy Taylor Landlord, Jennings Cumberland, Hawkshead Bitter and a range of guest beers from
other local brewers. On a one-a-day basis, a five-month stay would be necessary to sample each
of the bar's 165 malt whiskies! Seven en suite bedrooms provide good quality accommodation and
superb views.

Recommended in the area

Ravenglass & Eskdale Railway; Coniston Water; Scafell

The Punch Bowl Inn

★★★★★ ◉ INN

Address: CROSTHWAITE, Nr Kendal, LA8 8HR
Tel: 015395 68237
Fax: 015395 68875
Email: info@the-punchbowl.co.uk
Website: www.the-punchbowl.co.uk
Map ref: 6, SD49
Directions: M6 junct 36, A590 towards Barrow, A5074 & follow
signs for Crosthwaite. Pub by church on left
Open: 12–11 ᴸ L 12–6 D 6–9.30 ◉ L 12–2.30 D 6–9.15
Rooms: 9 en suite S £93.75–£232.50 D £125–£310
Facilities: Garden Parking **Notes:** ⊕ Free House ♀♂ ♞ ♟

The Punch Bowl is not only a bar and restaurant with excellent accommodation, it also serves as the
village post office. The slatefloored bar, with open fires and original beams, is the perfect spot to enjoy
a pint of Tag Lag from the Barngates Brewery. Leather chairs, gleaming wooden floors and a pale stone
fireplace make for an elegant dining room. The award-winning menu features the local suppliers.

Recommended in the area

Sizergh Castle; Beatrix Potter country; Cartmel Race Course

Bower House Inn

★★ 74% HOTEL

Address: ESKDALE GREEN, Holmrook, CA19 1TD
Tel: 019467 23244
Fax: 019467 23308
Email: info@bowerhouseinn.freeserve.co.uk
Website: www.bowerhouseinn.co.uk
Map ref: 5, NY10
Directions: 4m off A595, 0.5m W of Eskdale Green
Open: 11–2.30 6–11 ᴸ L 12.30–2.30 D 6–9
◉ D 7–9 **Rooms:** 29 (9 GF) S £55–£75
D £61–£92 **Facilities:** Garden Parking **Notes:** ⊕ Free House ♞

Located close to the main Cumbrian coast road in a scenic and unspoilt part of the Lake District, this
fine 17th-century former farmhouse still provides a sanctuary for weary travellers. Inside it oozes
traditional appeal, with its oak-beamed bar, warm fires and a warren of rooms. Hearty imaginative
dishes, such as Morecambe Bay potted shrimps followed by roast venison with red wine and juniper
sauce, are available in the charming restaurant. The inn also has a range of tasteful en suite bedrooms.

Recommended in the area

Ravenglass and Eskdale Railway; Muncaster Castle; Eskdale Water Mill

Queens Head Hotel

★★ 72% 🏵 HOTEL

Address: Main Street, HAWKSHEAD, LA22 0NS
Tel: 015394 36271
Fax: 015394 36722
Email: enquiries@queensheadhotel.co.uk
Website: www.queensheadhotel.co.uk
Map ref: 5, SD39
Directions: M6 junct 36, A590 to Newby Bridge, 1st right, 8m to Hawkshead
Open: 11–12 🍴 L 12–2.30 D 6.15–9.30 🍽 L 12–2.30 D 6.15–9.30 **Rooms:** 14 (2 GF) **S** £42.50–£50 **D** £90–£110
Facilities: Garden **Notes:** ⊕ FREDERIC ROBINSON 👫 🍷 11

This charming 16th-century hotel sits in the heart of historic Hawkshead, the village where William Wordsworth went to school and Beatrix Potter created Peter Rabbit. The surrounding area is a haven for walkers, and Esthwaite Water is a stone's throw away. Inside the hotel, you'll find low oak-beamed ceilings, wood-panelled walls, an original slate floor and a welcoming fire; one curiosity on display is the Girt Clog, a 20-inch-long shoe made for an elephantitis sufferer in the 1820s. As well as a range of well-appointed en suite bedrooms and self-catering accommodation, the hotel offers everything you could need for relaxed wining and dining. There's an extensive wine list and a selection of real ales, plus a full carte menu and an ever-changing specials board. Dishes draw from the wealth of quality produce on the doorstep: trout from Esthwaite Water, pheasant from Graythwaite, traditionally cured meats from Waberthwaite, and slow-maturing Herdwick lamb. For lunch there are sandwiches, salads or interesting light bites such as chicken liver pâté with orange and tequila served with toasted brioche. An evening meal might open with confit Barbary duck leg followed by baked brill.

Recommended in the area

Hill Top (NT); Go Ape at Grizedale Forest Park; Brantwood House and Gardens

The Horse & Farrier Inn

Address: Threlkeld Village, KESWICK, CA12 4SQ
Tel: 017687 79688
Fax: 017687 79823
Email: info@horseandfarrier.com
Website: www.horseandfarrier.com
Map ref: 5, NY22
Directions: M6 junct 40 follow Keswick (A66) signs, 12m, right signed Threlkeld. Pub in village centre
Open: 8am–12am ⓑ L 12–2 D 6–9 🍽 L 12–2 D 5–9 **Facilities:** Garden Parking
Notes: 🛢 JENNINGS BROTHERS PLC 👥 🐕 🍷 9

Within these whitewashed stone walls are all the essential features of an inn built over 300 years ago – slate-flagged floors, beamed ceilings, open fires. It stands in the picturesque village of Threlkeld, at the foot of 868-metre Blencathra, with views of the even higher Skiddaw in the west and Helvellyn to the south. The inn has an excellent reputation for good food in these parts, from hearty Lakeland breakfasts for those staying in the guest house, to meals served in either the bar, or the charming period restaurant. Making full use of local, seasonal produce, the kitchen offers a wide ranging menu. At lunch there are open sandwiches, baguettes and salads, as well as more substantial pan-fried 10oz steaks; poached smoked haddock; and spinach and ricotta cannelloni. The bar menu offers deep-fried breaded Whitby scampi; Mediterranean vegetable lasagne, and plenty more. At dinner, start with roasted fennel risotto; warm oriental duck leg confit; or duck liver and brandy paté. Particular house specials include lamb shoulder, where the meat is slowly braised in Jennings Cumberland ale, and seared yellow fin tuna steak in olive oil and fresh lime marinade; or warm red onion and cherry tomato tartlet. Typical desserts include chocolate pudding with chocolate sauce and ice cream; and hot sticky toffee pudding.

Recommended in the area

Theatre by the Lake; Rookin House Adventure Centre; Keswick Golf Club

The Kings Head

Address: Thirlspot, KESWICK, CA12 4TN
Tel: 017687 72393
Fax: 017687 72309
Email: stay@lakedistrictinns.co.uk
Website: www.lakedistrictinns.co.uk
Map ref: 5, NY22
Directions: From M6 take A66 to Keswick then A591, pub 4m S of Keswick
Open: 12–11 (Sun 12–10.30) 🍴 L 12–3 D 6–9.30 🍽 D 7–8.30 **Facilities:** Garden Parking
Notes: 🌐 Free House 👬 🐾 🍷 10

With 950-metre Helvellyn rearing up behind this 17th-century former coaching inn, it is not hard to describe the views as anything but truly sublime. Take our word for it, they really are. On sunny days, the garden is the most sought-after place to enjoy a meal or drink, although the wooden beams and inglenook fireplaces of the bar, restaurant and lounge areas could make it a tough call. Dark, strong Sneck Lifter is one of the Jennings beers on draught brewed in nearby Cockermouth. Favourites from the bar menu include home-made beefburgers, Waberthwaite Cumberland sausage, and peach, Blengdale Blue cheese and rocket salad, while soups and bloomer bread sandwiches are available all day. The elegant St John's Restaurant menu offers dishes such as home-cured gravadlax with celeriac rémoulade, followed by rack of lamb with roasted root vegetables, or monkfish tail fettucine with steamed mussels. Those with a sweet tooth will find it hard to resist sticky toffee pudding, or vanilla pod crème brûlée. The Lakeland Speciality Shop is well worth a visit for home-made preserves, Emma Bridgewater pottery, and local ale gift packs. All 17 well-appointed guest rooms are en suite and have stunning views of the surrounding fells.

Recommended in the area

Lake District National Park; Thirlmere; Aira Force Waterfall

Queens Head

★★★★ ⇔ INN

Address: Townhead, TROUTBECK, Windermere,
LA23 1PW
Tel: 015394 32174
Fax: 015394 31938
Email: enquiries@queensheadhotel.com
Website: www.queensheadhotel.com
Map ref: 5, NY40
Directions: M6 junct 36, A590/591, W towards
Windermere, right at mini-rdbt onto A592 signed
Penrith/Ullswater. Pub 2m on right
Open: 11–11 (Sun 12–10.30) ⓑ L 12–5 D 5–9 ⓘ L 12–2 D 6.30–9 **Closed:** 25 Dec
Rooms: 15 en suite (2 GF) **Facilities:** Parking **Notes:** ⊕ FREDERIC ROBINSON ⒤ ♟ 9

A classic 17th-century coaching inn, the Queen's Head offers stunning views across the Garburn
Pass. Just three miles from Windermere, it is little wonder that it is a magnet for ramblers. Today this
thriving pub, situated in the lovely, undulating valley of Troutbeck, continues to provide sustenance
and comfortable accommodation to its many visitors, both in the main hotel and in the converted barn.
The bars are full of nooks and crannies, and there are open fires and carved settles. With Robinson's
Brewery beers on the pumps, and a reputation for good food and varied menus, both at lunchtime and
in the evening, it draws regulars and travellers alike. Meals on offer range from home-made soups to
simple braised dishes, such as shank of lamb in red wine and rosemary, or roast fillet of local beef with
real ale and oxtail sauce and gratin potato, through to imaginative seafood options, including risotto
of crab and Parmesan served with chive salad; pan-fried sardines on lemon rocket; or mussels in a
fragrant Thai broth. A delicious dessert list follows, with mouthwatering choices.

Recommended in the area

Brockhole National Park Visitor Centre; The World of Beatrix Potter; Lake Windermere

The River Eamont near Penrith

The Yanwath Gate Inn

Address: YANWATH, Penrith, CA10 2LF
Tel: 01768 862386
Email: enquiries@yanwathgate.com
Website: www.yanwathgate.com
Map ref: 6, NY52
Directions: Telephone for directions
Open: 12–11 ⓑ L 12–2.30 D 6–9 ⓘ L 12–2.30
D 6–9 **Facilities:** Garden Parking
Notes: ⊕ Free House ⋔ ⋔ ♀ 12

The delightful 17th-century inn takes its name from its original function as a tollgate. It has a growing reputation for good food and has a beautiful garden with outdoor seating. At least three Cumbrian ales are served here at any one time. For lunch the starter might be a bowl of mussels, soup of the day or ham terrine followed by a main dish of fisherman's pie, venison burger or Cumberland sausage with Yanwarth Gate black pudding. For dinner the mains include red bream, crisp belly pork, smoked venison loin and an open lasagne of mushrooms and summer vegetables.

Recommended in the area

Rheged; Brougham Hall; steamer cruises on Ullswater

DEVON

Bowerman's Nose, Dartmoor National Park

The Masons Arms

★★ 79% ◉ HOTEL
Address: BRANSCOMBE, EX12 3DJ
Tel: 01297 680300
Fax: 01297 680500
Email: reception@masonsarms.co.uk
Website: www.masonsarms.co.uk
Map ref: 2, SY18
Directions: Turn off A3052 towards Branscombe, down hill, hotel at bottom of hill
Open: 11–11 Times vary, please phone ⬛ L 12–2 D 7–9 ⬤ D 7–9 Rooms: 21 S £80–£170 D £80–£170 Facilities: Garden Parking
Notes: ⬛ Free House ⬛⬛ ⬛ ⬛ 14

Originally a cider house, this fine creeper-clad inn dates from 1360 and was at one time a well-documented haunt of smugglers. It is set in the picturesque village of Branscombe, just a 10-minute stroll from the beach, and there are wonderful walks in the area, including the South West Coast Path. The charming bar features stone walls, ancient ships' timbers, slate floors and a splendid open fireplace, which is used for spit roasts on a weekly basis, including Sunday lunchtime. The bar offers an extensive menu supplemented by daily specials, and the restaurant has an AA Rosette award for its fine dining. The menus draw on quality local produce, specialising in Branscombe crab and lobster, and feature such dishes as confit of aromatic duck leg with truffle oil mash, pear compôte and baby carrots. Outside there is a walled terrace with seating for around 100 people – very popular in the summer months – and if you are tempted to stay over, there are rooms in the original building and separate cottage rooms, all beautifully presented with designer fabrics and antique furniture. The Masons Arms welcomes dogs and water is provided for them.

Recommended in the area

Old Bakery, Manor Mill and Forge (NT); Jurassic Coast World Heritage Site; Donkey Sanctuary

The Sandy Park Inn

★★★ INN

Address: CHAGFORD, Newton Abbott, TQ13 8JW
Tel: 01647 433267
Email: sandyparkinn@btconnect.com
Website: www.sandyparkinn.co.uk
Map ref: 2, SX78
Directions: From A30 exit at Whiddon Down, turn left towards Moretonhampstead. Inn 5m
Open: 11–11 **L** 12–2.30 **D** 6.30–9 **L** 12–2.30 **D** 6.30–9 **Rooms:** 5 (2 en suite) (3 pri facs) **S** £45 **D** £85 **Facilities:** Garden Parking **Notes:** Free House 14

Everything about the 17th-century, thatched Sandy Park is how you'd want it to be. Dogs are frequently to be found slumped in front of the fire, horse-brasses and sporting prints adorn the walls, and the beamed bar attracts locals and tourists alike, all happily setting the world to rights with the help of a jolly good wine list and a choice of local brews, including Otter, St Austell Tribute and Sharp's Doom Bar. The Inn has built a local following for good quality pub food, sourced in and around Dartmoor, such as the roasting joints used for Sunday lunch, which began life less than two miles away. The bar offers a creative brasserie-style menu, with daily choices on the blackboard; the candlelit restaurant is equally appealing. Dishes to consider include pork and herb sausages hand-made in Moretonhampstead; beer-battered cod and chips; pan-seared tuna with salad Niçoise; smoked haddock kedgeree; and John Dory with dry roasted tomatoes and warm buttered samphire. Vegetarians are not forgotten – check out the handmade spinach and goats' cheese filo parcels with basil and parmesan; or risotto with sauté courgettes and sweetcorn. Tastefully refurbished bedrooms all have private bathrooms and modern luxuries.

Recommended in the area

Dartmeet; Grimspound Bronze Age Settlement; Castle Drogo

The Old Thatch Inn

Address: CHERITON BISHOP, Nr Exeter, Devon
EX6 6JH
Tel: 01647 24204
Email: mail@theoldthatch.f9.co.uk
Website: www.theoldthatchinn.com
Map ref: 2, SX79
Directions: 0.5m off A30, 7m SW of Exeter
Open: 11.30–3 6–11 ⅂ L 12–2 D 6.30–9
⅂◯ L 12–2 D 6.30–9 **Closed:** 25–26 Dec
Facilities: Garden Parking
Notes: ⊕ Free House ⅰ⅏ ⅏ ⅏ 9

The Old Thatch Inn is a charming Grade II listed 16th-century free house located just inside the eastern
borders of Dartmoor National Park, and half a mile off the A30. It once welcomed stagecoaches on
the London to Penzance road and today it remains a popular halfway house for travellers on their way
to and from Cornwall. For a time during its long history, the inn passed into private hands and then
became a tea-room, before its licence was renewed in the early 1970s. Experienced owners David and
head chef Serena London pride themselves on their high standards, especially when it comes to food,
and all of the meals are prepared using fresh ingredients from the south-west, with seafood featuring
strongly. Dishes change daily, depending on supplies, and examples include pan seared pigeon breast
with a spinach mousse and mixed berry dressing; and baked fillet of seabass with a crayfish tail, lemon
and thyme risotto. Diners can choose from a number of real ales and a good range of wines, with
many available by the glass. For those wishing to stay over, the inn offers a number of well-equipped
en suite bedrooms.

Recommended in the area

Castle Drogo (NT); Fingle Bridge, Dartmoor; Exeter

The Five Bells Inn

Address: CLYST HYDON, Cullompton, EX15 2NT
Tel: 01884 277288
Email: info@fivebellsclysthydon.co.uk
Website: www.fivebellsclysthydon.co.uk
Map ref: 2, ST00
Directions: B3181 towards Cullompton, right at Hele Cross towards Clyst Hydon. 2m turn right, then sharp right at left bend at village sign
Open: 11.30–3 6.30–11 (Sun 12–3, 6.30–10.30)
🍴 L 11.30–2 D 7–9 ⭐️ L 11.30–2 D 7–9
Closed: Mon lunch (winter) **Facilities:** Garden Parking **Notes:** ⊕ Free House ♦♦ ♟ 8

Named after the number of bells in the village church, this beautiful white-painted, thatched former farmhouse is still surrounded by rolling East Devon countryside. It became a pub around a century ago, and in recent years accolades have been pouring in for the family-friendly atmosphere and the dedication to real ales and good food of the owners, Roger and Di Shenton. For warmer days there's a garden with a children's play area. The interior is welcoming, with old beams and an inglenook fireplace, gleaming copper and brass, watercolours, books and games, and there are four eating areas. Here you can choose from an interesting and well-balanced menu of dishes based on fresh local ingredients such as prime West Country steaks and fresh fish. The traditional dishes might include steak and kidney suet pudding, beef casserole, or plaice with chips and peas, and there are more eclectic offerings – perhaps salmon with pesto crust and tomato salsa; breast of chicken with a Stilton and apricot sauce; or citrus beef, leek and pickled kumquat pie in a potato pastry basket. There are always vegetarian choices, the children's menu is particularly good and you can even get take-away cod or sausage and chips. Real ales include Cotleigh Tawny Ale, Otter Bitter and O'Hanlon's.

Recommended in the area

Killerton Gardens; Exeter; Jurassic Coast World Heritage Site

The Tuckers Arms

Address: DALWOOD, Axminster,
EX13 7EG
Tel: 01404 881342
Fax: 01404 881138
Email: davidbeck@tuckersarms.freeserve.co.uk
Website: www.tuckersarms.co.uk
Map ref: 2, ST20
Directions: Off A35 between Honiton & Axminster
Open: 12–3 6.30–11 (Sun 12–10.30)
🛏 L 12–2 D 7–8.30 ⌖ L 12–2 D 7–9
Facilities: Garden Parking Notes: ⌗ Free House ♇ 8

Dating back eight centuries, this Devon longhouse enjoys a pretty setting between two ridges of the Blackdown Hills, with the Corry Brook trickling by a few yards away. It is overlooked by the ancient fort of Danes Hill, constructed by the Vikings who came to these parts long before the Norman Conquest. It was built either as a hunting lodge for the Duke of Beaulieu, or as accommodation for the builders of the local church across the way. You can take your pick, but frankly, it hardly matters when it is everything you would expect of a traditional, thatched inn – it has inglenook fireplaces, low beams and flagstone floors; real ales such as Otter Bitter and Old Speckled Hen are on tap; and the restaurant specialises in fresh fish and game. Locally caught crab, lobster, scallops, monkfish, sea bass and lemon sole feature regularly on the menu or specials board (Lyme Regis is only 15 minutes away, Brixham a bit further), and are supplemented by home-made sweets, local cheeses and clotted cream. Outside there is a lovely country garden and a more recently created covered patio. Comfortable guest rooms were added on the site of the old skittle alley.

Recommended in the area

Loughwood Meeting House; South West Coastal Path; West Dorset Heritage Coast

The coast near Tintagel Quay

The Nobody Inn

Address: DODDISCOMBSLEIGH, Exeter, EX6 7PS
Tel: 01647 252394
Fax: 01647 252978
Email: info@nobodyinn.co.uk
Website: www.nobodyinn.co.uk
Map ref: 2, SX88
Directions: 3m SW of Exeter Racecourse (A38)
Open: 11–11 (Sun 12–10.30) L 12–2 (Sun 12–3)
D Mon–Thu 6.30–9 (Fri–Sat 6.30–9.30, Sun 7–9)
Closed: 25–26 & 31 Dec **Facilities:** Garden Parking
Notes: ⊕ Free House ♦ ♂ ♀ 20

Dating from around 1591, this is a charming free house, with low ceilings, blackened beams, inglenook fireplace and antique furniture all contributing to the timeless and homely atmosphere. The great pub food here is based around fresh local produce – as well as unusual local ales, there are over 300 wines and 240 whiskies, not to mention 20 local cheeses.

Recommended in the area

Exeter Quay; Crealy Adventure Park; Haldon Forest Park

The Hoops Inn & Country Hotel

★★★ 71% 🏵 HOTEL

Address: Clovelly, HORN'S CROSS, Bideford,
EX39 5DL
Tel: 01237 451222
Fax: 01237 451247
Email: sales@hoopsinn.co.uk
Website: www.hoopsinn.co.uk
Map ref: 1, SS32
Directions: On A39 between Bideford & Clovelly
Open: 8–11 🍽 **L** 12–9.30 **D** 6–9.30 🍴 **L** 12–3

D 6–9.30 **Rooms:** 13 (1 GF) **S** £65–£120 **D** £95–£180 **Facilities:** Garden Parking
Notes: 🍺 Free House 🕴 🐾 🍷 20

A thatched, cob-walled, 13th-century inn, The Hoops is set in 2½ acres of gardens and terraces
on the rugged Atlantic coast. The inn was once a meeting place for smugglers who made their way
along precipitous footpaths to evade the revenue men and share their spoils. A cliff-top walk from
the inn takes in ancient oak woods, two visits to the sea shore and no main roads, all amid glorious
countryside. During your stay you can arrange to fly eagles and try your hand at falconry on site. The
inn has individually decorated, en suite bedrooms and suites with four-poster beds. Menus are based
on the freshest produce Devon can offer, including herbs, fruit and vegetables from the gardens, and a
wide choice of wines by the glass from more than 220 bins. The wine list has an AA Notable Wine List
Award. Beers brewed especially for the inn by a local brewery include Hoops Old Ale and Hoops Special
Ale, offered alongside guests like Atlantic IPA, Golden Pig and Grenville's Renown. Guests may eat in
the bars, courtyard, gardens or restaurant, where oak-panelled walls, period furniture and tables set
with crisp white napkins create just the right level of formality.

Recommended in the area

North Devon Maritime Museum; Dartington Crystal; RHS Rosemoor

Bickley Mill Inn

Address: KINGSKERSWELL, Newton Abbot,
TQ12 5LN
Tel: 01803 873201
Email: info@bickleymill.co.uk
Website: www.bickleymill.co.uk
Map ref: 2, SX86
Directions: From Newton Abbot on A380 towards
Torquay. Right at Barn Owl Inn, follow brown tourist
signs
Open: 11.30–3 6.30–11 ⬜ L 12–2 🍴 L 12–2
D 6.30–9 **Closed:** 27–28 Dec & 1 Jan
Facilities: Garden Parking **Notes:** 🛢 Free House 🚶 🐕 🍷 8

Once a flour mill, Bickley Mill Inn dating back to the 13th century, is a family-run free house with accommodation. Located in the beautiful wooded Stoneycombe Valley, it is within convenient reach of Torquay, Newton Abbot and Totnes. The mill was bought by David and Patricia Smith and reopened after a thorough refurbishment, which blends old and new in a fresh contemporary style. All the en suite bedrooms are individually styled and have many thoughtful extras such as flatscreen DVD TV and tea- and coffee-making facilities. In the restaurant, quality produce from the south-west is transformed by chef Bill Gott into a range of British dishes with an international influence. The seasonally changing menu might include crispy pork belly with smashed parsnips and apples; grilled sea bream fillets with roast vegetables and tomato sauce; and sweet potato and aubergine rogan josh, all accompanied by wine from a well-chosen list. Fresh fish is delivered every day from neighbouring Brixham. In the cosy bar, roaring log fires and comfortable sofas make it easy to relax over one of the locally brewed ales.

Recommended in the area

Dartmoor National Park; Paignton Zoo; Compton Castle (NT)

The Ring of Bells Inn

Address: NORTH BOVEY, Newton Abbot, TQ13 8RB
Tel: 01647 440375
Fax: 01647 440746
Email: info@ringofbellsinn.com
Website: www.ringofbellsinn.com
Map ref: 2, SX78
Directions: 1.5m from Moretonhampstead off
B3212. 7m S of Whiddon Down junct on A30
Open: 11–11 L 12–2.30 D 6.30–9.30
L 12–2.30 D 7–9.30 **Facilities:** Garden **Notes:**

This is one of Dartmoor's most historic inns, an attractive thatched property just off the village green. It was built in the 13th century for stonemasons working on the nearby church, and is still at the heart of the village's social life. Visitors are attracted by good Devon pub food and West Country ales, and there is certainly plenty to do and see in the area. Hearty appetites are catered for with classics like steak and ale pie, local bangers and mash, and lambs' liver and bacon. Alternatives range through local rabbit braised in red wine, and charred aubergine rolls stuffed with mushroom, olives and pine nuts.

Recommended in the area

Dartmoor National Park; Exeter; Dartmoor Railway

The Ship Inn

Address: NOSS MAYO, Plymouth, PL8 1EW
Tel: 01752 872387
Fax: 01752 873294
Email: ship@nossmayo.com
Website: www.nossmayo.com
Map ref: 2, SX58
Directions: 5m S of Yealmpton
Open: 11–11 L 12–9.30 D 12–9.30
L 12–9.30 D 12–9.30 **Facilities:** Garden Parking
Notes: Free House 10

The Ship is a waterside free house that has been beautifully renovated using reclaimed materials, including English oak and local stone, in a style that is simple and properly pub-like. The inn's tidal location is superb, making it a popular port of call for yachting enthusiasts (who can tie their boat up right outside) as well as walkers. The daily changing menu of home-made dishes majors on local produce, notably fish, and regional and local beers include Tamar, Jail Ale and Butcombe Blonde. Outside, there is a waterside garden with great views. Dogs are allowed, but only downstairs.

Recommended in the area

Dartmoor National Park; Plymouth; South Devon Coastal Path

Jack in the Green Inn

@@

Address: London Road, ROCKBEARE, Nr Exeter, EX5 2EE
Tel: 01404 822240
Fax: 01404 823445
Email: info@jackinthegreen.uk.com
Website: www.jackinthegreen.uk.com
Map ref: 2, SY09
Directions: From M5 take old A30 towards Honiton, signed Rockbeare
Open: 11–2.30 6–11 (Sun 12–10.30) 🛏 **L** 11–2 **D** 6–9.30
🍽 **L** 11–2 **D** 6–9.30 **Closed:** 25 Dec–5 Jan **Facilities:** Parking
Notes: ⊕ Free House ♦♦ ♇ 12

There has been an inn on this site for several centuries, but since Paul Parnell took over some 17 years ago, it has become a beacon of good food in a contemporary and relaxed atmosphere, earning it two AA Rosettes. The inn is set in four acres of grounds and within its whitewashed walls is a lounge bar furnished with comfy seating and dark wood tables, and a smart restaurant. The courtyard features herb beds, hanging baskets and country views. The simple philosophy here is to serve real food to real people, with a firm commitment from the kitchen to sourcing the best and freshest local produce and preparing it to a consistently high standard. Typical dishes on the bar menu range from venison sausages with spiced red cabbage and mash to tomato risotto with chorizo and basil; in the restaurant you will find dishes such as chicken breast with chestnuts, smoked bacon, shitake mushrooms and a juniper and Madeira jus; or pan-fried salmon with cucumber, dill and sauce mousseline. The inn is a free house, serving Cotleigh Tawny Ale, Hardy Country, Otter Ale and Yellowhammer and a list of nearly 100 wines. Dogs are welcome in the courtyard, with water provided outside and a field for walking them.

Recommended in the area

Bicton Park; Escot Park; Crealy Adventure Park

Dukes

★★★★ INN

Address: The Esplanade, SIDMOUTH, EX10 8AR
Tel: 01395 513320
Fax: 01395 519318
Email: dukes@hotels-sidmouth.co.uk
Website: www.hotels-sidmouth.co.uk
Map ref: 2, SY18
Directions: M5 junct 30 onto A3052, take 1st exit to Sidmouth on right then left onto Esplanade
Open: 10–11 L 12–9 D 12–9 L 12–9 D 12–9
Facilities: Garden Parking **Notes:** Free House 16

Situated at the heart of Sidmouth town centre on the Regency Esplanade, Dukes is a contemporary inn that successfully combines traditional values with an informal atmosphere. The interior is stylish and lively, with a relaxed continental feel in the bar and public areas, and there are comfortable en suite bedrooms to stay in, most of which have sea views and come with a range of home comforts, including Wi-fi. In fine weather, the patio garden overlooking the sea is the perfect place to bask in the sun with a smoothie or freshly ground mid-morning coffee and home-baked pastry, or to enjoy a pint and plate of your choice at lunchtime. Branscombe and O'Hanlons are among the real ale choices on offer, and over a dozen wines are served by the glass. Traditional English-style dishes vie with the specials board, where seafood from Brixham and Lyme Bay, and prime meats from West Country farms will be found. The head chef and his team aim to produce dishes that will suit all tastes: potted crab, crispy duck confit and home-made banoffee pie are typical examples. If just a snack is required, sandwiches, pizzas and Devon cream teas are among the options.

Recommended in the area

Jurassic Coast; Crealy Great Adventure Parks; Exeter Cathedral

The Tower Inn

Address: Church Road, SLAPTON, Kingsbridge,
TQ7 2PN
Tel: 01548 580216
Email: towerinn@slapton.org
Website: www.thetowerinn.com
Map ref: 2, SX84
Directions: Off A379 S of Dartmouth, turn left at
Slapton Sands
Open: 12–2.30 6–11 (Sun 7–10.30) ᕒ **L** 12–2.30
D 6–9 ᵀᴏ̵ **L** 12–2.30 **D** 6–9 **Closed:** Mon lunch
winter **Facilities:** Garden Parking **Notes:** ⊕ Free House ♙ ♖ ♟ 8

The Tower is a 14th-century inn set in the historic village of Slapton in Devon's lovely South Hams region. Its name comes from the ruined tower overlooking the pub's walled garden, which is all that remains of the Collegiate Chantry of St Mary, founded by Guy de Brian in 1373. Indeed, the inn may have been the college's guest house, beginning a centuries old tradition of hospitality. The approach to the inn is by a narrow lane and through the porch into a fascinating series of interconnecting rooms, with stone walls, beams, pillars and pews, flagstone floors, scrubbed oak tables and log fires. There's an excellent range of traditional beers, augmented by local cider and mulled wine in winter, and the wine list includes Old and New World wines. Food is available at lunchtime, ranging from sandwiches to full meals, and a separate evening menu is served by candlelight. Try the locally caught seafood platter or winter warmers of pheasant and caramelised pear, followed with a selection of home-made desserts, including the famous sticky toffee pudding. All of the food is sourced locally where at all possible, with a number of the suppliers being patrons themselves. The bedrooms, in a self-contained wing, have tea- and coffee-making facilities and TV. Dogs are allowed (water and biscuits provided).

Recommended in the area

Slapton Sands; Slapton Ley Nature Reserve; Cookworthy Museum of Rural Life

The Kings Arms Inn

Address: STOCKLAND, Nr Honiton, EX14 9BS
Tel: 01404 881361
Fax: 01404 881387
Email: info@thekingsarmsinn.org.uk
Website: www.thekingsarmsinn.org.uk
Map ref: 2, ST20
Directions: Off A30 to Chard, 6m NE of Honiton
Open: 12–3 6.30–11.30 ⓑ L 12–2 D 6.30–9
⑂ L 12–2 D 6.30–9 Closed: 25 Dec
Facilities: Garden Parking
Notes: ⊞ Free House ⑂⑂⑂ 15

Tucked away in the Blackdown Hills, this Grade II listed, thatched and whitewashed inn dates from the 16th century and has an impressive flagstone entrance, a medieval oak screen and an original bread oven. Local real ales are served and a good choice of food is offered, including exotic choices such as ostrich and squirrel fish. More cautious diners will be glad to find dishes like steak and kidney pie, tournedos Rossini, salmon hollandaise; plus vegetarian options. Three en suite guest rooms available.

Recommended in the area

Crealy Adventure Park; Jurassic Coast World Heritage Site; Bicton

---

Kings Arms

◎

Address: Dartmouth Road, STRETE, TQ6 0RW
Tel: 01803 770377
Fax: 01803 771008
Email: kingsarms_devon_fish@hotmail.com
Website: www.kingsarms-dartmouth.co.uk
Map ref: 2, SX84
Directions: On A379, 5m from Dartmouth
Open: 11.30–2.30 6.30–11 (Sun 12–3, 7–10.30)
ⓑ L 12–2 D 6.30–9 ⑂ L 12–2 D 6.30–9
Facilities: Garden Parking Notes: ⊞⑂⑂⑂ 15

When entering the only pub in the village, remember to stop and admire the intricate wrought-ironwork outside – it's quite delightful. Customers may eat in the terracotta-walled bar, with its old photographs, or in the contemporary dining room, enlivened by specially commissioned art. Menus are based around local and regional produce, with seafood playing a big part, including River Yealm oysters, grilled fillets of red mullet, and seared hand-dived scallops on braised Puy lentils with sherry dressing.

Recommended in the area

South West Coast Path; Woodlands Park; Dartmoor National Park

The Golden Lion Inn

Address: TIPTON ST JOHN, Sidmouth, EX10 0AA
Tel: 01404 812881
Email: info@goldenliontipton.co.uk
Website: www.goldenliontipton.co.uk
Map ref: 2, SY09
Open: 12–2.30 6–11 (Sat 12–3, Sun 12–3, 7–11)
🍴 L 12–2 D 6.30–8.30 🍽️ L 12–2 D 6.30–8.30
Closed: Sun eve (Sep–Mar) **Facilities:** Garden
Parking **Notes:** ⊕ 🍷 10

This inviting village pub, run by a French/Cornish husband-and-wife team, has a pleasingly eclectic decor, with art deco prints sitting alongside Tiffany lamps and paintings by Cornish artists. Yet it maintains its traditional atmosphere thanks to low wooden beams, stone walls and a log fire. The food is equally pleasing, combining rustic Mediterranean and British cuisine as seen in dishes such as pork tenderloin with prunes and Armagnac. Daily specials might include fresh fish and seafood landed at nearby Sidmouth or braised oxtail. Vegetarians have plenty to choose from, and there's a lighter lunch menu too, again based on good, local produce.

Recommended in the area

Bicton Park and Gardens; Sidmouth Regency town; Ottery St Mary Church

The Durant Arms

★★★★ 🛏️ INN
Address: Ashprington, TOTNES, TQ9 7UP
Tel: 01803 732240
Website: www.thedurantarms.com
Map ref: 2, SX86
Directions: Exit A38 at Totnes junct, to Dartington & Totnes, at 1st lights right for Knightsbridge on A381, in 1m left for Ashprington
Open: 11.30–2.30 6.30–11 🍴 L 12–2.30
D 7–9.15 🍽️ L 12–2 D 7–9.15
Rooms: 8 en suite (2 GF) **S** £50 **D** £80 **Facilities:** Garden Parking
Notes: ⊕ Free House 👥 🍷 8

A locally renowned dining pub set in a pretty South Hams village, the Durant Arms dates from the 18th century and was originally the counting house for the neighbouring 500-acre Sharpham Estate. Sharpham wines and cheese are among the culinary delights, offered alongside a choice of real ales and dishes cooked to order, using local produce where possible.

Recommended in the area

Sharpham Vineyard & Cheese Dairy; Elizabethan town of Totnes; River Dart

The White Hart

Address: Dartington Hall, TOTNES, TQ9 6EL
Tel: 01803 847111
Fax: 01803 847107
Website: www.dartingtonhall.com
Map ref: 2, SX86
Directions: From Totnes on A38 to Plymouth, approx 4m
Open: 11–11 ⓑ L 12–2 D 6–9 ⓘ L 12–2 D 6–9
Closed: 24–29 Dec **Facilities:** Garden Parking
Notes: ⓑ Free House ⓘ ⓨ 8

The White Hart is tucked away in the corner of the courtyard of 'the most spectacular mansion in Devon', the 14th-century Dartington Hall, famed for its advancement of the arts. Surrounding it are landscaped gardens, rolling farmland, an ancient deer park and woodland, through which the River Dart heads for Totnes and the sea. In the informal bar chunky beams, flagstone floors and log fires are balanced by light-oak furniture to create a stylish blend of old and new, while the restaurant, originally the hall's kitchen, retains its medieval architecture, original tapestry and huge fireplace. Here, you'll discover a menu prepared with diligently sourced, ethically produced ingredients from South Devon, even from the estate itself, such as single-suckled beef, grass-reared lamb, and additive-free and free-range chickens and eggs. Fish is sourced daily at the local fish market and interesting local cheeses come from speciality makers. Featuring might be Dartington beefburger, caramelised onions and melted Cheddar served with French fries and salad; local mussels cooked with curried leeks, cream and coriander; and aubergine, spinach and chickpea tagine with lemon-minted couscous. Overnight guests can wake to birdsong and views of the South Devon countryside. Walks wind through the gardens and along the Dart.

Recommended in the area

Dartington Cider Press Centre; South Devon Heritage Coast; Dartmoor National Park

The Digger's Rest

Address: WOODBURY SALTERTON,
          EX5 1PQ
Tel: 01395 232375
Fax: 01395 232711
Email: bar@diggersrest.co.uk
Website: www.diggersrest.co.uk
Map ref: 2, SY08
Directions: 2.5m from A3052. Signed from Westpoint
Open: 11–3 6–11 (All day Sat–Sun & in summer)
🍴 L 12–2 D 6.30–9.30 🍽 L 12–2 D 6.30–9.30
Facilities: Garden Parking Notes: ⊕ Free House ☕ 13

Originally a Devon cider house, this 500-year-old building has thick walls of stone and cob with heavy beams under a thatched roof. Whether you're after a drink by the fire or a relaxed meal, the Digger's Rest provides a perfect country pub ambiance, full of character. Real ales are available on tap, alongside fine wines from a local merchant and Italian Fairtrade coffee. A great deal of care is shown in sourcing top quality West Country and English produce for the freshly prepared dishes. The menu and specials board offer pub classics, including nice nibbles (olives, hummus, breads); West Country steaks, hung for a minimum of 21 days, and a good choice of fish and vegetarian dishes. With the Digger's Rest's one-hour lunch promise you can be assured of good food promptly served to fit into your schedule. Highchairs and baby changing facilities are provided, and there's a children's menu of proper food that kids actually like, from Marmite sandwiches to organic sausages or fresh cod in batter with chips. A meeting room with full facilities (flipchart, wireless broadband, datacoms/telephone lines, fax and photocopier) is available for parties of 12–20, and can also be hired for private and family functions.

Recommended in the area

Jurassic Coast; Powderham Castle; Fairlynch Museum

Hengistbury Head

Shave Cross Inn

★★★★★ ➠ INN

Address: Shave Cross, Marshwood Vale,
BRIDPORT, DT6 6HW
Tel: 01308 868358
Fax: 01308 867064
Email: roy.warburton@virgin.net
Website: www.theshavecrossinn.co.uk
Map ref: 2, SY49
Directions: From Bridport take B3162, 2m left
signed 'Broadoak/Shave Cross' then Marshwood

Open: 11–3 6–11 (All day Tue–Sun in Summer & BH Mons) ♨ L 12–2.30 D 5–9.30 ⊙ L 12–2.30
D 7–9.30 **Closed:** Mon (ex BHs) **Rooms:** 7 en suite (3 GF) **Facilities:** Garden Parking
Notes: ⊕ Free House ♦♦ ⌂ ♚ 8

The name of this friendly, family-run pub goes back to the 13th century, when pilgrims and monks
on their way to the church of St Candida and St Cross in nearby Whitchurch Canonicorum would stop
here for a quick haircut. Tucked away down narrow lanes, time seems to stand still here, though
the Caribbean-inspired cooking might surprise: owners Roy and Mel Warburton spent a long time in
Tobago, and on returning they brought with them their head chef, who adds authentically Caribbean
touches to the menu. Examples include roast Creole duck with cherry compote, and Dorset prime fillet
steak with a rum, brandy and Caribbean peppercorn sauce. Fans of traditional British food won't be
disappointed, though, with battered haddock or cheese ploughman's, while local beers come from
Quay Brewery in Weymouth and Devon's Branscombe Vale. The garden has a play area and a thatched
wishing well. In addition, the inn houses the oldest thatched skittle alley in the country, and maintains
such traditions as Morris dancing. Luxurious en suite rooms are available, including four-poster beds.
Recommended in the area
Chesil Beach; Jurassic Coast World Heritage Site; Lyme Regis

Stapleton Arms

Address: Church Hill, BUCKHORN WESTON,
SP8 5HS
Tel: 01963 370396
Email: relax@thestapletonarms.com
Website: www.thestapletonarms.com
Map ref: 2, ST72
Directions: 3.5m from Wincanton in village centre
Open: 11–3 6–11 (Sat–Sun 11–11) ♿ L 12–3
D 6–10 ⅼ⊙ℓ L 12–3 D 6–10 **Facilities:** Garden
Parking **Notes:** ⊕ ⅰⅰ 🐾 ♟ 12

At this stylish country pub you can relax by the fire or in the sunny garden to enjoy hand-pumped ales and farm ciders on draught; or book a table in the elegant dining room to feast on locally sourced food, crafted into such innovative dishes as pan-fried Dorset red mullet with tiger prawn and coriander green curry, or perhaps local venison with root mash and rosemary sauce. There's also a selection of tapas and an interesting wine list. It's well worth planning to stay overnight in one of the individually designed bedrooms, with a mix of contemporary and antique furnishings and state-of-the-art bathrooms.

Recommended in the area

Wincanton Racecourse; Stourhead (NT); Longleat

The Anchor Inn

Address: High Street, BURTON BRADSTOCK,
DT6 4QF
Tel: 01308 897228
Email: info@dorset-seafood-restaurant.co.uk
Website: www.dorset-seafood-restaurant.co.uk
Map ref: 2, SY48
Directions: 2m SE of Bridport on B3157
Open: 11–11 (Sun 12–10.30) ♿ L 12–2 D 6–9
ⅼ⊙ℓ L 12–2 D 6–9 **Facilities:** Parking
Notes: ⊕ PUNCH TAVERNS ⅰⅰ ♟ 10

A 300-year-old coaching inn just inland from a stretch of the Jurassic Coast World Heritage Site, and near the amazing shingle feature known as Chesil Beach. In keeping with its name, the pub is full of marine memorabilia, fishing tools and shellfish adorn the walls. The house speciality is seafood, and there are 20 main fish courses on offer, plus Catch of the Day specials. Look out for fillet of brill stuffed with local crab; red bream and red mullet grilled with Cajun seasoning; and lobster Thermidor. Meat dishes include Barbary duck; beef Stroganoff; peppered pork fillet; and fillet steak Rossini.

Recommended in the area

Coastline from Chesil Beach to Lyme Regis; West Bay Harbour; Abbotsbury Sub-Tropical Gardens

Ruins of Corfe Castle

The Cock & Bottle

Address: EAST MORDEN, Wareham, BH20 7DL
Tel: 01929 459238
Map ref: 2, SY99
Directions: From A35 W of Poole turn right B3075, pub 0.5m on left
Open: 11–3 6–11 (Sun 12–3, 7–10.30) ⌷ L 12–2 D 6–9 ⌷ L 12–2 D 6–9 **Facilities:** Garden Parking
Notes: ⌷ HALL & WOODHOUSE ⌷ ⌷ ⌷ 6

From the outside, the brick façades of this pub conceal the fact that it is a cob-walled Dorset longhouse, built some 400 years ago – the brick skin was added around 1800. Inside it is as rustic and charming as one could hope for, with a plethora of nooks and crannies around the log fires. Outside, the pub has a paddock where vintage car rallies are occasionally hosted in summer. In addition to the popular locals' bar, there's a cosy lounge bar and an attractive restaurant extension. The kitchen produces an eclectic mix of traditional and inventive cooking, using local produce where possible: confit of potted pheasant could be followed by steamed sea bass fillets with Poole Bay mussel and saffron broth.

Recommended in the area

Monkey World; Farmer Palmer's Farm; Bovington Tank Museum

The Acorn Inn

★★★★ ◉ INN

Address: EVERSHOT, Dorchester, DT2 0JW
Tel: 01935 83228
Fax: 01935 83707
Email: stay@acorn-inn.co.uk
Website: www.acorn-inn.co.uk
Map ref: 2, ST25
Directions: A303 to Yeovil, Dorchester Rd, on A37
right to Evershot
Open: 11–11 L 12–2 D 7–9 L 12–2 D 7–9
Rooms: 10 en suite Facilities: Garden Parking Notes: ⊞ Free House 11

Thomas Hardy immortalised this 16th-century stone-built inn as the Sow and Acorn in *Tess of the d'Urbervilles*, and the carefully restored building stands in the pretty village of Evershot (Hardy's Evershead), in a designated Area of Outstanding Natural Beauty. It is thought that the notorious 'Hanging Judge' Jeffreys used the Grand Hall – now the stylish Hardy Restaurant – as a court house, while a skittle alley occupies the former stables. There are two oak-panelled bars, one with a flagstone floor and the other tiled, and log fires blaze in carved Hamstone fireplaces. Meals and drinks can be taken outside in the lawned gardens. Several of the bedrooms feature interesting four-poster beds, and two rooms are suitable for families. Rooms are equipped with satellite television and facilities for making hot drinks. Most of the inn's food is sourced within a 15-mile radius. Bar meals include hearty soups, open sandwiches and steak and ale pie, and go down well with a pint of Draymans ale. Typical dishes in the restaurant include a starter of pan-fried pigeon breasts with butternut squash and sage risotto, drizzled with red wine jus, and such main courses as roast fillet of beef, poached in red wine with thyme and garlic. Scallops, seabass and bream also feature among a decent selection of fish.

Recommended in the area

Mapperton House and Gardens; Jurassic Coast World Heritage Site; Dorchester

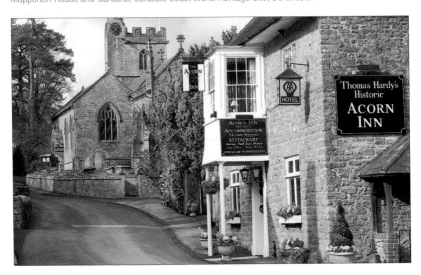

Fontmell and Melbury Downs

The Bottle Inn

Address: MARSHWOOD, Bridport, DT6 5QJ
Tel: 01297 678254
Fax: 01297 678739
Email: thebottleinn@msn.com
Website: www.thebottleinn.co.uk
Map ref: 2, SY39
Directions: On B3165 (Crewkerne to Lyme Regis)
Open: 12–3 6.30–11 ≞ L 12–2 D 6.30–9
Facilities: Garden Parking
Notes: ⊞ Free House ♦♦ ♟ 7

This thatched inn, first mentioned as an ale house in the 17th century, was the first pub in the area to serve bottled beer – hence the name. On the edge of Marshwood Vale, its rustic interior has simple wooden settles, scrubbed tables and a blazing fire. Landlord Rory MacLeod offers a good choice of food, from beef and ale pie to tagines, much of it with local and organic provenance. Taking the organic food theme to its furthest reaches, the pub is home to the annual World Stinging-Nettle Eating Championships, featured in the 2008 TV show *Rory and Paddy's Great British Adventure*.
Recommended in the area
Lyme Regis; Jurassic Coast World Heritage Site; Forde Abbey

The Cricketers

Address: SHROTON OR IWERNE COURTNEY,
Blandford Forum, DT11 8QD
Tel: 01258 860421
Fax: 01258 861800
Email: cricketers@heartstoneinns.co.uk
Website: heartstoneinns.co.uk
Map ref: 2, ST81
Directions: 7m S of Shaftesbury on A350, turn right after
Iwerne Minster. 5m N of Blandford Forum on A360, past
Stourpaine, in 2m left into Shroton. Pub in village centre
Open: 12–3 6–11 ⓑ L 12–2.30 D 6.30–9.30
🍴◎ L 12–2.30 D 6.30–9.30
Facilities: Garden Parking **Notes:** 🛢 Free House ⁑ 🍷 10

The Cricketers lies at the foot of Hambledon Hill in the heart of the beautiful Dorset countryside, with The Wessex Ridgeway nearby. At The Cricketers you will find great pub food, a selection of real ales, and a warm welcome from hosts Andy and Natasha and their team. Daily deliveries of fresh fish, meat and local produce, combined with a choice of well kept real ales, mean that The Cricketers is the perfect choice for food or just to enjoy a quiet pint. Although proud of their food, The Cricketers is a real village pub and customers are equally welcome to drop by for a pint of real ale or a glass of wine. The pub lies between the cricket pitch and the village green. A right of way passes through the pub garden which provides a delightful spot for weary walkers to take refreshment. Andy and Natasha are proud of their long association with Shroton Cricket Club from which the pub takes its name. (The club celebrated its 150th anniversary in 2007.)

Recommended in the area

Cavalcade of Costume Museum; Gold Hill Museum and Garden; Royal Signals Museum

Castle Hedingham

Axe & Compasses

Address: High St, ARKESDEN, CB11 4EX
Tel: 01799 550272
Fax: 01799 550906
Map ref: 4, TL43
Directions: From Buntingford take B1038 towards Newport. Then left for Arkesden
Open: 11.30–2.30 6–11 ﹩ L 12–2 D 6.45–9.30
🍴 L 12–2 D 6.45–9.30 **Facilities:** Garden Parking
Notes: ⊕ GREENE KING ♟ 14

Picture postcard perfect, this historic inn is located in the narrow main street of a captivating village. A stream called Wicken Water runs alongside, criss-crossed by footbridges leading to white, cream and pink colour-washed thatched cottages. The central section of the inn – the thatched part – dates from approximately 1650, but the building has since been extended to utilise the old stable block, which accommodated horses until the 1920s, and into a 19th-century addition that now houses the public bar. The beamed interior is full of character and includes the welcoming bar, a comfortable and softly lit restaurant, and a cosy lounge furnished with antiques, and displaying horse brasses and old agricultural implements. During winter there may well be a warming fire blazing in the hearth, and in summer there is further seating outside on the patio. Beer lovers will enjoy the real ales on tap, which include Greene King IPA, Abbot Ale and Old Speckled Hen. For those who prefer the juice of the vine, there is a wine list that's split almost evenly between France and the rest of the world. The restaurant offers a full carte, while an extensive blackboard menu is available in either the lounge or bar. Dishes range from an authentic moussaka on the bar menu to a restaurant dish of beef fillet served with pâté on a Madeira and red wine sauce with horseradish mash quenelles.

Recommended in the area

Audley End House and Gardens; Imperial War Museum Duxford; Mountfitchet Castle

The Green Dragon at Young's End

Address: Upper London Road, Young's End,
BRAINTREE, CM77 8QN
Tel: 01245 361030
Fax: 01245 362575
Email: info@thegreendragonyoungsend.co.uk
Website: www.thegreendragonyoungsend.co.uk
Map ref: 4, TL72
Directions: At Braintree bypass take A131 S towards
Chelmsford, exit at Youngs End on Great Leighs
bypass

Open: 12–3 5.30–11 (Sun–BHs 12–11) 🍴 L 12–2.30 D 6.30–9.30 🍽 L 12–2.15 D 6–9.30
Facilities: Garden Parking **Notes:** 🍺 GREENE KING 🍷 10

The Green Dragon is a comfortable venue for eating and drinking. As well as a wide range of ales,
international lagers and fine wines, it provides good facilities, including cosy bar areas with relaxed
seating, winter fires, exposed beams and traditional furnishings. Outside, the large garden is a great
place to enjoy a drink or a meal in summer, and there's a heated patio area if it turns chilly; inside,
Great Leigh's Room, with its leather sofas and low-level lighting, is the ideal place to relax and soak
up the warm ambience. For an extensive menu of well-cooked, simple food, the barn and hayloft
restaurants provide plenty of space, and maintain the rustic theme with bare brick walls and more old
beams. Full meals and light snacks are available throughout, including blackboard specials; tempting
choices are game in season and excellent dishes such as Gloucester Old Spot pork. Seafood is a real
speciality here, from oysters, dressed crab and moules marinière to halibut steak with prawns and lime
and lemon butter. Vegetarian options are also available and there's a children's menu with imaginative
choices such as planet spaghetti. On Sunday, a traditional lunch offers a choice of farmhouse meats.
Recommended in the area
Great Leigh's Racecourse; Audley End House and Gardens; Mountfitchet Castle and Norman Village

The Swan at Felsted

Address: Station Road, FELSTED, Dunmow,
CM6 3DG
Tel: 01371 820245
Fax: 01371 821393
Email: info@theswanatfelsted.co.uk
Website: www.theswanatfelsted.co.uk
Map ref: 4, TL62
Directions: Exit M11 junct 8 onto A120 signed Felsted. Pub in village centre
Open: 11–11(Sun 12–4) 🍴 L 12–3 D 6–10 🍴 L 12–3 D 6–10
Facilities: Garden Parking **Notes:** ⊕ GREENE KING 🚻 🅿 🍷 9

Ideally situated for exploring the pretty north Essex countryside, and only a short drive from Stansted Airport, the Swan is an imposing building and was for many years the village bank. It was rebuilt after a disastrous fire in the early 20th century, and the interior decoration has a fresh, contemporary feel. A pretty courtyard garden to the rear provides a tranquil, sheltered eating area overlooked by the village church, and during winter a roaring log fire greets guests as they cross the threshold. The kitchen has a great commitment to quality local produce, with dishes ranging from beer battered fish and chips or Swan bacon and cheese burger to game and Guinness casserole with dumplings and roast root vegetables, or pan-fried monkfish wrapped in Parma ham on sautéed new potatoes, with pak choi and spiced coconut cream. Fine wines, including a good selection by the glass, and well-kept cask ales also help to achieve a fine balance between the traditional English pub and a high quality restaurant. A stylish function room with its own entrance and bespoke menus is available for private parties of up to 20 people.

Recommended in the area

Hatfield Forest National Nature Reserve; Mountfitchet Castle Experience; Paycockes House

Colne Valley Country Park, Hedingham

Bell Inn & Hill House

Address: High Road, HORNDON ON THE HILL,
SS17 8LD
Tel: 01375 642463
Fax: 01375 361611
Email: info@bell-inn.co.uk
Website: www.bell-inn.co.uk
Map ref: 4, TQ68
Directions: M25 junct 30/31 signed Thurrock
Open: 11–2.30 5.30–11 (Sun 12–4, 7–10.30)
 L 12–1.45 D 6.45–9.45 L 12–1.45
D 6.45–9.45 **Closed:** 25–26 Dec **Facilities:** Garden Parking **Notes:** Free House   16

When the present family acquired this coaching inn in 1938 it had no running water or electricity.
Today there are plenty of mod cons, but the restoration has retained such features as the courtyard
balcony where luggage was lifted from coach roofs. There's a good range of real ales, a lengthy wine
list, and dishes such as poached leg of lamb with olive polenta are among the intriguing food options.
Recommended in the area
Tilbury Fort; Hadleigh Castle; Southend Museum, Planetarium and Discovery Centre

The Compasses at Pattiswick

Address: Compasses Road, PATTISWICK, Braintree, CM77 8BG
Tel: 01376 561322
Fax: 01376 564343
Email: info@thecompassesatpattiswick.co.uk
Website: www.thecompassesatpattiswick.co.uk
Map ref: 4, TL82
Directions: From Braintree take A120 E towards Colchester. After Bradwell 1st left to Pattiswick
Open: 11–3 5–12 (all day Etr–Sep) L 12–2.45 D 6–9.30 L 12–2.45 D 6–9.45 **Facilities:** Garden Parking
Notes: Free House 12

Tucked away in delightful countryside, this renovated gastro-pub offers a contemporary take on country style, with a flagstone floor in the bar, an open fire and rustic furniture. The menu of light bar meals and à la carte dishes is packed with quality produce, including pheasant, partridge, venison and rabbit from the surrounding woods. Dishes range through fillets of sea bass, wilted spinach and parmentier potatoes; braised lamb shank with peppered mash and fine beans; and wild mushroom potato cakes with ruby chard and courgette salsa. Similarly, the children's menu concentrates on simple classics popular with younger guests. The balance between bar, restaurant and private dining room enables the Compasses to cater for any occasion, and it is popular with locals, walkers and cyclists as well as those willing to travel in search of quality. Outside, extensive patios offer separate areas allowing families a clear view of the children's play area, while locals can enjoy the glorious Pattiswick sunsets with a well-kept pint of Woodforde's Wherry, from Norfolk, or one of a range of local ales from Nethergate Brewery. Weekly changing guest ales range from St Austell's Tribute to Everards Tiger.

Recommended in the area

Paycockes House; Beth Chatto Gardens; Colchester Zoo

Farmington

The Kilkeney Inn

Address: Kilkeney, ANDOVERSFORD, Cheltenham, GL54 4LN
Tel: 01242 820341
Fax: 01242 820133
Website: www.kilkeneyinn.co.uk
Map ref: 3, SP01
Directions: On A436 1m W of Andoversford
Open: 11–3 5–11 ⓑ L 12–2.30 D 6.30–9
ⓘ L 12–2 D 6.30–9 **Facilities:** Garden Parking
Notes: ⓫ Free House ⓨ 9

With the rolling Cotswold landscape stretching away on all sides, the roads leading to this charming country dining pub can be an absolute pleasure to drive along. Some fine views may also be had from the front of the pub, and from the mature garden with bench seating at the rear. This site was once individual plots belonging to the terrace of mid-19th-century stone cottages lived in by agricultural workers and their families. Inside are fresh flowers, polished quarry tiles, twinkling lights illuminating the impressive display of wines, and a sparkling bar area with comfortable, colourful seats – resist if you can the temptation to sit down and relax! Looking around the bar you'll see pastel coloured walls complementing the abundant exposed beams and Cotswold stone. In the light and airy Conservatory Restaurant are wicker tables and chairs, and prints on the walls, just the place for lunch or dinner, especially on a warm day when the doors to the patio are open. Menus are likely to list beef pie topped with cheese mash, sea bass with crayfish and bacon butter, slow-roasted shoulder of lamb with thyme, fillet steak with grilled tomatoes, and leek and walnut tart with gruyère.

Recommended in the area

Cotswold Farm Park; Notgrove Long Barrow; Hales Owen Abbey

The Old Passage Inn

★★★★ ◎ ◎ 🏛 RESTAURANT WITH ROOMS
Address: Passage Road, ARLINGHAM, GL2 7JR
Tel: 01452 740547
Fax: 01452 741871
Email: oldpassage@ukonline.co.uk
Website: www.theoldpassage.com
Map ref: 2, SO82
Directions: 5m from A38 adjacent M5 junct 13
Open: 12–3 7–11 (closed Sun eve) 🍴 **L** 12–2 **D** 7–9.30
🍽 **L** 12–2 **D** 7–9.30 **Closed:** 25 Dec, Mon **Rooms:** 3 en suite
S £75–£130 **D** £95–£130 **Facilities:** Garden Parking
Notes: ⊕ Free House 🐾 🍷 14

The 'old passage' in the name refers to the ford and later ferry service that crossed the River Severn here. The rich harvest of salmon and elvers that once came from the river is now sadly depleted, but chef Mark Redwood's seafood menu features local, sustainable ingredients, such as freshwater crayfish, whenever possible. Fresh lobster from Pembrokeshire (sometimes from Cornwall) is always available from the tank, and freshly shucked oysters and Fruits de Mer are specialities. The simple but innovative menus often change daily to reflect what is available, but might include such dishes as roast tranche of turbot served with parsley new potatoes and hollandaise. The large dining room has a fresh and airy appeal, and in summer you can eat out on the garden terrace, with views across a bend in the river towards Newnham-on-Severn and the distant Forest of Dean. The three stunning en suite bedrooms enjoy the same views and enable guests to enjoy not only an exceptional breakfast, but also take full advantage of the excellent wine list at dinner, which includes plenty of half bottles and wines by the glass, and features wines from the Three Choirs Vineyard at Newent.

Recommended in the area

Wildfowl and Wetlands Trust, Slimbridge; Owlpen Manor; Berkeley Castle

Ruined priory and the tower of Gloucester Cathedral

The Queens Arms

Address: The Village, ASHLEWORTH, GL19 4HT
Tel: 01452 700395
Map ref: 10, SO82
Directions: From Gloucester N on A417 for 5m. At Hartpury, opposite Royal Exchange turn right at Broad St to Ashleworth. Pub 100yds past village green
Open: 12–3 7–11   L 12–2 D 7–9   L 12–2 D 7–9 **Closed:** 25–26 Dec & 1 Jan, Sun eve (ex BH wknds) **Facilities:** Garden Parking
Notes: Free House ☗ ☗ 14

South African-born Tony Burreddu and his wife Gill ran a Durban steakhouse before coming to England in 1995, viewing 250 pubs before settling on The Queens Arms. They believe the building dates from the 16th century, and although the Victorians left their mark, the original beams and iron fireplaces remain, and the interior is a treat. Two separate rooms make up the dining area, with regular pub food from a blackboard menu, and specials that might include roasted local partridge, pan-fried Gressingham duck breast with black cherry and kirsch sauce, and a couple of South African dishes.

Recommended in the area

Ashleworth Tithe Barn; Gloucester Docks and Museum; Slimbridge Wildfowl & Wetlands Trust

The Kings Head Inn

★★★★ INN

Address: The Green, BLEDINGTON, Chipping Norton, OX7 6XQ
Tel: 01608 658365
Fax: 01608 658902
Email: kingshead@orr-ewing.com
Website: www.kingsheadinn.net
Map ref: 3, SP22
Directions: On B4450 4m from Stow-on-the-Wold
Open: 11.30–3 6–11 (Wknds & BHs 12–11) L 12–2 D 7–9 L 12–2 D 7–9.30 **Closed:** 24–25 Dec **Rooms:** 12 en suite (3 GF) **Facilities:** Garden Parking **Notes:** Free House 8

This award-winning 16th-century inn is set off the village green, complete with a little brook and crossed by a rustic bridge. Much of the original building has survived complete with low ceilings, sturdy beams, flagstone floors, exposed stone walls and big open fireplaces. Solid oak furniture, and in the winter, warm roaring fires in the inglenook, result in that unmistakeable English country pub look. But this is no museum piece, and in recent years the pub has acquired considerable renown for its excellent beer, the quality of the food, its 12 comfortable rooms and a wine list with more than 40 bins. All of the food on the menu is prepared in-house and is organic and locally sourced as far as is practical. A meal could begin with tiger prawns cooked in lemongrass, ginger and garlic; home made duck spring roll with sweet chilli sauce; or chargrilled courgette, watercress and cous cous salad with harissa dressing. This might be followed by grilled mustard and herb chicken breast with purple sprouting broccoli and chorizo parmentier potatoes, chargrilled tuna steak with ginger and leek salad, or spicy green vegetable curry.

Recommended in the area

Blenheim Palace; Cotswold Wildlife Park; Hook Norton Brewery

Eight Bells

Address: Church Street, CHIPPING CAMPDEN,
GL55 6JG
Tel: 01386 840371
Fax: 01386 841669
Email: neilhargreaves@bellinn.fsnet.co.uk
Website: www.eightbellsinn.co.uk
Map ref: 3, SP13
Directions: 8m from Stratford-upon-Avon
Open: 12–11 ₺ L 12–2.30 D 6.30–9
🍴 L 12–2.30 D 6.30–9 Closed: 25 Dec
Facilities: Garden Notes: ⊕ Free House ♦♦ ♂ ♀ 8

This beautiful 14th-century Cotswold stone inn was built to house stonemasons working on the nearby church and to store the eight church bells. There is an atmospheric bar and a candlelit dining room with oak beams, open fires and a priest's hole. Traditional ales and ciders are served and there's a daily-changing menu of freshly prepared local food. Outside is a courtyard garden and a terrace where you are allowed to smoke.

Recommended in the area

The Cotswold Way; Hidcote Manor (NT); Stratford-upon-Avon

The Crown of Crucis

★★★★ 73% HOTEL
Address: Ampney Crucis, CIRENCESTER, GL7 5RS
Tel: 01285 851806
Fax: 01285 851735
Email: reception@thecrownofcrucis.co.uk
Website: www.thecrownofcrucis.co.uk
Map ref: 3, SP00
Directions: On A417 to Lechlade
Open: 10.30–11 ₺ L 12–10 D 12–10
🍴 L 12–2.30 D 7–9.30 Closed: 25 Dec

Rooms: 25 (13 GF) S £60–£89 D £80–£138 Facilities: Garden Parking Notes: ⊕ Free House ♦♦ ♂ ♀ 10

A beautiful South Cotswolds village not far from Cirencester is the setting for this 16th-century inn, overlooking the village cricket green, with the Ampney Brook running by. An extensive menu is offered alongside the real ales in the beamed bar, supplemented by blackboard specials. Alternatively you can dine more formally in the restaurant, where an innovative menu is prepared by a team of young chefs. Seats are available outside in the Mediterranean courtyard or riverside garden.

Recommended in the area

Cotswold Water Park; Corinium Museum; Westonbirt The National Arboretum

The Yew Tree

Address: Cliffords Mesne, NEWENT, GL18 1JS
Tel: 01531 820719
Fax: 01531 820912
Email: cass@yewtreeinn.com
Website: www.yewtreeinn.com
Map ref: 2, SO72
Directions: From Newent High Street follow signs to Cliffords Mesne. Pub at far end of village on road to Glasshouse.
Open: 12–2.30 6–11 (Sun 12–4) ≞ L 12–2 D 6–9
Closed: Mon all day, Tue lunch & Sun eve **Facilities:** Garden Parking **Notes:** ⊕ Free House ⅋ ㅅ 🍷 16

Originally a cider house, the Yew Tree is a pretty inn dating from the 16th century with traditional bars floored with quarry tiles and warmed by a crackling log fire. A good range of local cider and perry is still stocked, alongide Wye Valley Butty Bach, Wye Valley Best, Fuller's London Pride and Whittingtons Nine Lives ales. The inn is situated on the slopes of the National Trust's May Hill, and were you to climb to the 971ft summit you would be able to glimpse the bluish outlines of the Welsh Mountains, Malvern Hills and the River Severn. It is, naturally enough, a popular place with walkers in search of rest and refreshment, and there is plenty of hearty fare on offer. An appealing daily changing menu might include mussels in saffron and cider; chargrilled Gloucester Old Spot loin steak; and marmalade pudding with custard. Seasonal and local ingredients are used whenever possible – much from the owner's garden. The wine list is lengthy, detailed and entirely French, taking in the best of regional specialities. Look out for the cider and perry festival in March, and the in-house wine shop, which sells bottles imported from France under the name of Premier Crew wines.

Recommended in the area

Shambles Victorian Village; National Birds of Prey Centre; Eastnor Castle

The Tunnel House Inn

Address: COATES, Cirencester, GL7 6PW
Tel: 01285 770280
Fax: 01285 700040
Email: bookings@tunnelhouse.com
Website: www.tunnelhouse.com
Map ref: 2, SO90
Directions: From A433 (Cirencester–Tetbury) follow
signs to Coates, then 'Canal Tunnel & Inn'
Open: 11–3 6–11 (Open all day Fri–Sun)
🍺 L 12–2.15 D 6.45–9.15 ⏚ L 12–2.15
D 6.45–9.15 Facilities: Garden Parking Notes: ⊕ ⫯ 🐾

The Tunnel House Inn, steeped in history and enjoying a glorious rural location, is reached down a
bumpy track by Sapperton Tunnel on the Thames and Severn Canal. The garden is ideal for relaxing
with a drink or a meal, while log fires warm the welcoming bar in winter months. A children's play area
and spectacular local walks add to its popularity. The monthly-changing menu features good home-
cooked dishes such as Gloucester Old Spot sausages with mash, red onion marmalade and gravy.
Recommended in the area
Thames and Severn Canal; Westonbirt Arboretum; Corinium Museum, Cirencester

The Colesbourne Inn

Address: COLESBOURNE, Cheltenham, GL53 9NP
Tel: 01242 870376
Email: info@thecolesbourneinn.co.uk
Website: www.thecolesbourneinn.co.uk
Map ref: 3, SP01
Directions: Midway between Cirencester &
Cheltenham on A435
Open: 12–3 6–11 (Sat–Sun 12–11, Nov–Feb
12–11) 🍺 L 12–1.45 D 6–8.45 ⏚ L 12–1.45
D 6.30–8.45 Facilities: Garden Parking
Notes: ⊕ WADWORTH ⫯ 🐾 🍷 20

This handsome 19th-century stone coaching inn is set in the heart of the Cotswolds, midway between
Cheltenham and Cirencester. All the food is home made with ingredients sourced locally wherever
possible, and cooked to order by the owner/chef Richard Johnson, and his team. Diners can eat in
any one of four different areas, which include log fires and a magnificent terrace with stunning country
views. The bar serves a range of Wadworth ales, and has an extensive wine list.
Recommended in the area
Holst Birthplace Museum; National Waterways Museum; Cirencester

The Green Dragon Inn

★★★★ 🛏 INN

Address: Cockleford, COWLEY, Cheltenham,
GL53 9NW
Tel: 01242 870271
Fax: 01242 870171
Email: green-dragon@buccaneer.co.uk
Website: www.buccaneer.co.uk
Map ref: 2, SO91
Directions: Telephone for directions
Open: 11–11(Sun 12–10.30) 🛏 L 12–2.30 D 6–10
Rooms: 9 en suite (4 GF) S £70 D £95–£150
Facilities: Garden Parking **Notes:** ⊞ Free House ♦♦ 🛏 🍷 9

A handsome stone-built inn dating from the 17th century, the Green Dragon is located in the hamlet of Cockleford at the heart of the picturesque Cotswolds. It is a popular retreat for those who appreciate good food, fine wine and real ales. The fittings and furniture are the work of Robert Thompson, the Mouse Man of Kilburn (so-called for his trademark mouse) who lends his name to the Mouse Bar, with its stone-flagged floors, beamed ceilings and crackling log fires. Nine cottage-style, en suite bedrooms are available, including a suite. All rooms are equipped with direct dial telephones and colour televisions, and breakfast is included, along with the newspaper of your choice. The menu takes in lunchtime sandwiches, children's favourites, and starters/light meals such as smoked halibut on Thai marinated vegetable tagliatelle or Caesar salad. The daily specials board might offer local Cockleford trout with garlic and caper butter, or pavé of venison on sweet potato mash with a wild mushroom sauce. The choice of real ales includes Hook Norton, Directors, Butcombe and a monthly changing guest beer. Additional features are the heated dining terrace and the function room/skittle alley.
Recommended in the area
Holst Birthplace Museum; Gloucester Cathedral; Witcombe Roman Villa

The Inn at Fossebridge

★ ★ ★ ★ INN

Address: FOSSEBRIDGE, nr Cheltenham, GL54 3JS
Tel: 01285 720721
Fax: 01285 720793
Email: info@fossebridgeinn.co.uk
Website: www.fossebridgeinn.co.uk
Map ref: 3, SP01
Directions: From M4 junct 15, A419 towards
Cirencester, then A429 towards Stow. Pub approx
7m on left

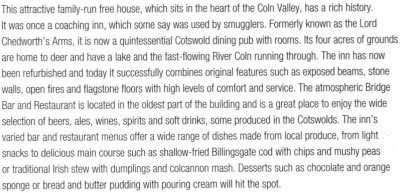

Open: 12–12 (Sun 12–11.30) 🍺 L 12–3 D 6–10 🍽 L 12–3 D 6–10 **Rooms:** 8 en suite
S £110–£130 **D** £135–£160 **Facilities:** Garden Parking **Notes:** ⊕ Free House 👫 🐕 🍷 8

This attractive family-run free house, which sits in the heart of the Coln Valley, has a rich history.
It was once a coaching inn, which some say was used by smugglers. Formerly known as the Lord
Chedworth's Arms, it is now a quintessential Cotswold dining pub with rooms. Its four acres of grounds
are home to deer and have a lake and the fast-flowing River Coln running through. The inn has now
been refurbished and today it successfully combines original features such as exposed beams, stone
walls, open fires and flagstone floors with high levels of comfort and service. The atmospheric Bridge
Bar and Restaurant is located in the oldest part of the building and is a great place to enjoy the wide
selection of beers, ales, wines, spirits and soft drinks, some produced in the Cotswolds. The inn's
varied bar and restaurant menus offer a wide range of dishes made from local produce, from light
snacks to delicious main course such as shallow-fried Billingsgate cod with chips and mushy peas
or traditional Irish stew with dumplings and colcannon mash. Desserts such as chocolate and orange
sponge or bread and butter pudding with pouring cream will hit the spot.

Recommended in the area

Chedworth Roman Villa (NT); Warwick Castle; Oxford

Sudeley Castle

The Britannia

Address: Cossack Square, NAILSWORTH, GL6 0DG
Tel: 01453 832501
Email: pheasantpluckers2003@yahoo.co.uk
Website: www.food-club.com
Map ref: 2, ST89
Directions: From A46 S'bound right at town centre rdbt. 1st left. Pub directly ahead
Open: 11–11 (Fri–Sat 11–12) ⓑ L 11–2.45 D 5.30–10 ⓞ L 11–2.45 D 5.30–10
Closed: 25 Dec **Facilities:** Garden Parking
Notes: ⓦ Free House ⓘ ⓡ ⓟ 10

This impressive 17th-century manor house occupies a delightful position. The open plan interior is bright and uncluttered with low ceilings, a blue slate floor and cosy fires, while outside there's a pretty garden with plenty of tables. Inside or out, a pint of well-kept London Pride or Abbot Ale is sure to go down well. The wine list is also worthy of attention. Modern British and continental food is offered on the brasserie-style menu, with ingredients from local suppliers and Smithfield Market.

Recommended in the area

Chavenage; Owlpen Manor; Woodchester Park (NT)

The Butchers Arms

Address: SHEEPSCOMBE, Nr Painswick, GL6 7RH
Tel: 01452 812113
Fax: 01452 814358
Email: mark@butchers-arms.co.uk
Website: www.butchers-arms.co.uk
Map ref: 2, SO81
Directions: 1.5m S of A46 (Cheltenham to Stroud Rd), N of Painswick
Open: 11.30–2.30 6.30–11.30 (Sat–Sun all day summer)   L 12–2.30 D 7–9.30   L 12–2.30 D 7–9.30 **Facilities:** Garden Parking **Notes:** Free House   10

The Butchers Arms dates from 1670 and remains a solid symbol of continuity at the centre of village life, with thick stone walls, mullioned windows and the famous carved inn sign, depicting a butcher sipping a pint of beer with a pig tied to his leg. The pub is set in the heart of *Cider with Rosie* country, in the beautiful Sheepscombe Valley, and author Laurie Lee, who lived in nearby Slad, was a regular visitor. The terraces and gardens afford magnificent views of the beech-wooded slopes, and the location, on the sunny side of the valley, is particularly sheltered. There is a passion for real ale here, with three classic ales permanently available. Stowford Press draught cider comes from family producers, Westons of Much Marcle, and among the many wines is a small selection from the nearby Strawberry Hill. The restaurant serves home-made fare, freshly prepared from local produce, including an extensive choice of fish and vegetarian dishes. The regular menu of pub food is supplemented by ever changing blackboard specials. Children are welcome, and can choose half portions from the main menu or from a selection of children's favourites.

Recommended in the area

Painswick Rococo Gardens; Prinknash Abbey; Prinknash Bird and Deer Park

The Swan at Southrop

Address: SOUTHROP, Nr Lechlade,
GL7 3NU
Tel: 01367 850205
Fax: 01367 850517
Map ref: 3, SP10
Directions: Off A361 between Lechlade & Burford
Open: 12–3 6–11 ⓫ L 12–3 D 6–10.30
⑩ L 12–3 D 6–10.30
Notes: ⊞ Free House ⫯ ⫟ ⚇ 10

A beautifully kept, foliage-covered, early 17th-century Cotswold inn on the village green. The interior is light and airy in summer, yet in the colder months, with log fires burning, you couldn't wish for a cosier place. In the quarry-tiled Snug, old Penguin paperbacks line the mantelpiece over the open fire, while in the restaurant modern art lines the white walls. Antony Worrall-Thompson protégé Sebastian Snow and his wife Lana relaunched the Swan in September 2008; he cooks 'turf to table' food, while Lana looks after front of house. Menus include a carte, a simpler bar menu and a weekend roast.

Recommended in the area

Bibury; Buscot Park; Cotswold Water Park

The Eagle and Child

★★★ 74% ⑳ ⑳ HOTEL
Address: STOW ON THE WOLD, GL54 1HY
Tel: 01451 830670
Fax: 01451 870048
Email: stay@theroyalisthotel.com
Website: www.theroyalisthotel.com
Map ref: 3, SP12
Directions: A429 from Moreton-in-Marsh rail station to Stow-on-the-Wold. At 2nd lights turn left onto Sheep St. (A436). 100yds on left

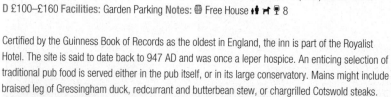

Open: 11–11 ⓫ L 12–2.30 D 6–9.30 ⑩ L 12–2.30 D 7–9.30 Rooms: 14 (2 GF) S £65–£110 D £100–£160 Facilities: Garden Parking Notes: ⊞ Free House ⫯ ⫟ ⚇ 8

Certified by the Guinness Book of Records as the oldest in England, the inn is part of the Royalist Hotel. The site is said to date back to 947 AD and was once a leper hospice. An enticing selection of traditional pub food is served either in the pub itself, or in its large conservatory. Mains might include braised leg of Gressingham duck, redcurrant and butterbean stew, or chargrilled Cotswold steaks.

Recommended in the area

Cotswold Farm Park; Cotswold Falconry Centre; Broadway

The Bear of Rodborough

★★★ 77% HOTEL

Address: Rodborough Common, STROUD, GL5 5DE
Tel: 01453 878522
Fax: 01453 872523
Email: info@bearofrodborough.co.uk
Website: www.cotswold-inns-hotels.co.uk/bear
Map ref: 2, SO80
Directions: From M5 junct 13 follow signs for
Stonehouse then Rodborough
Open: 10.30–11 ⓑ L 12–2.30 D 6.30–10
ⓘ D 7–9.30 Rooms: 46S £75–£105 D £120–£240 Facilities: Garden Parking
Notes: ⓦ Free House ⅰⅰ ⅰ ⅰ 6

Set at the top of a steep hill and surrounded by 300 acres of National Trust land, The Bear of Rodborough is situated in the historic south west corner of the Cotswolds. This 17th-century former coaching inn has 46 bedrooms and is worth seeking out for all sorts of reasons: comfortable accommodation, open log fires, stone walls and solid wooden floors, and provides a luxurious retreat where you can enjoy fine food and drink while relaxing in a homely, friendly atmosphere. The delightful Yorkstone terrace area and the walled croquet lawn and gardens provide the perfect spot for relaxing with friends or just catching the sun in the afternoon or on a warm summer's evening. The restaurant with its stone-arched dining room is a great setting for the contemporary English cuisine with strong traditional influences, which uses the finest fresh ingredients, many produced locally. The seasonal menu might include caramelised loin of Old Spot pork wrapped in Parma ham or roasted pumpkin and parmesan risotto. Enjoy fine traditional British ales in the Grizzly Bar, where there is an extensive menu if you wish to lunch or dine in a more relaxed atmosphere.

Recommended in the area

Owlpen Manor; Westonbirt Arboretum; Stroud House Gallery

Gumstool Inn

Address: Calcot Manor, TETBURY, GL8 8YJ
Tel: 01666 890391
Fax: 01666 890394
Email: reception@calcotmanor.co.uk
Website: www.calcotmanor.co.uk
Map ref: 2, ST89
Directions: 3m W of Tetbury
Open: 11.30–2.30 5.30–11 (Sat 11.30–11, Sun
12–10.30) ♿ L 12–2 D 5.30–9.30 ⓘ L 12–2
D 7–9.30 **Facilities:** Garden Parking
Notes: ⌨ Free House ♦♦ ♟ 12

The cheerful and cosy Gumstool is part of Calcot Manor Hotel, set in 220 acres of Cotswold countryside. The hotel is a successfully converted 14th-century stone farmhouse built by Cistercian monks, its ancient courtyard flower-filled. As a free house, Gumstool stocks a good selection of real ales, mostly from the West Country, and an excellent choice of wines. The food is top-notch – no wonder, as it comes from the same kitchen as its 'big sister', the hotel's Conservatory restaurant, meticulously supervised by Chef-Director Michael Croft. Monthly menus offer a good choice, with typical starters of devilled lambs' kidneys in a pastry case; crisp goats' cheese parcel with roasted beetroot salad; and twice-baked Arbroath smokie soufflé. Then perhaps beer-battered cod, chips and 'proper' tartare sauce; roasted pheasant with bacon, bread sauce and roasted root vegetables; or braised local lamb hotpot. Among the desserts are bread and butter pudding with clotted cream; baked toffee apple and nut cheesecake; and homemade sorbets and ice creams. There is a pretty sun terrace outside, while dark winter evenings are warmed with cosy log fires. The bedrooms, some in the original farmhouse, others in a converted old barn, all have luxurious en suite bathrooms.

Recommended in the area

Westonbirt Arboretum; Cotswold Water Park; Horton Court

The Farriers Arms

Address: Main Street, TODENHAM,
Moreton-in-Marsh, GL56 9PF
Tel: 01608 650901
Fax: 01608 650403
Email: info@farriersarms.com
Website: www.farriersarms.com
Map ref: 3, SP23
Directions: Right to Todenham at N end of Moreton-in-Marsh. 2.5m from Shipston-on-Stour
Open: 12–3 6.30–11 (Sun 7–10.30) ⓑ L 12–2
D 7–9 ⓘ L 12–2 D 7–9 **Facilities:** Garden Parking **Notes:** ⌗ Free House ⓘⓘ ⓘ ⓘ 11

Just three miles from Moreton-in-Marsh, stands this traditional Cotswold pub, next door to the old village smithy. The Farriers Arms dates from 1650 and has all the features you'd associate with a country local: a large inglenook fireplace, exposed stonework, beams, and horse brasses and cider flagons adorning the walls. Award-winning food is served in the bar and restaurant, which includes a secluded library area, and there's a great choice of real ales. For warmer days there is a patio garden.
Recommended in the area
Batsford Arboretum; Chastleton House; Cotswold Falconry Centre

The Old Fleece

Address: Bath Road, Rooksmoor, WOODCHESTER,
GL5 5NB
Tel: 01453 872582
Email: pheasantpluckers2003@yahoo.co.uk
Website: www.food-club.com
Map ref: 2, SO80
Directions: 2m S of Stroud on A46
Open: 11–11 ⓑ L 11–2.45 D 5.30–10
ⓘ L 11–2.45 D 5.30–10 **Closed:** 25 Dec
Facilities: Garden Parking
Notes: ⌗ PHEASANT PLUCKERS LTD ⓘⓘ ⓘ ⓘ 12

This is a delightful coaching inn, dating back to the 18th century and built of Cotswold stone with a traditional stone roof. The interior has had a complete makeover in the last couple of years, and the atmosphere has been enhanced with wooden floors, wood panelling and exposed stone. Predominantly French chefs prepare quality, freshly produced dishes and ingredients are sourced locally or directly. Main courses such as venison fillet with rich chocolate and balsamic sauce set the style.
Recommended in the area
Woodchester Park (NT); Owlpen Manor; Cotswold Way

Tatton Park

The Victoria

Address: Stamford Street, ALTRINCHAM, WA14 1EX
Tel: 0161 613 1855
Email: the.victoria@yahoo.co.uk
Map ref: 6, SJ78
Directions: Telephone for directions
Open: 12–11(Sun 12–6) ☕ L 12–3 D 5.30–9.30
🍽 L 12–3 D 5.30–9.30
Closed: 26 Dec & 1–2 Jan
Notes: ⊕ ♟ 9

Situated in the Stamford quarter of Altrincham, tucked away behind the main shopping street, the Victoria has been carefully restored as a traditional food-led tavern. This small, one-roomed pub now offers a wood-panelled dining area to one side, and a more casual bar area on the other. As well as the main menu, which changes every six to eight weeks according to seasonal availability and majors on locally sourced ingredients, there's a lighter lunch menu. Starters might include Morecambe Bay brown shrimp and battered prawn cocktail; Bury black pudding Scotch egg topped with locally smoked bacon; or Blacksticks Blue cheese and broad bean rice pudding. Among the main courses may be naturally raised Cumbrian pink veal and mushroom steamed pudding; and oven-roasted monkfish on a bed of pease pudding. On Sunday, a traditional roast is also available, usually including locally raised rib of beef. The wine list features over 30 carefully chosen bottles, while there are a range of hand-pulled cask ales, as well as many non-alcoholic drinks from the temperance bar, such as Dandelion and Burdock. The search is on for products no longer seen on menus, and future delights may include dishes such as tripe, smoked eel and pressed tongue.

Recommended in the area

Dunham Massey Hall Park and Garden (NT); Altrincham Market; Altrincham Ice Dome

The Metropolitan

Address: 2 Lapwing Lane, WEST DIDSBURY,
Manchester, M20 2WS
Tel: 0161 438 2332
Fax: 0161 282 6544
Email: info@the-metropolitan.co.uk
Website: www.the-metropolitan.co.uk
Map ref: 6, SJ89
Directions: M60 junct 5, A5103 turn right onto
Barlow Moor Rd, then left onto Burton Rd. Pub at the
x-rds. Right onto Lapwing Lane for car park

Open: 11.30–11 (Fri–Sat 11.30–12am) ⅙ L 12–6 D 6–7 ⅩⓄ L 12–6 D 6–9.30 **Closed:** 25 Dec
Facilities: Garden Parking **Notes:** ⊞ ⅋ 20

The Metropolitan, originally a Victorian railway hotel, is an architectural triumph, with decorative floor tiling, ornate windows, impressive roof timbering and delicate plasterwork. In the decade since it first opened its doors as a gastro-pub, the Met has grown with the community and provides the well-travelled residents with a local comparable to anything in the country. The imposing building comprises an eclectic collection of smaller spaces, each with its own identity; from the red room to the library, from the snug to the conservatory, there is a space to suit each and every visitor. The bar with its 20-metre span and 5-metre high wall of wines and malt whiskies, reached by means of a swinging ladder, is undoubtedly impressive, as is the al fresco bar, with cover, heaters and comfortable seating plus an attendant to look after your car. The food has gained national acclaim, and the beer's not bad either, with Timothy Taylor Landlord and Jennings Cumberland Ale among the favourites. Dishes range from 'famous' 100% prime beef burger topped with bacon, mature cheddar and red onion relish to baked whole sea bream stuffed with fresh herbs and garlic.

Recommended in the area

Fletcher Moss Gardens; People's History Museum; Manchester Art Gallery

HAMPSHIRE

Butser Hill

The Wellington Arms

Address: Baughurst Road, BAUGHURST, RG26 5LP
Tel: 0118 982 0110
Email: info@thewellingtonarms.com
Website: www.thewellingtonarms.com
Map ref: 3, SU56
Directions: M4 junct 12 follow Newbury signs on A4. At rdbt left to Aldermaston. At rdbt at top of hill 2nd exit, at T-junct left, pub 1m
Open: 12–2.30 6.30–9.30 ❧ L 12–2.30 D 6.30–9.30 **Closed:** Sun eve, Mon & Tue am **Facilities:** Garden Parking **Notes:** ⊕ PUNCH TAVERNS ♀ 12

An exceptionally pretty whitewashed building, The Wellington Arms is set amid well-tended gardens, surrounded by fields and woodland. This is Jason King and Simon Page's first venture in the pub trade and after three years their elegantly furnished dining room has a well-deserved reputation for its impressive daily changing menus and very good-value lunches. The board is chalked up daily with many of the pub's home-grown favourites; crispy fried pumpkin flowers stuffed with ricotta and parmesan on young leaves and lemon dressing; roast rack of home-reared pork with crackling on bashed parsnips and thyme with caramelised crabapples; wild elderflower and honey jelly with strawberries and thick cream. Further evidence of the commitment to quality are the pub's three Langstroth beehives, 110 free-range rare breed and rescue hens, four pedigree saddleback pigs, working herb and vegetable gardens, home-made jams, chutneys and pickles together with careful sourcing of organic and home-grown produce. Fish is delivered direct from the market in Brixham and English meat comes from Vicars family butchers in Reading.

Recommended in the area

The Vyne (NT); Basing House; Roman Silchester

The Red Lion

Address: Rope Hill, BOLDRE, Lymington, SO41 8NE
Tel: 01590 673177
Fax: 01590 674036
Website: www.theredlionboldre.co.uk
Map ref: 3, SZ39
Directions: M27 junct 1, A337 through Lyndhurst &
Brockenhurst towards Lymington, follow Boldre signs
Open: 11–3 5.30–11 (Sun 12–3.30, 6–10.30)
 L 12–2.30 D 6–9.30 L 12–2.30 D 6–9.30
Facilities: Garden Parking
Notes: Free House 18

There was a Domesday Book mention for this quintessential New Forest pub, although today's building
dates from the 15th century. Inside you'll find rambling beamed rooms packed with rural memorabilia.
Head chef Stuart Lancaster creates traditional dishes based around the bounty of the excellent local
produce, such as venison from Forest herds and fish from local catches. Begin with pan-fried black
pudding with caramelised apple, before home-made steak and Ringwood Ale pie. Booking is advisable.
Recommended in the area
Bucklers Hard; Hurst Castle; Beaulieu

The Bell Inn

★★★ 83% ◉ ◉ HOTEL
Address: BROOK, nr Lyndhurst, SO43 7HE
Tel: 023 8081 2214
Fax: 023 808 13958
Email: bell@bramshaw.co.uk
Website: www.bellinnbramshaw.co.uk
Map ref: 3, SU21
Directions: From M27 junct 1 (Cadnam) take
B3078 signed Brook, 0.5m on right
Open: 11–11 L 12–9.30 L 12–3

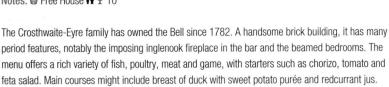

D 7.30–9.30 Rooms: 27 (8 GF) S £50–£80 D £90–£120 Facilities: Garden Parking
Notes: Free House 10

The Crosthwaite-Eyre family has owned the Bell since 1782. A handsome brick building, it has many
period features, notably the imposing inglenook fireplace in the bar and the beamed bedrooms. The
menu offers a rich variety of fish, poultry, meat and game, with starters such as chorizo, tomato and
feta salad. Main courses might include breast of duck with sweet potato purée and redcurrant jus.
Recommended in the area
New Forest National Park; National Motor Museum; Paulton's Park

The Hampshire at Crondall

Address: Pankridge Street, CRONDALL, GU10 5QU
Tel/Fax: 01252 850418
Email: info@thehampshireatcrondall.co.uk
Website: www.thehampshireatcrondall.co.uk
Map ref: 3, SU74
Directions: From M3 junct 5 take A287 S towards Farnham. Follow signs to Crondall on right
Open: All day **L** 12–2.30 **D** 6.30–9.30 (Sun 12–6.30)
Facilities: Garden Parking **Notes:** ⊕ GREENE KING ♦♦ ♟ 10

This notorious gastro-pub offers open fires, candelit dining and a menu that is frequently changing. An old 18th-century courthouse, the pub is set in the beautiful village of Crondall and has a warm and welcoming country atmosphere. The locals bar at the front is cosy, where you can enjoy a sandwich and a pint of real ale. Walking through to the restaurant area there are 40 covers in a traditional style and a separate snug for group bookings and private dining. The kitchen team prepare bread on site, smoke their own meats, and have their own sausage recipes, as well as offering pre-booked Victorian style feasting for groups. This country dining pub offers traditional fresh food at restaurant standards and specialises in seasonal game and local produce. Popping in you may see: haunch of venison, suckling pig, potted crab, saddle of hare and the occasional classic French influence appearing on the menu. Daily menus are posted online (Starters £5–7, Mains £10–20, Feasting menus £24–37). Feasting menus and private dining are available by booking in advance. From lighter dishes to fuller, richer flavours, the team are consistently competent. And with their flavour combinations and eye for detail, the overall experience is relaxed and very noteworthy. Their passion for food is matched by a wine list that is difficult to fault. You could easily lose a few hours here.

Recommended in the area

Birdworld; Winchester Cathedral; Jane Austen's House

New Forest National Park

The Chestnut Horse

Address: EASTON, Winchester, SO21 1EG
Tel: 01962 779257
Fax: 01962 779037
Website: www.thechestnuthorse.com
Map ref: 3, SU53
Directions: M3 junct 9, A33 towards Basingstoke, then B3047. 2nd right, then 1st left
Open: 11–3 5.30–11 (Sat all day, Winter Sun 11–6)
🍴 L 12–2.30 D 6–9.30 🍽 L 12–2.30 D 6–9.30
Facilities: Garden Parking
Notes: ⊕ HALL & WOODHOUSE 👫 🐕 🍷 9

This 16th-century dining pub has a well-earned local reputation for the quality of its food. Old tankards and teapots hang from the low-beamed ceilings in the two bar areas, where a large open fire is the central focus in winter. The candlelit restaurants are equally inviting: the light, panelled Green Room, and the darker low-beamed Red Room with a wood-burning stove. There's an excellent set price menu offering mains like lamb navarin with pomme purée, and seared salmon darne with red lentil dahl.

Recommended in the area

Winchester; New Forest National Park

The Bugle

Address: High Street, HAMBLE-LE-RICE, SO31 4HA
Tel: 023 8045 3000
Fax: 023 8045 3051
Email: manager@buglehamble.co.uk
Website: www.buglehamble.co.uk
Map ref: 3, SU40
Directions: M27 junct 8, follow Hamble signs. In village right at
mini-rdbt into one-way cobbled street, pub at end
Open: 11–11 (Fri–Sat 11–12, Sun 12–10.30) ▣ L 12–2.30
D 6–9.30 ▣ L 12–2.30 D 6–9.30 Notes: ⊕ ⋔ ♇ 8

Restored using traditional materials and methods, The Bugle is
at the heart of village life. The Grade II listed building features
natural flagstone floors, exposed beams and brickwork, a solid oak bar and real open fires. In addition
to the restaurant area, a private dining room, the Captain's Table, is available upstairs, accommodating
up to 12 guests. The seasonal menu is based on fresh, top quality ingredients, using local produce
wherever possible, with meals served alongside well-kept real ales, wines and speciality rums. The
menu offers a good range of bar bites such as home-made soup with crusty bread; salt and pepper
ribs with sweet chilli dip; and a half pint of prawns with Marie rose sauce. For something a bit more
substantial, the 'Classics' section offers beer-battered fish and chips with minted mushy peas; wild
mushroom and pea risotto; char-grilled Angus steak burger; and sirloin steak with Béarnaise sauce.
Fresh seafood and other home-made dishes are offered from the daily specials board, and there is
a tempting range of desserts. At weekends, The Bugle's brunches, all day breakfasts and traditional
roasts are popular, and once a month the Wine Club offers an evening of wine tastings and a two-
course meal. Dogs are allowed, except in the restaurant.

Recommended in the area

Hamble River boat trips; Royal Victoria Country Park; Netley Abbey

The Vine at Hannington

Address: HANNINGTON, Tadley, RG26 5TX
Tel: 01635 298525
Fax: 01635 298027
Email: info@thevineathannington.co.uk
Website: www.thevineathannington.co.uk
Map ref: 3, SU55
Directions: Hannington signed from A339 between Basingstoke & Newbury
Open: 12–3 6–11 (Sat–Sun all day) **Closed:** Sun eve in winter ♨ L 12–2 D 6–9 ⦿ L 12–2 D 6–9
Facilities: Garden Parking **Notes:** ⊞ ♦ ⌁ ⚑ 10

This traditional village pub sits high up on the beautiful Hampshire Downs – a delightful establishment where visitors can enjoy a warm welcome and delicious home-made food. The menu changes with the seasons and includes daily specials. Many of the ingredients come from the pub's own large garden, and typical dishes are mozzarella cheese and roasted vegetable crumble or locally reared Aberdeen Angus steak. From the specials board come roast pheasant and grilled skate wing.

Recommended in the area

Highclere Castle; The Wayfarers Walk; Milestones Museum, Basingstoke

The Running Horse

★★★★ ⊛ ⊛ INN
Address: 88 Main Road, LITTLETON, SO22 6QS
Tel: 01962 880218
Fax: 01962 886596
Email: runninghorseinn@btconnect.com
Website: www.runninghorseinn.co.uk
Map ref: 3, SU43
Directions: signed from Stockbridge Rd
Open: 11–3 5.30–11 ♨ L 12–2 D 6.30–9.30 ⦿ L 12–2 D 6.30–9.30
Rooms: 9 en suite (9 GF) **S** £65 **D** £85 **Facilities:** Garden Parking **Notes:** ⊞ ♦ ⌁ ⚑ 15

This pretty pub has a stylish interior, with warm modern decor blending well with traditional fixtures. The food has sophistication, too, with international influences in such dishes as pan-fried lamb's liver with wilted spinach, mash, and port and pancetta jus. You can eat informally in the bar, in the restaurant, or, in summer, on the outside terraces (the one at the rear overlooking the large garden). Bedrooms are elegant, with en suite bath or shower room, flat-screen TV and other home comforts.

Recommended in the area

Winchester; The South Downs; Mottisfont Abbey

Highcliffe Castle

The Black Swan

Address: High Street, MONXTON, SP11 8AW
Tel: 01264 710260
Fax: 01264 710961
Map ref: 3, SU34
Directions: Exit A303, at rdbt follow signs for Monxton, pub on main road
Open: 12–11 ⓑ L 12–2.30 D 6–9.30 ⓘ L 12–2.30 D 6–9.30 **Facilities:** Garden Parking
Notes: ⊕ ENTERPRISE INNS ♟ 🐾 ♟ 9

Passing through Monxton it is as if time hasn't touched the village, and a mixture of thatched and clay tiled buildings, some dating back to the 16th century, create a wonderful backdrop to this popular destination inn. The inn itself dates from at least 1662, and the restaurant was once the stables. This restaurant is rapidly earning itself a well-deserved reputation for its fine food, with quality and simplicity of flavours being the bywords in the kitchen. The menu is predominantly French/English with some New World influences, and the dishes change regularly. All the ingredients are locally sourced to ensure freshness and quality. Watch out for the monthly seafood nights.

Recommended in the area

Museum of Army Flying; Hawk Conservancy; Finkley Down Farm Park

The Bush

Address: OVINGTON, Alresford, SO24 0RE
Tel: 01962 732764
Fax: 01962 735130
Email: thebushinn@wadworth.co.uk
Website: www.wadworth.co.uk
Map ref: 3, SU53
Directions: A31 from Winchester, E to Alton &
Farnham, approx 6m turn left off dual carriageway to
Ovington. 0.5m to pub
Open: 11–3 6–11 (Sun 12–3, 7–10.30)

L 12–2.30 D 6.30–9.30 **Closed:** 25 Dec **Facilities:** Garden Parking **Notes:** ⊕ WADWORTH 🐾 ♀ 12

A rose-covered vision of a bygone age, The Bush is as delightful as it is hard to find, tucked away just off a meandering lane and overhung by trees. Once a refreshment stop on the Pilgrim's Way linking Winchester and Canterbury, these days the pub is more likely to attract walkers exploring the Itchen Way. A gentle riverside stroll along the Itchen, which flows past the pretty garden, will certainly set you up for a leisurely drink or a lingering meal. The pub's interior is dark and atmospheric; there's a central wooden bar, high backed seats and pews, stuffed animals on the wall and a real fire. Ales on offer include Wadworth 6X, IPA and Farmers Glory, JCB, Summersault, Old Timer and guest beers. The regularly-changing menu makes good use of local produce. Choices range from bar snacks, sandwiches and ploughman's lunches through to satisfying gastro-pub meals, taking in the likes of organic smoked trout mousse with warm toast, and slow-roasted belly pork on braised Savoy cabbage with organic cider jus. Finish with a traditional pudding such as Eton mess or rhubarb crumble. Not surprisingly, film crews love this location.

Recommended in the area

Avington Park; Winchester Cathedral; Mid-Hants Railway

The Rose & Thistle

Address: ROCKBOURNE, Fordingbridge, SP6 3NL
Tel: 01725 518236
Email: enquiries@roseandthistle.co.uk
Website: www.roseandthistle.co.uk
Map ref: 3, SU11
Directions: Follow Rockbourne signs from either A354 or from A338 at Fordingbridge
Open: 11–3 6–11 (Sun Oct–Apr closes at 8) ⓑ L 12–2.30 D 6.30–9.30 ⓘⓞⓘ L 12–2.30 D 6.30–9.30 **Facilities:** Garden Parking **Notes:** ⊕ Free House ⦙⦙ ♇ 18

Nestling in one of the most picturesque villages in the county, on the edge of the New Forest, the Rose & Thistle has everything you'd expect from the quintessential English pub: a tranquil setting, flowers around the door and a beautiful old building dating back to the 16th century. It has a welcoming low-ceilinged interior with oak beams and furniture, fresh flowers, magazines and an open fireplace. In summer, you can enjoy the delightful country garden. Well-kept real ales – Fuller's London Pride, Timothy Taylor Landlord and Palmers Copper Ale – are on offer, along with Scrumpy (cider), a carefully selected wine list and other drinks. Fresh seasonal food is cooked to order and includes fish such as skate, turbot and Cornish crab when available. The restaurant menu, available at lunch and dinner, offers dishes such as venison steak with sloe gin and blackberries, Gressingham duck with red onion marmalade, and tagliatelle with feta, spinach and sun blush tomatoes. Lighter lunch choices might include scrambled eggs with smoked salmon, locally-made pork and sausages with wholegrain mustard mash, and wild mushroom stroganoff; the Sunday lunch of rare roast sirloin of beef is also very popular. Desserts are all homemade – even the ice cream, which includes apple pie flavour.

Recommended in the area

Rockbourne Roman Villa and Trout Fishery; Breamore House; Salisbury

The Plough Inn

Address: Main Road, SPARSHOLT, Nr Winchester,
SO21 2NW
Tel: 01962 776353
Fax: 01962 776400
Map ref: 3, SU43
Directions: From Winchester take B3049 (A272) W,
left to Sparsholt, Inn 1m
Open: 11–3 6–11 (Sun 12–3, 6–10.30)
🍴 L 12–2 D 6–9 🍽 L 12–2 D 6–9 **Closed:** 25 Dec
Facilities: Garden Parking **Notes:** ⊕ WADWORTH ♦♦ 🐾 🍷 14

Set in beautiful countryside, just a stone's throw from
Winchester, this inn is a great place to refresh yourself after a
walk in the nearby Farley Mount Country Park. Owners Richard and Kathryn Crawford have a simple
philosophy: to serve customers with good quality food and drink in a friendly atmosphere. The Plough
was built about 200 years ago as a coach house for Sparsholt Manor, but within 50 years it had already
become an alehouse. Since then it has been much extended, yet from the inside it all blends together
very well, helped by the farmhouse-style furniture and the adornment with agricultural implements,
stone jars and dried hops. The Wadworth brewery supplies all of the real ales, and there's a good wine
selection. The left-hand dining area is served by a blackboard menu offering such light dishes as feta
and spinach filo parcels with a Thai pesto dressing or a beef, ale and mushroom pie with vegetables.
To the right, a separate board offers meals that reflect a more serious approach – perhaps breast of
chicken filled with mushrooms on a garlic and bacon sauce; lamb shank with braised red cabbage and
rosemary jus; and several fish dishes. Booking is always advisable.

Recommended in the area

Winchester Cathedral; Mottisfont Abbey (NT); Sir Harold Hillier Gardens and Arboretum

Carnarvon Arms

Address: Winchester Road, WHITWAY, Burghclere, Newbury RG20 9LE
Tel: 01635 278222
Fax: 01635 278444
Email: info@carnarvonarms.com
Website: www.carnarvonarms.com
Map ref: 3, SU45
Directions: Exit A34 at Tothill Services follow Highclere Castle signs, pub on right
Open: All day 🍺 L 12–2.30 🍽 L 12–2.30
D 6.30–9 **Facilities:** Garden Parking **Notes:** ⊞ MERCHANT INNS PLC 👫 🐾 🍷 15

This stylish country inn was built in the mid-1800s as a coaching inn for travellers to nearby Highclere Castle, which has been the home of the Earls of Carnarvon since the late 17th century. Now completely refurbished, the inn's interior strongly reflects its history, in particular its relationship with one of the 20th century's most famous archaeologists, the 5th Earl, who in 1922 discovered Tutankhamen's tomb in the Valley of the Kings. In the dining room, with its impressive vaulted ceiling, Egyptian-inspired wall motifs pay homage to his work; in the friendly bar rich leather upholstery is offset by natural colours. From his kitchen, executive chef Rob Clayton oversees modern British cooking interlaced with plenty of pub classics, all with a strong emphasis on local seasonal produce, and menus change accordingly. Examples of what to expect are pan-fried scallops with buttered samphire and herb fish cream, rump of English lamb with fine beans, sun-blushed tomatoes and rosemary sauce, and Mr Parsons' local sausages with mash and shallot sauce. The bedrooms offer home-from-home comfort, which here means wide-screen plasma TV, free Wi-fi, high quality toiletries and beverage-making facilities. Comfortable private rooms are available for business meetings, corporate events and private parties.

Recommended in the area

Newbury Races; Watermill Theatre; Kennet & Avon Canal

HEREFORDSHIRE

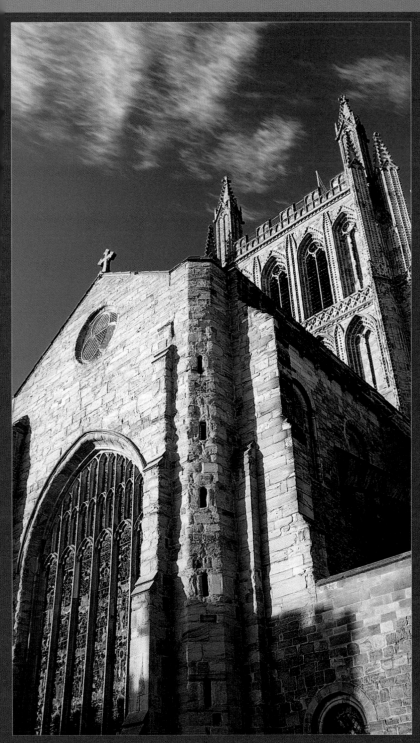

Hereford Cathedral

The Riverside Inn

Address: AYMESTREY, nr Leominster, HR6 9ST
Tel: 01568 708440
Fax: 01568 709058
Email: theriverside@btconnect.com
Website: www.theriversideinn.org
Map ref: 2, SO46
Directions: On A4110, 18m N of Hereford
Open: 11–3 6–11 Open all day in summer
L 12.30–2.15 D 7–9.15 L 12–2.15 D 7–9.15
Facilities: Garden Parking
Notes: Free House 7

Alongside the lovely River Lugg, overlooking an old stone bridge, this delightful black-and-white inn is surrounded by wooded hills and meadowland. Anglers will certainly appreciate the mile of private fly fishing for brown trout and grayling on the river here. It is located halfway along the Mortimer Way, making it great for walkers, too, and there are a number of circular walks in the vicinity. Walking packages are offered at the inn, with accommodation and free transport provided to and from the start/finish points. The interior of the building, with its low beams and log fires, provides a relaxing atmosphere, reflecting the 400 years of hospitality that have been carried out on this spot. Richard and Liz Gresko are the current hosts, who take a serious approach to food. Locally-grown produce is used wherever possible, including vegetables, salads and herbs from their own gardens, and home-made preserves. The type of cuisine here is English, but with a new and interesting twist. Real ales and ciders from local brewers match bar food specialities such as home-made steak and kidney pudding, while the restaurant menu might include a roasted haunch of local venison on sweet and sour red cabbage. On a summer's day, sit outside in the terraced and landscaped garden, watching the river flow by.

Recommended in the area

Hergest Croft Gardens; Berrington Hall, Ashton; Croft Castle

The Pandy Inn

Address: DORSTONE, Golden Valley, HR3 6AN
Tel: 01981 550273
Fax: 01981 550277
Email: magdalena@pandyinn.wanadoo.co.uk
Website: www.pandyinn.co.uk
Map ref: 2, SO34
Directions: Off B4348 W of Hereford
Open: 12–3 6–11 Closed: Mon (Oct–Jun)
L 12–3 D 6–9.30 L 12–3 D 6–11 Facilities:
Garden Parking Notes: Free House

In 1170 Richard de Brito assisted in the murder of Thomas à Becket in Canterbury Cathedral. To atone for this terrible deed, he erected a chapel at Dorstone and for its builders what is now The Pandy. Today's visitors walk on the same flagstone floors as Oliver Cromwell did when he took refuge here during the Civil War. Cask ales and farmhouse cider come from local small producers, just as food products do for Pandy pies, lamb shank with red wine and redcurrant sauce, Hungarian goulash, fish and vegetarian dishes, home-made puddings, and baguettes. The garden has views of Dorstone Hill.

Recommended in the area

Arthur's Stone; Hay-on-Wye; Black Mountains

Stockton Cross Inn

Address: KIMBOLTON, Leominster, HR6 0HD
Tel: 01568 612509
Email: info@stocktoncrossinn.co.uk
Website: www.stocktoncrossinn.co.uk
Map ref: 2, SO56
Directions: On A4112, 0.5m off A49, between
Leominster & Ludlow
Open: 12–3 7–11 L 12–2.15 D 7–9
L 12–2.15 D 7–9 Closed: Sun & Mon eve
Facilities: Garden Parking
Notes: Free House

Stockton Cross is a 16th-century drovers' inn with real log fires, its picturesque black and white exterior regularly photographed by tourists and for calendars etc. Its peace and beauty are belied by the historical fact that alleged witches were once hanged here. There is a serious interest in good food, with much produce locally sourced to provide an interesting and varied menu. The relaxed and friendly atmosphere, real ales and fine wines add to the charm, and there is also a pretty country garden.

Recommended in the area

Hergest Croft Gardens; Croft Castle; Berrington Hall (NT)

Leintwardine's Church of St Mary Magdalene

The Stagg Inn and Restaurant

◈ ◈

Address: Titley, KINGTON, HR5 3RL
Tel: 01544 230221
Email: reservations@thestagg.co.uk
Website: www.thestagg.co.uk
Map ref: 2, SO25
Directions: Between Kington & Presteigne on B4355
Open: 12–3 6.30–11 ♨ **L** 12–2 **D** 6.30–9
⍟ **L** 12–2 **D** 6.30–9 **Closed:** Sun eve & Mon
Facilities: Garden Parking
Notes: ⊞ Free House ♞ ♟ 10

A popular gastro-pub surrounded by lovely countryside, the Stagg is part medieval and part Victorian with later additions. The decor has an authentic feel, with local stone and furniture from the area's antique markets. A collection of 200 jugs adorns the bar, and there are three additional dining rooms. Chef patron Steve Reynolds makes great use of locally sourced ingredients in dishes such as pigeon breast on herb risotto, and saddle of venison with horseradish gnocchi and kummel.

Recommended in the area

Presteigne; Offa's Dyke Visitor Centre, Knighton; Hay-on-Wye

The Saracens Head Inn

★★★★ INN

Address: Ross-on-Wye, SYMONDS YAT [EAST],
HR9 6JL
Tel: 01600 890435
Fax: 01600 890034
Email: contact@saracensheadinn.co.uk
Website: www.saracensheadinn.co.uk
Map ref: 2, SO51
Directions: From Ross-on-Wye take A40 to
Monmouth. In 4m take Symonds Yat East turn.
1st right before bridge. Right in 0.5m. Right in 1m

Open: 11–11 🍺 L 12–2.30 D 6.30–9 🍴 L 12–2.30 D 6.30–9 Rooms: 10 en suite (1 GF) S £55
D £79–£130 Facilities: Garden Parking Notes: ⊞ Free House 🍴 ⏺ 7

Symonds Yat is a spectacular natural attraction, and the Saracens Head is located in an Area of
Outstanding Natural Beauty on the east bank of the Wye where the river meets the Royal Forest of
Dean. Formerly a cider mill, the 17th-century inn is just over a mile from the Welsh border and makes
a convenient base for exploring an area ideal for walking and cycling. An ancient hand ferry carries
passengers across the Wye as it has for many years. The inn's atmosphere is informal and relaxed,
with two eating areas inside and two riverside terraces outside, with views of the Wye Valley. A great
choice of food majors on popular bar fare and restaurant main courses, including many traditional
home-made dishes with modern touches. Old Speckled Hen and ales from Theakstons and the Wye
Valley Brewery are served in the flagstoned bar. Eight standard bedrooms are offered in the main house
and two superior rooms are available in the boathouse annexe. All the rooms are centrally heated, and
furnished with antique pine.

Recommended in the area

Goodrich Castle; Symonds Yat Rock; Forest of Dean

Carvings in Royston Caves

The Bricklayers Arms

Address: Hogpits Bottom, FLAUNDEN,
Nr Hemel Hempstead, HP3 0PH
Tel: 01442 833322
Fax: 01442 834841
Email: goodfood@bricklayersarms.com
Website: www.bricklayersarms.com
Map ref: 3, TL00
Directions: M25 junct 18 onto A404 (Amersham road). Right at Chenies for Flaunden
Open: 12–11.30 ᵇ L 12–2.30 D 6.30–9.30

🍴 L 12–2.30 D 6.30–9.30 **Facilities:** Garden Parking **Notes:** ⊕ Free House ♦ ⚞ ♇ 12

This award-winning country pub, owned and managed by Alvin and Sally Michaels, has become a foodie destination thanks to its happy pairing of British traditions and French classics. Tucked away in deepest rural Hertfordshire, it's popular with walkers, locals, and all those who seek a sunny and secluded garden to relax in during the summer months. Rambling and ivy-covered on the outside, the interior provides the expected low beams, exposed brickwork, candlelight and open fires. The French influence comes from chef Claude Paillet, who trained in Paris at the three Michelin-starred Pierre Gagnaire restaurant. His passion for food is reflected in a menu that marries French sophistication, with great respect for the traditions of this old English pub. A meal here might start with brochette of tiger prawns on a rosemary stick or a selection of their home-smoked fish with coriander butter and tomato chutney. Continue, perhaps, with best end of lamb with pea flan and rosemary and Madeira jus, quail stuffed with mushrooms, or pan-fried sea bass with a creamy Chardonnay, red pepper, shallot and basil sauce. Be sure to check out the dessert menu, which might include a crepe filled with Cointreau-flavoured mascarpone with citrus fruits, chocolate layered mousse, crème brûlée or fresh fruit crumble.

Recommended in the area

Chenies Manor House; Berkhamsted Castle; Ashridge Estate (NT)

Alford Arms

Address: Frithsden, HEMEL HEMPSTEAD, HP1 3DD
Tel: 01442 864480
Fax: 01422 876893
Email: info@alfordarmsfrithsden.co.uk
Website: www.alfordarmsfrithsden.co.uk
Map ref: 3, TL00
Directions: From Hemel Hempstead on A4146 take 2nd left at Water End. In 1m left at T-junct, right after 0.75m. Pub 100yds on right
Open: 11–11 (Sun 12–10.30) **L** 12–2.30 (Sat 12–3, Sun 12–4) **D** 6.30–9.30 (Mon–Thurs) (Fri-Sat 6.30–10.30, Sun 7–9.30) **Closed:** 26 Dec **Facilities:** Garden Parking **Notes:** ⊕ SALISBURY PUBS LTD ♦ ♦ ♀ 19

An attractive Victorian pub in the unruffled hamlet of Frithsden, surrounded by National Trust woodland. The flower-filled garden overlooks the village green, and historic Ashridge Forest is nearby. Cross the threshold and in the dining room and bar you'll pick up on the warm and lively atmosphere, derived partly from the buzz of conversation, partly from the discreet background jazz, and partly from the rich colours and eclectic mixture of old furniture and pictures, mostly acquired from Tring salerooms. The seasonal menu and daily specials balance modern British with more traditional fare, mostly prepared from fresh, local produce. A good choice of 'small plates' ranges from rustic breads with roast garlic and olive oil, to oak-smoked bacon on bubble and squeak with hollandaise sauce and poached egg. Main meals with a similarly imaginative approach include Moroccan spiced lamb shank on sweet potato mash, pan juices and cumin yoghurt; Cornish fish stew with saffron potatoes, rouille and gruyère; and pumpkin gnocchi with roast beetroot, porcini, watercress and walnut pesto. Puddings are interestingly tweaked too, such as crispy banana and almond spring roll with lemongrass caramel.

Recommended in the area

Berkhamsted Castle; Walter Rothschild Zoological Museum; Whipsnade Wild Animal Park

The Privy Garden, Hatfield House

The Fox and Hounds

Address: 2 High Street, HUNSDON, SG12 8NH
Tel: 01279 843999
Fax: 01279 841092
Email: info@foxandhounds-hunsdon.co.uk
Website: www.foxandhounds-hunsdon.co.uk
Map ref: 3, TL41
Directions: From A414 between Ware & Harlow take B180 in Stanstead Abbotts N to Hunsdon
Open: 12–4 6–11 ⓓ **L** 12–3 **D** 6–10.30
🍽 **L** 12–3 **D** 7–10 **Closed:** All day Mon, Sun eve
Facilities: Garden Parking **Notes:** ⊕ Free House ♦♦ 🐾 ♟ 10

The pub is set in a pretty village surrounded by Hertfordshire countryside. It has a comfy, laid-back bar featuring a log fire, leather sofas and local ales. There's a large separate dining room and an outside terrace in the large garden. Chef owner James Rix, who trained under some of the industry's top chefs, has quickly made a name for himself at this family-run establishment, with a seasonal menu that changes twice a day. Dogs are permitted.

Recommended in the area

Henry Moore Foundation; Paradise Wildlife Park; Lee Valley Park

The Cabinet Free House and Restaurant

Address: High Street, Reed, ROYSTON, SG8 8AH
Tel: 01763 848366
Email: thecabinet@btconnect.com
Website: www.thecabinetatreed.co.uk
Map ref: 3, TL34
Directions: 2m S of Royston, just off A10
Open: 12–3 5.30–12 (all day Sat–Sun) L 12–3 D 5–9 L 12–3 D 5–9 **Closed:** 1 Jan
Facilities: Garden Parking **Notes:** 8

The village of Reed lies just off what the Romans knew as Ermine Street, but which today, rather more prosaically, we call the A10. The word 'cabinet' in the pub's name came into use in the 16th century to describe a small room used as a study, retreat or meeting place. This ties in with the age of this country inn and restaurant, which has a white-painted clapboard exterior, low beams and an open fire. The lovely surroundings lend themselves to special occasions, particularly weddings, and the premises are licensed for civil ceremonies. Food is prepared from the best local produce, while drawing inspiration from around the world to offer an interesting variety of dishes, including traditional favourites. There is a good choice of menus too, with a seasonal carte, and fixed-price lunch and dinner menus of two or three courses. A meal might begin with gravadlax with beetroot compôte and dressed leaves, followed by dry-aged fillet of beef with potato rösti. To round off, try baked bitter chocolate fondant with raspberry ice cream. Lunchtime snacks available at the bar include tian of crab with aïoli and horseradish dressing, and pan-fried steak and onion confit with salad and chips.

Recommended in the area

Imperial War Museum Duxford; City of Cambridge; Shuttleworth Collection

ISLE OF WIGHT

Freshwater Bay

The Seaview Hotel & Restaurant

★★★ 82% ◉ ◉ HOTEL

Address: High Street, SEAVIEW, PO34 5EX
Tel: 01983 612711
Fax: 01983 613729
Email: reception@seaviewhotel.co.uk
Website: www.seaviewhotel.co.uk
Map ref: 3, SZ69
Directions: B3330 (Ryde to Seaview road), left via Puckpool along seafront road, hotel on left
Open: 11–2.30 6–11 ⌂ L 12–2 D 7–9.30
◉ L 12–1.30 D 7.30–9.30 **Rooms:** 27 (4 GF) **S** £100–£199 **D** £120–£245 **Notes:** ⊕ Free House ♦♦

In a sailing-mad Victorian village, this smart, sea-facing hotel is crammed with nautical associations. There are ships' wheels, oars, model ships, and lots of polished wood and brass. The Front Bar & Lounge resembles a naval wardroom and is home to a collection of naval artefacts, while the Pump Bar at the back is like a traditional pub, but with a more fish-focused menu than you'd find in most. You may also eat in the small Victorian dining room, or the Sunshine restaurant and conservatory, both of which share a modern European (with a hint of British) menu that offers the very best of the season, caught or grown around the island – fish straight from the sea; pork and beef from its lush grazing land; venison from the hotel's own farm; and tomatoes, garlic and herbs from its garden. If the menu offers it, consider spider crab risotto with fennel sauce as a starter; Wight lamb shepherd's pie, carrot purée and beef sauce; or lightly curried cod, spiced lentils, buttered spring greens, and herb crème fraîche sauce as a main course; and pineapple parfait, black pepper ice cream, and sweet red pepper and chilli syrup for dessert.

Recommended in the area

Seaview Wildlife Encounter (Flamingo Park); Osborne House; Isle of Wight Steam Railway

KENT

South Foreland Lighthouse, Saxon Shore Way, Dover

Castle Inn

Address: CHIDDINGSTONE, TN8 7AH
Tel: 01892 870247
Fax: 01892 871420
Email: info@castleinn.co.uk
Website: www.castleinn.co.uk
Map ref: 3, TQ54
Directions: 1.5m S of B2027 between Tonbridge
& Edenbridge
Open: 11–11 ♒ L 11–7 D 7–9.30 ﷯ L 12–2
D 7–9.30 Facilities: Garden
Notes: ⊕ Free House ♦♦ ♖ ♟ 10

The unique row of timbered houses known as Chiddingstone contains, tucked away in one corner, in the lea of Chiddingstone Castle, the Castle Inn. It was first documented in 1420, and started selling ale around 1730. Today, one glance at its mellow exterior makes it easy to see why this charming old building has starred in films as diverse as *Elizabeth R* and *Room with a View*. The interior is equally photogenic, with its heavy beams, nooks and crannies, period furniture and curios. Thirsty visitors can sample Larkins Traditional and Larkins Porter, brewed just up the road at Larkins Farm, while the wine list runs to well over 100 bins, and whisky lovers can, given time, work their way through 30 malts from Aberlour to Tomintoul. Diners have the option of lighter bar meals or a more sophisticated restaurant menu, which contains an eclectic range of dishes such as grilled goats' cheese on baked field mushroom, chargrilled pigeon breast, grilled swordfish Niçoise with a poached egg, and rounds off with puddings or and a list of 15 or so British cheeses. On sunny days, both bar and restaurant meals can be taken al fresco, in the Castle's vine-hung courtyard garden.

Recommended in the area

Hever Castle; Penshurst Place and Gardens; Knole Park (NT)

The fortress of Dover Castle

Griffins Head

Address: CHILLENDEN, Canterbury, CT3 1PS
Tel: 01304 840325
Fax: 01304 841290
Map ref: 4, TR25
Directions: A2 from Canterbury towards Dover,
then B2046. Village on right
Open: 10.30–11 ⓑ L 12–2 D 7–9.30 ⓘ L 12–2
D 7–9.30 Facilities: Garden Parking
Notes: ⓦ SHEPHERD NEAME ⓨ 10

Dating from 1286, this Kentish Wealden hall has great historical character, with beamed bars and inglenook fireplaces. Fine Kentish ales from Shepherd Neame and home-made food have helped the old inn to make its mark with visitors as well as locals, among them Kent's cricketing fraternity. The menu is typically English and specialises in game from local estates in season and locally caught fish where possible. Outside there's a very pretty garden where drinkers can linger at their leisure, and a bat and trap pitch (an ancient relative of cricket, still popular in Kent). A vintage car club meets here on the first Sunday of every month.

Recommended in the area

Canterbury; Wingham Bird Park; Howletts Wild Animal Park

The Bottle House Inn

Address: Coldharbour Road, PENSHURST,
Tonbridge, TN11 8ET
Tel: 01892 870306
Fax: 01892 871094
Email: info@thebottlehouseinnpenshurst.co.uk
Website: www.thebottlehouseinnpenshurst.co.uk
Map ref: 4, TQ54
Directions: From Tunbridge Wells take A264 W, then
B2188 N. After Fordcombe left towards Edenbridge &
Hever. Pub 500yds after staggered x-rds
Open: 11–11 (Sun 11–10.30) ⅃ L 12–10 D 12–10 ⅃ L 12–10 D 12–10 **Closed:** 25 Dec
Facilities: Garden Parking **Notes:** ⊞ Free House ⅃ ⅃ ⅃ 8

The year 1492 was historically significant. Not only was Christopher Columbus 'discovering' America,
but also, in this pretty corner of Kent, craftsmen were putting the finishing touches to the farmhouse
that was later to become the Bottle House Inn. This cosy beamed building retains its original stone
fireplace pillars, which bear the marks of centuries of tool sharpening. A polished copper counter top
adds to the warmth of the atmosphere in the bar. Here a selection of local hand pumped beers, such as
Larkins Ale and Harveys Sussex Best Bitter, accompanies the ploughman's lunches, filled baguettes and
light meals. In the dining room there's a daily changing menu offering a wide choice of dishes, made
from produce sourced locally where possible. After a starter such as spicy Thai fishcakes with sweet
chilli jam, main course selections might include the local Speldhurst sausages; or stuffed pig's trotter
with Puy lentils. The Bottle House is reputedly haunted, and there have been claims of sightings and
items having moved in the bar area overnight, but don't let this put you off. The pub is family friendly,
with high chairs provided and a children's menu. Dogs are welcome too, except in the dining room.

Recommended in the area

Hever Castle; Royal Tunbridge Wells; Penshurst Place and Gardens

The Beacon

★★★★ INN

Address: Tea Garden Lane, Rusthall,
ROYAL TUNBRIDGE WELLS, TN3 9JH
Tel: 01892 524252
Fax: 01892 534288
Email: beaconhotel@btopenworld.com
Website: www.the-beacon.co.uk
Map ref: 4, TQ53
Directions: From Tunbridge Wells take A264
towards East Grinstead. Pub 1m on left
Open: 11–11 (Sun 12–10.30) L 12–2.30 D 6.30–9.30 L 12–2.30 D 6–9.30
Rooms: 3 en suite S £68.50 D £97 Facilities: Garden Parking Notes: ⊕ Free House 12

High up on a sandstone outcrop just 1.5 miles from Tunbridge Wells, The Beacon has one of the best views in southeast England. Formerly a grand country home, it retains impressive architectural features, including stained glass, moulded ceilings and an oak-panelled bar in which you can select from a fine range of beers and wine to complement the food. As members of Kentish Fare, the proprietors are strongly committed to using county-produced ingredients, and in the restaurant you can choose from starters such as layered pork and chicken liver terrine with grape and apple chutney, or crispy fried calamari with chilli pickled cucumber and passionfruit sauce. Your meal could continue with slow braised Kentish lamb shoulder with toasted pinenut mashed potato and elderberry jus, or pan-fried halibut with king scallops, calamari and mussel casserole. Try to save room for dessert, notably the sticky toffee pudding or a vanilla and apple bavaroise. Any culinary excesses can be walked off in the 17 acres of grounds, which include lakes, woodland paths and a chalybeate spring. There's also a lovely terrace that's perfect for a pre-dinner drink in summer.

Recommended in the area

Tunbridge Wells; Penshurst Place & Gardens; Spa Valley Railway

LANCASHIRE

Forest of Bowland at Whitewell

The Red Pump Inn

Address: Clitheroe Road, BASHALL EAVES,
BB7 3DA
Tel: 01254 826227
Fax: 01254 826750
Email: info@theredpumpinn.co.uk
Website: www.theredpumpinn.co.uk
Map ref: 6, SD64
Directions: 3m from Clitheroe
Open: 12–2.30 6–11 (Sun 12–9.30, BHs 12–5)
 L 12–2 D 6–9 ❍ L 12–2 D 6–9 **Closed:** Mon
(winter) **Facilities:** Garden Parking **Notes:** ⊕ Free House ❦ ♇ 10

With superb views of the Ribble Valley, on the edge of the Forest of Bowland's Area of Outstanding Natural Beauty, the Red Pump Inn boasts two dining rooms, a bar, a snug with roaring real fire, sunny lounges, a courtyard and garden, two outside dining areas and three lovely guest bedrooms with big hand-made beds and en suite or private bathrooms. An owner-run free house, it maintains a commitment to high standards and environmentally-friendly sustainability. The short but fresh menu is compiled to reflect the passion for superb food held by owners Jonathan and Martina Myerscough and their chefs. Extra-matured local beef features on the weekly steak night, and Fridays bring a celebration of seafood in which dishes such as potted crayfish tails, calamari with aïoli, hake, sea bass and snapper are offered. Herbs and vegetables come from the garden, and bread, sausages and desserts are all home-made. The children's menu is both appealing and healthy, and special diets can be catered for. Local, regional and national cask ales – including Timothy Taylor Landlord, Black Sheep, Moorhouses and Grindleton Brewhouse – are kept in tip-top condition and there's an impressive and varied wine list. The owners aptly sum it all up: 'Three miles from Clitheroe; a million miles from hectic'.

Recommended in the area

Forest of Bowland; Gawthorpe Hall; Pendle Hill

Clog and Billycock

Address: Billinge End Road, Pleasington, BLACKBURN, BB2 6QB
Tel: 01254 201163
Email: enquiries@clogandbillycock.com
Website: www.clogandbillycock.com
Map ref: 6, SD62
Directions: M6 junct 29 onto M65 junct 3, follow signs for Pleasington
Open: 12–11 (Sun 12–10.30) ⓑ L 12–2 D 6–9
🍴 L 12–2 D 6–9 **Closed:** 25 Dec
Facilities: Garden Parking **Notes:** ⊕ ⅰ♦ ⅰ⌐ ♀ 8

The Clog and Billycock has been part of Pleasington's history for over 150 years, although this new venture opened only in August 2008. Its name comes from the attire of an early landlord (a billycock is black felt hat, a predecessor of the bowler). Set in the quaint village of Pleasington on the quiet edges of Blackburn's western suburbs, the building has undergone an expensive renovation, and the result is a warm and relaxing pub in which to enjoy Thwaites ales, draught ciders, fine wines and superb food. Sharrock's Lancashire cheese on toast with local cured streaky bacon makes an excellent light lunch, while the ploughman's highlights the pub's real food objectives, consisting of an impressive plate of Blackstick's Blue, Sandham's Creamy Lancashire, honey roast ham, Forager's collared pork, pickled free-range egg, celeriac and walnut salad, home-made pickles, piccalilli and organic bread. Hot options from chef Nigel Haworth's locally sourced menu, which introduces a contemporary twist to traditional favourites, may include cornfed Goosnargh chicken with chunky chips and garlic and herb sauce; Simpson's Dairy rice pudding could complete a meal to remember. Children are welcomed with fun educational sheets and competitions, as well as equally well thought-out children's meals.

Recommended in the area

Pleasington Priory; Pleasington Old Hall Wood and Wildlife Garden; Witton Country Park

The Millstone at Mellor

★★ 85% ◉◉ HOTEL

Address: Church Lane, Mellor, BLACKBURN, BB2 7JR
Tel: 01254 813333
Fax: 01254 812628
Email: info@millstonehotel.com
Website: www.millstonehotel.co.uk
Map ref: 6, SD62
Directions: M6 junct 31, A59 towards Clitheroe, past British Aerospace. Right at rdbt signed Blackburn/Mellor. Next rdbt 2nd left. Hotel at top of hill on right
Open: 11–11 (Fri–Sat 11–12, Sun 12–10.30)
🍴 L 12–9.30 D 12–9.30 ◉ L 12–2.15 D 6.30–9.30
Rooms: 23 (8 GF) S £74.50–£124 D £99–£155
Facilities: Parking **Notes:** ⊞ SHIRE HOTELS ♥ 12

The Millstone at Mellor has retained the charm of the coaching inn it once was, yet has added all of the comforts of a modern hotel. This award-winning establishment, which was once a tithe barn, sits in the heart of the glorious Ribble Valley. Inside, it maintains a traditional bar and an elegant restaurant, with wood-panelling and a beamed ceiling, as well as a grandfather clock and country prints setting the scene. Chef-Patron Anson Bolton and his team offer a flexible approach to dining, with the daily bar and restaurant menus available in either venue, complemented by a number of real ales and a wide-ranging wine list. The freshest produce from around Lancashire and the north-west is used to create a range of simple but classic dishes, which might include glazed Pendle lamb shank or pan-fried fillet of sea bass. Sunday roasts with all the trimmings are another draw. The hotel makes a good base for visiting the area, and has a number of well-equipped en suite bedrooms.

Recommended in the area

Ribble Valley; Blackpool; Samlesbury Hall

The Highwayman

Address: BURROW, Nr Kirkby Lonsdale, LA6 2RJ
Tel: 01524 273338
Email: enquiries@highwaymaninn.co.uk
Website: www.highwaymaninn.co.uk
Map ref: 6, SD67
Directions: M6 junct 36, A65 to Kirkby Lonsdale. Then A683 south. Burrow approx 2m
Open: 12–11(Sun 12–10.30) **L** 12–2 **D** 6–9
L 12–2 **D** 6–9 **Closed:** 25 Dec
Facilities: Garden Parking **Notes:** 8

Starting life as a coaching inn during the 18th century, a legend surrounds this establishment regarding its use as a midnight haunt of notorious Lancashire highwaymen. The inn is set in a delightful country area close to the historic market town of Kirkby Lonsdale, popular for its pretty cottages, quaint streets and attractive shops and tea rooms. The refurbished Highwayman has a stone-floored interior with solid wood furniture and welcoming open fires. There is also a beautifully landscaped terraced garden, planted to attract local butterflies and birds. Thwaites cask ales, ciders and guest beers are served alongside a list of fine wines, and the menus are a tribute to regional specialities and local producers and suppliers. Typical dishes are Port of Lancaster Smokehouse kipper fillet, with boiled egg and watercress salad; slow cooked leg of Highwayman mutton pudding with purée potatoes, roasted root vegetables and juniper berry gravy; and Cartmel sticky toffee pudding with butterscotch sauce and vanilla ice cream. Don't miss the tri-counties cheeseboard, with the best from Lancashire, Yorkshire and Cumbria. The children's menu offers real food in smaller portions, and seasonal fun sheets are available to keep younger customers amused.

Recommended in the area

Sizergh Castle; Levens Hall; White Scar Caves

Cartford Country Inn & Hotel

Address: Little Eccleston, PRESTON,
PR3 0YP
Tel: 01995 670166
Email: info@thecartfordinn.co.uk
Website: www.thecartfordinn.co.uk
Map ref: 6, SD52
Directions: Off A586
Open: 11–11 L 12–2 D 5.30–9 L 12–2
D 5.30–9 **Closed:** 25 Dec **Facilities:** Parking
Notes: Free House

The refurbished Cartford Inn is a 17th-century coaching inn nestling on the banks of the River Wyre on Lancashire's Fylde Coast; it combines traditional features with contemporary style. As a result of the extensive refurbishment the owners, Patrick and Julie Beaume have achieved a unique ambience where a warm welcome is always assured. An open wood fire welcomes guests in the bar lounge area where there are several cosy corners to enjoy a quiet drink. Food, from an informal snack to a three-course meal, is served throughout the lounge, alcoves and games room (where dominos, cards, chess, backgammon and other board games are available). Alternatively the same menu is available in the first-floor restaurant, Mushrooms, for those seeking a more traditional dining experience. There is also a charming beer garden overlooking the River Wyre with stunning views of the surrounding countryside with Beacon Fell and the Trough of Bowland as a backdrop. Although in the heart of the Fylde Coast countryside, the Cartford is less than ten minutes from the M55 junction 3 and an equal distance from nearby Blackpool.

Recommended in the area

Blackpool; Wyre Estuary Country Park; Marsh Mill

The Three Fishes

Address: Mitton Road, Mitton, WHALLEY, BB7 9PQ
Tel: 01254 826888
Fax: 01254 826026
Email: enquiries@thethreefishes.com
Website: www.thethreefishes.com
Map ref: 6, SD73
Directions: M6 junct 31, A59 to Clitheroe. Follow signs for Whalley, take B6246 for 2m
Open: 12–11 ☕ **L** 12–2 **D** 6–9 **Closed:** 25 Dec
Facilities: Garden Parking **Notes:** ⊕ Free House ⛺ 🐕 ☕ 8

The Three Fishes is over 400 years old and has been a pub for most of that time, providing refreshment to travellers on the old road from the 16th-century bridge at Lower Hodder and the ferry at Mitton. The place was supposedly named after the three fishes pendant in the coat of arms of John Paslew, last abbot of nearby Whalley Abbey (look above the entrance to see them carved in stone). The tiny hamlet of Mitton is set on a limestone rise above the River Ribble and is surrounded by beautiful countryside. The multi award-winning pub prides itself on its genuine Lancashire hospitality, real ales, and the best food ever in its long history. The menu demonstrates a passionate commitment to regional food, with dishes such as Morecambe Bay shrimps, served with blade mace butter and toasted muffin; heather reared Bowland lamb Lancashire hotpot; and aged sirloin of Ribble Valley beef with proper chips. You might finish your meal with Lancashire curd tart with organic lemon cream, or the excellent Lancashire cheese board with biscuits and fireside chutney. Photographs of local 'food hero' producers and suppliers line the walls, in tribute to their contribution to the success of the Three Fishes. A great place for visitors to relax amidst beautiful countryside.

Recommended in the area

Stonyhurst College; Clitheroe Castle; All Hallows Medieval Church

Blackpool's Central Pier and Ferris Wheel

The Inn at Whitewell

★★★★★ ◉ INN

Address: Forest of Bowland, WHITEWELL,
Nr Clitheroe, BB7 3AT
Tel: 01200 448222
Fax: 01200 448298
Email: reception@innatwhitewell.com
Website: www.innatwhitewell.com
Map ref: 6, SD64
Directions: From B6243 follow Whitewell signs
Open: 11–3 6–11 ⓑ L 12–2 D 7.30–9.30
🍽 D 7.30–9.30 **Rooms:** 23 en suite (1 GF) S £70–£135 D £96–£172 **Facilities:** Garden Parking
Notes: ⓦ Free House ⊁ ♇ 20

Commanding wonderful views this is a delightful 16th-century inn, a former deer keeper's cottage, set high up on the banks of the River Hodder in the Forest of Bowland. The bar – just one area where the family passion for antiques is evident – serves local real ales, and bottled organic beers and ciders from around the world, and food at lunchtime and evening. For formal dining, try the riverside restaurant.

Recommended in the area

Ribchester Roman Museum; Browsholme Hall; Yorkshire Dales National Park

Beacon Hill, near Woodhouse Eaves

Town Hall Square, Leicester

The Queen's Head

★★★★ ◎ ◎ RESTAURANT WITH ROOMS

Address: 2 Long Street, BELTON, Loughborough, LE12 9TP
Tel: 01530 222359
Fax: 01530 224860
Email: enquiries@thequeenshead.org
Website: www.thequeenshead.org
Map ref: 3, SK42
Directions: On B5324 between Coalville & Loughborough
Open: Mon–Sun 7am–late ⓑ **L** 12–2.30 **D** 7–9.30
⓪ **L** 12–2.30 **D** 7–9.30 **Closed:** 25–26 Dec
Rooms: 6 en suite **S** £65 **D** £70–£110
Facilities: Garden Parking **Notes:** ⓦ Free House ⓘ ⓡ ⓨ 14

A stunning contemporary gastro-pub with bedrooms, located in the very heart of the East Midlands. Whether you just want to enjoy a drink in the comfortable bar or try the culinary creations of Head Chef David Ferguson in the bistro or the restaurant, The Queen's Head has something to offer for all. There's a bar menu available nearly all week, and a set menu offers impressive dishes using local produce.

Recommended in the area

National Forest; Conkers; The Great Central Railway

The Staff of Life

Address: Main Street, MOWSLEY, LE17 6NT
Tel: 0116 240 2359
Website: www.staffoflifeinn.co.uk
Map ref: 3, SP68
Directions: M1 junct 20, A4304 to Market Harborough. Left in Husbands Bosworth onto A5199. Pub 3m
Open: 12–3 6–11 (Sun 12–close) ⓑ L 12–2.30 D 6.30–9.15 ⓧ L 12–2.30 D 6.30–9.15
Closed: Mon lunch (ex BHs) **Facilities:** Garden Parking **Notes:** ⊕ Free House ⚱ 19

An integral part of the rich heritage of the beautiful village in which it stands, the Staff of Life captures the true essence of a good country pub while delivering the standards and qualities of a fine restaurant. The atmosphere is warm and convivial, with traditional features such as high-backed settles, a wood-panelled ceiling and flagstone floors, warmed by a roaring open fire in winter. In the warmer seasons you can enjoy the inviting front patio, surrounded by herbs and flowers, or the garden at the rear.
In the dining area overlooking the garden, the interesting menu includes a good mix of British pub classics and dishes with more of an international influence. Recent examples from the daily-changing blackboard lunch menu have included Joseph Morris faggots on mash with rich gravy, and Aberdeen Angus cottage pie with Black Bomber cheddar topping. The evening carte might include starters such as seared king scallops on tarragon-scented black pudding, followed perhaps by roast chicken breast stuffed with chargrilled red peppers on thyme courgettes. The wine list is extensive, with many offered by the glass. Sunday lunch here is a great favourite – and great value – featuring roasts of meat sourced from local farms.

Recommended in the area

Stanford Hall; Mallory Park; Wicksteed Park

Bust of George III in Lincoln

Old Hall in Gainsborough

The Chequers Inn

★★★★ ⬡ INN

Address: Main Street, WOOLSTHORPE, NG32 1LU
Tel: 01476 870701
Email: justinnabar@yahoo.co.uk
Website: www.chequersinn.net
Map ref: 3, SK83
Directions: From Grantham on A607. Right for Woolsthorpe. Follow heritage signs to Belvoir Castle
Open: 12–3 5.30–11 🍺 **L** 12–2.30 **D** 6–9.30
🍽️ **L** 12–2.30 **D** 6–9.30 **Rooms:** 4 en suite (3 GF)
S £49 **D** £59 **Facilities:** Garden Parking **Notes:** ⊕ Free House 👫 🐾 🍷 25

The Chequers Inn combines the rustic charm of a 17th-century inn with sympathetic modern touches and fine, seasonal British cuisine. As well as occupying a unique location – Belvoir Castle is just a stone's throw away – it delights visitors with its own cricket pitch and gardens. Inside, the fully stocked bar meets every taste. The Bakehouse Restaurant has a strong emphasis on home cooking and quality local ingredients, with an excellent value fixed-price lunch menu or a range of a la carte choices.

Recommended in the area

Belvoir Castle; Belton House (NT); Vale of Belvoir

LONDON

Parliament Square towards the Houses of Parliament and Big Ben

The Bleeding Heart Tavern

Address: 19 Greville Street, LONDON, EC1N 8SQ
Tel: 020 7242 8238
Fax: 020 7831 1402
Email: bookings@bleedingheart.co.uk
Website: www.bleedingheart.co.uk
Map ref: 3, TQ38
Directions: Close to Farringdon tube station,
at corner of Greville St & Bleeding Heart Yard
Open: 7am–11pm (breakfast 7–10.30am)
L from 11 D 6–10.30 L 12–3 D 6–10.30 Closed: BHs, 10 days at Xmas, Sat–Sun
Notes: Free House 17

The Tavern has guarded the entrance to Bleeding Heart Yard since 1746. Today it offers a traditional neighbourhood bar with Adnams real ales and a light lunchtime menu. Downstairs is the Dining Room, an open rotisserie and grill providing free-range, organic British meats, game and poultry. On the menu: braised mutton hotpot; and smoked haddock with poached egg. The Tavern also opens for breakfast.
Recommended in the area
St Paul's Cathedral; Tower of London; Museum of London

The Fire Station

Address: 150 Waterloo Road, LONDON, SE1 8SB
Tel: 020 7620 2226
Email: firestation.waterloo@marstons.co.uk
Map ref: 3, TQ38
Directions: Turn right at exit 2 of Waterloo Station
Open: 11–11 (From 9am Tue–Sat) 9am–11pm
9am–11pm Closed: 25–26 Dec, 1 Jan
Notes: MARSTONS INNS & TAVERNS 8

Built in 1910, this former Fire Brigade Station is especially popular with travellers, given that Waterloo Station is next door. Inside is a big room with shiny red brick walls and an assortment of old domestic dining tables, from which you can see into the open-plan kitchen. This is the source of traditional British/European dishes, such as calves' liver with bacon and mustard mash, and lemon sole with Jerusalem artichokes. Drinks include a wide range of draught beers, cask ales and New and Old World wines.
Recommended in the area
London Eye; Royal Festival Hall; London Aquarium

The Bountiful Cow

Address: 51 Eagle Street, Holborn, LONDON, WC1R 4AP
Tel: 020 7404 0200
Email: manager@roxybeaujolais.com
Website: www.thebountifulcow.co.uk
Map ref: 3, TQ38
Directions: via Procter St. Through 2 arches into Eagle St. Pub between High Holborn & Red Lion Square
Open: 11–11 🍴 L 12–3 D 5–10.30 🍽 L 12–3 D 5–10.30
Closed: BHs Sun **Notes:** ⊕ ♟ ♟

Roxy Beaujolais, proprietor of the ancient Seven Stars in WC2, found a 1960s pub nearby and turned it into a 'public house devoted to beef', The Bountiful Cow, located on quiet Eagle Street in the heart of Holborn. The redesign, by Roxy's architect husband Nathan Silver, achieves a balance between funky bistro and stylish saloon, seating up to 70 diners and eight in the bar. The interior is uniquely bedecked with posters of beef, cowboys, rustlers, cowgirls and cattle drives, plus antique and contemporary film posters, all of which glorify the cow and all things cow related. Food-wise, the emphasis is on exceptionally large and well-made hamburgers and, of course, steak, alongside cask-conditioned ales and excellent wines. As executive chef, Roxy has plenty of form; she is author of the pub cookbook Home from the Inn Contented and was co-presenter of the BBC's Full On Food. Five cuts of meat feature on the menus: onglet (for steak sandwiches), rib-eye, sirloin, filet and T-bone, all aged many weeks for tenderness and flavour. Steaks can be served à la Capricorn (with melted goats' cheese), or with Béarnaise or green peppercorn sauce. Starters, chips, salads and desserts are appropriately simple and the meat is accurately cooked by the grill chef. The sights and tourist destinations of central London are all a short walk away.

Recommended in the area

British Museum; Dr Johnson's House; Dickens House Museum; Sir John Soame's Museum

The Seven Stars

Address: 53 Carey Street, LONDON,
WC2A 2JB
Tel: 020 7242 8521
Email: roxy@roxybeaujolais.com
Map ref: 3, TQ38
Directions: From Temple N via The Strand & Bell Yard to
Carey St. From Holborn SE via Lincoln's Inn Fields & Searle St
to Carey St
Open: 11–11 (Sat 12–11, Sun 12–10.30) 🍴 L 12–5 D 5–9.30
Closed: 25–26 Dec, 1 Jan, Good Fri, Etr Sun
Notes: ⊕ Free House

Since sometime cookbook author and TV food show presenter
Roxy Beaujolais took over this Grade II listed pub behind the Royal Courts of Justice, she has given it
a super-sensitive facelift. She has even expanded into the tiny former wig shop next door, where its
stock-in-trade is still displayed. Her architect husband managed the improvements with such respect
that some think his glazed, mahogany-mullioned dumbwaiter is ancient. The small bar and snug are
simply but comfortably furnished, with wooden settles and a few tables and chairs. Roxy is guided by
market availability for her simple, but good, blackboard-listed meals, which might include Dorset crab,
partridge pie, bruschetta of Piquillo peppers, tomato and toasted seeds (V). There's a good selection
of wines and real ales from the Adnams and Dark Star breweries. To the delight of customers, many
of them barristers and legal journalists (covering cases over the road), the venerable pub cat, Tom
Paine, struts about wearing a chorister's ruff. A chalkboard outside lists offences that will get one
barred, including 'no poodle-faking' and 'no alewife worrying'. Even if you don't need the loo, pretend
otherwise for the opportunity to use the ridiculously narrow stairs!

Recommended in the area

The Soane Museum; The Hunterian Museum; Lincoln's Inn

TO THE TRAITORS' GATE

The Tower of London

NORFOLK

West Newton

Church of St Peter and St Paul, Burgh Castle

Kings Head

Address: Harts Lane, BAWBURGH, NR9 3LS
Tel: 01603 744977
Fax: 01603 744990
Email: anton@kingshead-bawburgh.co.uk
Website: www.kingshead-bawburgh.co.uk
Map ref: 4, TG10
Directions: From A47 W of Norwich take B1108 W
Open: 11.30–11(Sun 12–10.30) ⓛ L 12–2
D 5.30–9 ⓘ L 12–2 D 6.30–9 Closed: 25–27 Dec
eve, 1 Jan eve Facilities: Garden Parking
Notes: ⊕ Free House ⓟ 18

A peaceful setting by the banks of the River Yare is perfect for visitors who want to head out of Norwich and enjoy the relaxing atmosphere of a genuine village pub, complete with heavy timbers and bulging walls. Standing opposite the village green, the pub is big on traditional charm, with wooden floors, log fires, comfy leather seating and pine dining furniture. Daily changing menus offer a wide choice of modern British, European and Oriental dishes, all from the best quality local produce.

Recommended in the area

Norwich Cathedral; Norfolk Broads; Norwich Theatre Royal

The Buckinghamshire Arms

Address: Blickling Road, BLICKLING, Nr Aylsham,
NR11 6NF
Tel: 01263 732133
Email: bucksarms@tiscali.co.uk
Website: www.bucks-arms.co.uk
Map ref: 4, TG12
Directions: From Cromer (A140) take exit at Aylsham
onto B1354, follow signs to Blickling Hall
Open: 11.30–3 6–11 (Sun 12–3, 7–10.30)
L 12–2.30 D 7–9 L 12–2 D 7–9
Closed: 25 Dec **Facilities:** Garden **Parking Notes:** ⊕ Free House ♦♦ ♇ 10

Its owners consider the late 17th-century 'Bucks' the 'most beautiful inn in Norfolk'. Cream-washed, elegant, and with only a swinging sign declaring its function, they have a point. It stands right by the gates of the National Trust's magnificent Jacobean Blickling Hall, the ancestral home of Anne Boleyn, whose headless ghost is said to wander the grounds on the anniversary of her execution. The inn's Victorian cellar houses barrels of Adnams, Woodforde's and Fuller's real ales, ready to accompany meals taken in either the lounge bar and restaurant, with their solid furniture and wood-burning stoves, the intimate Snug, or in the garden. Menus offer fresh local food served in both traditional and modern ways, with starters such as home-made fishcakes with dill and fresh tomato sauce; and smoked chicken, chorizo, red pepper and lentil salad with honey mustard dressing. Sample main courses include griddled Norfolk-reared, 10oz rib-eye steak with watercress and mustard sauce, roast tomato and home-cut chips; natural-smoked haddock with white bean, tomato, Brancaster mussels and chorizo cassoulet; and home-made spinach, lentil and feta pie with cumin, fresh herbs, puff pastry and green bean salad. Spacious guest rooms offer outstanding views of Blickling Hall.

Recommended in the area

Bure Valley Railway; Felbrigg Hall; Norwich Cathedral

The Hoste Arms

★★★ 86% ◉◉ HOTEL

Address: The Green, BURNHAM MARKET,
PE31 8HD
Tel: 01328 738777
Fax: 01328 730103
Email: reception@hostearms.co.uk
Website: www.hostearms.co.uk
Map ref: 4, TF84
Directions: Signed off B1155, 5m W of
Wells-next-the-Sea
Open: 11–11 ⓑ L 12–2 D 6–9 ⓘ L 12–2 D 6–9 Rooms: 35 (7 GF) S £114–£119 D £145–£160
Facilities: Garden Parking Notes: ⓗ Free House ⌀ ♇ 11

A 17th-century coaching inn turned stunningly presented hotel, The Hoste Arms is still very much
the social hub of Burnham Market, a lovely village close to the North Norfolk Coast, renowned for
its independent shops. Horatio Nelson was once a regular, and the bar retains a traditional feel
with its abundance of wood and log fire. Alternatively, you can sink into the accommodating leather
armchairs of the comfortable conservatory. Downstairs there is a private dining room, and the loos are
spectacularly extravagant. For the full Hoste experience, stay over in one of the stylish and luxuriously
decorated rooms, by Jeanne Whittome. The exotic Zulu wing reflects Jeanne's South African heritage,
with intimations of wild animals and tribal art. In addition, seven-bedroom, boutique sister hotel, Vine
House, is just opposite the Hoste. The stylish restaurants, serving imaginative cuisine, are favoured by
locals and guests alike. Breakfast, morning coffee and cream teas are also served to non-residents.
The Hoste offers over 100 wines, including some of the world's finest, and prides itself on its keen
pricing policy. Real ales include the best from Woodforde's, Greene King and Adnams breweries.

Recommended in the area

Titchwell Bird Reserve; Holkham Hall; The Sandringham Estate

The beach at Cromer

The Lord Nelson

Address: Walsingham Road, BURNHAM THORPE,
King's Lynn, PE31 8HN
Tel/Fax: 01328 738241
Email: simon@nelsonslocal.co.uk
Website: www.nelsonslocal.co.uk
Map ref: 4, TF84
Directions: B1355, pub 9m from Fakenham &
1.75m from Burnham Market
Open: 12–3 6–11 (Sun 12–10.30, Summer hols
12–11) ⓑ L 12–2.30 D 6–9 ⑩ L 12–2.30 D 6–9
Closed: Mon evenings ex school hols **Facilities:** Garden Parking **Notes:** ⊕ GREENE KING ♦♦ ☞ ☕ 15

Dating back 400 years, this pub is in the village where Lord Nelson was born, and the great Admiral used to eat and drink here, hosting a farewell meal for the whole village here in 1793. There is no bar – all drinks are served from the tap room, and the pub is famous for its real ales, direct from the cask. It also has a popular menu of freshly prepared food. Outside, the massive garden has seating, a barbecue, and wooden play equipment. Dogs are allowed, except in the restaurant.

Recommended in the area

Holkham Hall; Titchwell Nature Reserve; Sandringham House

The George Hotel

Address: High Street, CLEY NEXT THE SEA, Holt,
NR25 7RN
Tel: 01263 740652
Fax: 01263 741275
Email: thegeorge@cleynextthesea.com
Website: www.thegeorgehotelcley.com
Map ref: 4, TG04
Directions: On A149 through Cley next the Sea,
approx 4m from Holt
Open: 11–11 (Sun & BHs 11–10.30) 🍴 L 12–2
D 6.30–9 🍽 L 12–2 D 6.30–9 **Facilities:** Garden Parking **Notes:** ⊕ Free House 👍 🐾 🍷 8

Set within the pretty and historic village of Cley next the Sea, not far from Cley's famous old windmill, the George Hotel is a classic Edwardian Norfolk inn. This is walking and birdwatching country par excellence, and the wonderful sunsets are also renowned. The first naturalist trust was formed here, and the area's wildlife reserves boast abundant birdlife and local seal colonies. Across the road are the atmospheric marshes, with the sea beyond. The inn has been modernised to create tasteful seating and decor where visitors can mingle comfortably with locals. It has an excellent reputation for its wide selection of real ales and for freshly prepared food made from finest ingredients, supplied from the local area. Locally caught fish and shellfish are a highlight, including smoked salmon and prawns from the Cley Smoke House. The dinner menu includes starters such as pastrami-style smoked salmon with citrus oil; and oysters served with lemon and tarragon olive oil. Main dishes include grilled fillet of red snapper with roasted fennel; Dijon peppered chicken with tagliatelle; and pan-fried strips of lambs' liver served with crispy bacon and Madeira. Puddings might be sticky toffee pudding; lemon and lime posset; or honey and lavender crème brûlée. There are vegetarian options and a kids' menu.

Recommended in the area

Henry Blogg Museum; Felbrigg Hall (NT); North Norfolk Railway

The Gin Trap Inn

★★★★ ❀ INN

Address: High Street, RINGSTEAD, PE36 5JU
Tel: 01485 525264
Email: thegintrap@hotmail.co.uk
Website: www.gintrapinn.co.uk
Map ref: 4, TF74
Directions: A149 from King's Lynn towards
Hunstanton. In 15m turn right at Heacham
Open: 11.30–2.30 6–11 (Open all day summer)
🛏 L 12–2 D 6–9 ۞ L 12–2 D 6–9

Rooms: 3 en suite S £49–£80 D £78–£140 Facilities: Garden Parking Notes: ⊕ Free House 🐕 🍷 8

Just two miles inland from the north Norfolk coast, this sprawling, white-painted pub dates back to 1667. It is now very much a gastro-pub, offering neatly-presented dishes with clear flavours, served in a relaxed but attentive manner in the candlelit restaurant. You might start with seared Loch Duart salmon with citrus salad and sorrel velouté, or six Thornham oysters on ice, with shallot and red wine vinegar dressing, then choose roast Norfolk partridge with sarladaise potato, crispy pancetta, slow-roasted red onions and Madeira jus; handmade fresh dolcelatte and potato ravioli with fresh sage and white truffle oil; or Arthur Howell's traditional pork sausages with mashed potato and red onion gravy. The Gin Trap Burger is a succulent cut above your average burger, made from Courtyard Farm organic minced beef and dressed up with home-made relish and Monterey Jack cheese. Head chef Ethan Rodgers rounds off the menu choices with an irresistible selection of desserts, including baked Turkish black fig and almond galette with clotted cream and spiced honey, and a rich chocolate and black cherry marquise with kirsch and crème Anglaise. Three bedrooms are available, featuring wrought iron beds, country-style fabrics and lovely views.

Recommended in the area

Peddar's Way and Norfolk Coast Path; Sandringham; Norfolk Lavender

Horsey, Norfolk Broads National Park

Lifeboat Inn

★★ 78% ❀ HOTEL
Address: Ship Lane, THORNHAM, PE36 6LT
Tel: 01485 512236
Fax: 01485 512323
Email: reception@lifeboatinn.co.uk
Website: www.maypolehotels.com
Map ref: 4, TF74
Directions: A149 to Hunstanton, follow coast road to Thornham, pub 1st left
Open: 11–11 ⚬ L 11–11 ⚬ D 6.30–9.30
Facilities: Garden Parking **Notes:** ⊕ Free House ⚬⚬ ⚬ ⚬ 10

Retaining many original features, this 16th-century inn overlooks the salt marshes and Thornham Harbour. Inside, the warm glow of paraffin lamps enhances the welcoming atmosphere, while the adjoining conservatory has an ancient vine. The best available fish and game feature on the frequently changing menus of traditional country fare. Bowls of steaming mussels are legendary, harvested daily by local fishermen. Popular bar meals include roast loin of pork and Lifeboat fish pie.

Recommended in the area

Peddars Way and Norfolk Coast Path; Sandringham; Norfolk Lavender

The Crown

Address: The Buttlands, WELLS-NEXT-THE-SEA,
NR23 1EX
Tel: 01328 710209
Fax: 01328 711432
Email: reception@thecrownhotelwells.co.uk
Website: www.thecrownhotelwells.co.uk
Map ref: 4, TF94
Directions: 10m from Fakenham on B1105
Open: 11–11 ₺ L 12–2.30 D 6.30–9.30 ⦿ D 7–9
Facilities: Garden Parking Notes: ⊕ Free House ♦ ⚞ ♟ 14

The Crown is a handsome former coaching inn overlooking the tree-lined green known as the Buttlands in Wells-next-the-Sea. This superb location is just a few minutes from the beach on the north Norfolk coast. Striking contemporary furnishings work well with the old-world charm of the 17th-century building, and the bar, with its open fire and ancient beams, is an appealing place for a drink – Adnams Ales, Woodforde's Wherry, 12 wines by the glass – or light meal from the interesting bar menu. This might include marinated pork belly with stir-fried noodles and hot-and-sour sauce; smoked haddock chowder; or beef burger with Gruyére cheese, sweet onions and pepper relish. The Crown Restaurant, awarded an AA Rosette for the quality of its food, offers dishes freshly prepared from the finest ingredients, in modern and traditional styles with a hint of Pacific Rim. A recent menu included such starters as flash-fried squid, bacon and black pudding; cream of curried parsnip soup; and grilled goat's cheese. Main courses featured Thai marinated duck breast with seared scallops and chilli jam; steamed North Sea cod with ginger, lemongrass and lime; and roast partridge breasts and confit legs. A private dining room is also available.

Recommended in the area

Holkham Hall; Wells and Walsingham Light Railway; Blakeney Point (NT)

Wiveton Bell

Address: Blakeney Road, WIVETON, Holt, NR25 7TL
Tel: 01263 740101
Email: enquiries@wivetonbell.co.uk
Website: www.wivetonbell.com
Map ref: 4, TG04
Directions: 1m from Blakeney. Wiverton Rd off A149
Open: 12–3 5.30–11 (Sun eve closed Oct–Etr)
L 12–3 D 6–9.30 L 12–3 D 6–9.30
Facilities: Garden Parking
Notes: Free House 18

This pretty, 17th-century inn overlooks the village green just a mile from Blakeney on Norfolk's beautiful north coast. Inside, an inglenook fireplace, settles, scrubbed wooden tables and oil paintings create a relaxed atmosphere where customers are just as likely to be walkers with muddy boots (and muddy dogs) as members of the area's business community. The award-winning restaurant is strong on local produce such as mussels, crabs, oysters and lobster, as well as game from the Holkham Hall Estate. Other dishes might include slow-roast Norfolk pork belly or braised oxtail with venison faggots. At lunchtime, lighter dishes are on offer, including chicken and bacon bruschetta, omelette Arnold Bennett, or a fine steak sandwich. Some of the Norfolk beers come from neighbouring brewery Yetmans, whose owner regards the Bell as his brewery taproom. In summer, the sheltered gardens, with their fine views of the village church and countryside, come into their own. Nice touches are the wind-up torches and umbrellas left in the bus shelter on the green for customers to use on the way to and from their cars. For those who wish to stay in the area, the Bell has two well-equipped rooms and a tastefully restored fisherman's cottage.

Recommended in the area

Holkham Beach; seal-watching trips to Blakeney Point; Wells Beach

Brixworth's All Saint's Church

The Queen's Head

Address: Main Street, BULWICK, NN17 3DY
Tel: 01780 450272
Email: queenshead-bulwick@tiscali.co.uk
Map ref: 3, SP99
Directions: Just off A43, between Corby & Stamford
Open: 12–3 6–11 (Sun 7–10.30) ▄ L 12–2.30
D 6–9.30 ▐◉▌ L 12–2.30 D 6–9.30 Closed: Mon
Facilities: Garden Parking
Notes: ⊕ Free House ▐▌ ▅ ☘ 9

The Queen's Head is believed to have been a pub since 1647, but its history goes back even further, with parts of the building dating back to 1400. It was named after Charles II's wife, Catherine of Braganza (known, apparently, for her very elaborate hair styles), and is the only pub in this charming village. Its cosy interior is a warren of small rooms, with low beamed ceilings, flagstone floors and four open fireplaces, and the lively local social life adds greatly to the atmosphere. The pub has a resident darts and dominos team, and a group of bellringers who each Wednesday show off their skills at the 12th-century church opposite the pub. Special events and themed nights are also organised, including the popular Hog Roast for Spring Bank Holiday. The landlord is very keen on real ale, and always keeps Shepherd Neame's Spitfire, Rockingham Ales and Newby Wyke on tap, plus guest ales. Hearty pub food includes some interesting and unusual dishes, such as chicken and goats' cheese wontons with lemon and mixed herb cous cous; vanilla roasted monkfish tail with spinach, fondant potato and spiced port jus; and noisettes of roasted lamb with red pepper and Savoy cabbage. All ingredients are fresh and locally sourced where possible, with an emphasis on fish and game when in season. Outside there is a very pretty patio, candlelit at night, which is a great place to enjoy lunch or dinner in the summer, when it echoes with the sounds of peacocks from Bulwick Hall.

Recommended in the area

Kirby Hall; Deene Park; Rockingham Raceway

The Red Lion

Address: 43 Welland Rise, SIBBERTOFT, Nr Market
Harborough, Leicester LE16 9UD
Tel: 01858 880011
Email: andrew@redlionwinepub.co.uk
Website: www.redlionwinepub.co.uk
Map ref: 3, SP68
Directions: From Market Harborough take A4304,
straight through Lubenham, then left through
Marston Trussell up to Sibbertoft
Open: 12–2 6–11 (Sun 12–5) **Closed:** Mon & Tue
lunch ▶ L 12–2 D 6.30–9.45 ⊚ L 12–2 D 6.30–9.45 **Facilities:** Garden Parking
Notes: ⊕ Free House ♦♦ ♈ 20

A giant wine bottle outside proclaims: 'Top food, top wines, at pub prices!' Andrew and Sarah Banks have spent much time rejuvenating this 300-year-old, friendly, contemporary-style pub/restaurant; they call it 'A little bit of London in the sticks'. Certainly, it offers an appealing blend of contemporary and classic decor, with oak beams and leather upholstery inside and a quiet garden outside. In the buzzy bar, reliable real ales from Adnams and Timothy Taylor vie with European imports. In the smartly turned-out restaurant, enthusiastic and clued-up staff know about organic ingredients and things like when and where the asparagus was picked. The menu changes monthly to offer, for instance, roasted cod on a bed of leeks with bacon butter; trio of pork casserole slowly cooked in cider; roasted pheasant breast wrapped in bacon with cranberry mash; and wild mushroom risotto, while Monday night is curry night. The game is shot on the farm next door, and the beef cattle are reared in the surrounding area and prepared for the kitchen in the next village. More than 200 wine bins reflect Andrew's particular passion.

Recommended in the area

Coton Manor; Mallory Park; Rutland Water

The Crown

Address: Helmdon Road, WESTON, nr Towcester,
NN12 8PX
Tel: 01295 760310
Fax: 01295 760310
Email: thecrown-weston@tiscali.co.uk
Website: www.thecrownweston.co.uk
Map ref: 3, SP54
Directions: Accessed from A43 or B4525
Open: 12–3 6–12 (Sun 6–11.30) ⓑ L 12–2.30 D 6–9.30
Closed: 25 Dec, Mon–Tue lunch **Facilities:** Garden Parking
Notes: ⊞ Free House ⚑ ♟ 7

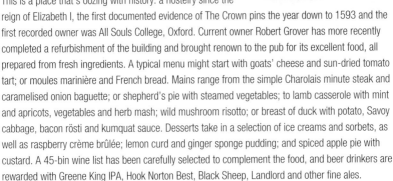

This is a place that's oozing with history: a hostelry since the
reign of Elizabeth I, the first documented evidence of The Crown pins the year down to 1593 and the
first recorded owner was All Souls College, Oxford. Current owner Robert Grover has more recently
completed a refurbishment of the building and brought renown to the pub for its excellent food, all
prepared from fresh ingredients. A typical menu might start with goats' cheese and sun-dried tomato
tart; or moules marinière and French bread. Mains range from the simple Charolais minute steak and
caramelised onion baguette; or shepherd's pie with steamed vegetables; to lamb casserole with mint
and apricots, vegetables and herb mash; wild mushroom risotto; or breast of duck with potato, Savoy
cabbage, bacon rösti and kumquat sauce. Desserts take in a selection of ice creams and sorbets, as
well as raspberry crème brûlée; lemon curd and ginger sponge pudding; and spiced apple pie with
custard. A 45-bin wine list has been carefully selected to complement the food, and beer drinkers are
rewarded with Greene King IPA, Hook Norton Best, Black Sheep, Landlord and other fine ales.

Recommended in the area

Sulgrave Manor; Silverstone; Canons Ashby House (NT)

The Wollaston Inn

Address: 87 London Road, WOLLASTON, NN29 7QS
Tel: 01933 663161
Email: info@wollaston-inn.co.uk
Website: www.wollaston-inn.co.uk
Map ref: 3, SP96
Directions: From Wellingborough, onto A507 towards Wollaston. After 2m, over rdbt, then immediately left. Inn at top of hill
Open: 11–11(Sun 11–10.30) ☕ L 11–7 D 5–10
🍴 L 11–7 D 5–10 **Facilities:** Garden Parking **Notes:** ⊕ ☐

Chris Spencer took over this historical pub, once the Sunday night venue of the late DJ John Peel, in 2003, reinventing it as a restaurant within a pub and giving it a new name. His loving restoration of the 350-year-old building's original features sits comfortably with the Italian leather sofas and casual tables and chairs. A commitment to please both formal and casual diners is reflected in the reasonably priced set lunch menus (available until 7pm), and an evening carte of seasonal dishes, with everything from the bread and infused oils to the ice creams and dark chocolate truffles made in the kitchen. Daily-changing selections, with ingredients coming from regional suppliers, might include venison haunch steak; Thai red chicken curry; slow roasted pork belly with pancetta and cannellini bean cassoulet; Mediterranean vegetable and buffalo mozzarella stack; and lots of fresh fish and seafood, such as lobster and monkfish thermidor; baked mackerel, sunblush tomato and courgette risotto; and organic sustainable cod, braised oxtail and caramelised apple. There is also a traditional Sunday roast. Service is attentive wherever you eat – choose from the bar, restaurant, patio or garden – and there is a good selection of real ales and an extensive wine list.

Recommended in the area

Summer Leys Nature Reserve; Santa Pod Raceway; Silverstone

Remains of Lindisfarne Priory

The Pheasant Inn

★★★★ INN
Address: Stannersburn, FALSTONE, NE48 1DD
Tel: 01434 240382
Fax: 01434 240382
Email: enquiries@thepheasantinn.com
Website: www.thepheasantinn.com
Map ref: 6, NY78
Directions: A69, B6079, B6320, follow signs for Kielder Water
Open: 11–3 6–11 (Opening times vary, ring for details) ♨ L 12–2.30 D 7–9 ♥ L 12–2.30 D 7–9 Closed: 25–26 Dec, Mon–Tue (Nov–Mar) Rooms: 8 en suite (5 GF) S £50–£55 D £90–£95 Facilities: Garden Parking Notes: ⊕ Free House ♠ ↬

Set close by the magnificent Kielder Water, this classic country inn, built in 1624, has exposed stone walls, original beams, low ceilings, open fires and a display of old farm implements in the bar. Run by the welcoming Kershaw family since 1985, the inn was originally a farmhouse and has been refurbished to a very high standard. The bright, modern en suite bedrooms, some with their own entrances, are all contained in stone buildings adjoining the inn and are set round a pretty courtyard. All the rooms, including one family room, are spotless, well equipped, and have tea and coffee facilities, hairdryer, colour TV and radio alarm clock; all enjoy delightful country views. Delicious home-cooked breakfasts and evening meals are served in the bar or in the attractive dining room, or may be taken in the pretty garden courtyard if the weather permits. Irene and her son Robin are responsible for the traditional home cooking using local produce and featuring delights such as game pie and roast Northumbrian lamb, as well as imaginative vegetarian choices. Drying and laundry facilities are available and, for energetic guests, cycle hire can be arranged.

Recommended in the area

Hadrian's Wall; Scottish Borders; Northumbrian castles and stately homes

Hadrian's Wall, Northumberland National Park

The Queen's Head

Address: GREAT WHITTINGTON, NE19 2HP
Tel: 01434 672267
Map ref: 7, NZ07
Website: www.the-queens-head-inn.co.uk
Directions: Exit A69 on A68. Then B6318, 1st left
Open: 12–3 5.30–1am (Fri–Sat 12–12, Sun
12–10.30) ⓑ L 12–2.30 D 6–9 ⓘ L 12–2.30
D 6–9 Facilities: Garden Parking
Notes: ⊕ Free House ⦿⦿ ⦿ 11

Just to the north of Hadrian's Wall country, surrounded by beautiful wooded countryside, stands this stone-built village pub. It holds plenty of character with its exposed stone walls, open fireplaces and old English fixtures, and the atmosphere is inviting and unpretentious in the bar and lounge. Here, displays of bric-a-brac and a mixture of banquette, pew and old spoke-back chair seating make a fine setting for enjoying a pint of locally-produced ale from Matfen Brewery. Cooking with Northumberland flair is offered in the dining room, where recent menus have included such dishes as pork tenderloin on an orange and onion marmalade, with black pudding fritters and cider and sage jus.

Recommended in the area

Hadrian's Wall and Roman Forts; Northumberland National Park; Belsay Hall, Castle and Gardens

Battlesteads Hotel & Restaurant

Address: Wark, HEXHAM,
NE48 3LS
Tel: 01434 230209
Fax: 01434 230039
Email: info@battlesteads.com
Website: www.battlesteads.com
Map ref: 7, NY96
Directions: 10m N of Hexham on B6320
(Kielder road)
Open: 11–11 **Closed:** winter Mon–Fri between 3–6
⮟ L 12–3 D 6.30–9.30 ⊙ L 12–3 D 6.30–9.30 **Facilities:** Garden Parking
Notes: ⊕ Free House ♯♯ ⋈

Originally built in 1747, this traditional Northumbrian inn and restaurant features a cosy bar with wood-burning stove, sunny conservatory and secret walled garden, excellent bar meals and a la carte menus (including vegetarian) using fresh, local produce, and a choice of 20 wines and five cask ales. Taken over in 2005 by Richard and Dee Slade, Battlesteads has quickly gained a reputation for its character and warm welcome as a friendly, family run establishment. Chefs source the best of local ingredients (within a 30 mile radius) to ensure freshness and flavour – including top quality Northumbrian lamb, prime Cumbrian beef and seasonal game. Fish and seafood is sourced from North Shields Fish Quay. A range of traditional roast dinners featuring locally reared beef, lamb and pork are available at the popular Sunday Carvery, all at set prices. Battlesteads has 17 en suite rooms with colour television, freeview, ironing boards and hairdryer. Four ground floor rooms have facilities for the disabled. Broadband access is available in all rooms.

Recommended in the Area

Hadrian's Wall; Kielder Forest and Lake; Alnwick Castle

The Olde Ship Hotel

★★ 84% SMALL HOTEL
Address: 9 Main Street, SEAHOUSES, NE68 7RD
Tel: 01665 720200
Fax: 01665 721383
Email: theoldeship@seahouses.co.uk
Website: www.seahouses.co.uk
Map ref: 10, NU23
Directions: Lower end of main street above harbour
Open: 11–11 (Sun 12–11) ᴇ **L** 12–2 **D** 7–8.30
I○I L 12–2 **D** 7–8.15 **Rooms:** 18 (3 GF) **S** £50–£58

D £100–£116 **Facilities:** Garden Parking **Notes:** ⊕ Free House ♗ 10

A former farmhouse dating from 1745, the inn stands overlooking the harbour in the tiny port of Seahouses, from where grain was once exported. The Olde Ship was first licensed in 1812 and has been in the same family for over 90 years, and these days it is a fully residential hotel. Boat trips run from the pier and there are wonderful coastal walks and attractive villages in the vicinity. The corridors, the boat gallery and the bars of the hotel are bulging at the seams with nautical memorabilia, creating a wonderful atmosphere, full of character, and the main saloon bar is warmed by an open fire and lit by stained glass windows. The overnight accommodation ranges through a self-catering fisherman's house, an all ground-floor self-catering cottage, adjoining executive suites and bedrooms in the hotel itself, including two four-poster rooms. They are all en suite, offering televisions, refreshment facilities and direct dial telephones. Some have marvellous views over to the bird and sea sanctuary on the nearby Farne Islands. Good home cooking features locally caught seafood and majors on soups, pastries, puddings and pies. Meals are served in the Restaurant, the Cabin Bar and the Locker Room.

Recommended in the area

Farne Islands; Bamburgh Castle; Lindisfarne

Statue of Robin Hood and Little John, Sherwood Forest Visitor Centre

The Martins Arms Inn

Address: School Lane, COLSTON BASSETT, NG12 3FD
Tel: 01949 81361
Fax: 01949 81039
Email: dinner@themartinsarms.co.uk
Website: www.themartinsarms.co.uk
Map ref: 8, SK73
Directions: Off A46 between Leicester & Newark
Open: 12–3 6–11 (Sun 7–10.30) ⓛ L 12–2 D 6–10
ⓨ L 12–2 D 6–9 **Closed:** 25 Dec eve
Facilities: Garden Parking **Notes:** ⊞ Free House ♦♦ ♯ ♛ 7

So popular is this award-winning inn that it has made appearances on both regional and national television. It is a listed 18th-century building, set close to the old market cross in this stunning village in the Vale of Belvoir, an area that is renowned for its Stilton cheese. The interior has a real country house feel to it, with period furnishings, traditional hunting prints and seasonal fires in the Jacobean fireplace. Outside there is an acre of landscaped grounds, which includes a herb garden and well established lawns, backing on to National Trust land. The inn is a free house, serving a good range of real ales – Marston's Pedigree, Interbrew Bass, Greene King Abbot Ale, Timothy Taylor Landlord – from hand pumps. The wine list also offers seven wines by the glass. Good regional ingredients are a feature of the menu. Take, for example, the classic ploughman's lunch comprising Melton Mowbray pork pie, Colston Bassett Stilton or cheddar, home-cured ham, pickles and bread. Alternatives in the bar include game pie, or fresh gnocchi with oven roasted tomatoes, peppers, spinach and parmesan cream. Typical restaurant dishes are cod fillet with lobster ravioli, potato rösti and creamed leek sauce; and bacon-wrapped rump of lamb with potato fondant and Puy lentils. Dogs are allowed in the garden only.

Recommended in the area

Belvoir Castle; Grantham Canal; National Watersports Centre

The Full Moon Inn

Address: Main Street, FISKERTON, Morton, Southwell
NG25 0UT
Tel: 01636 830251
Fax: 01636 830554
Email: info@thefullmoonmorton.co.uk
Website: www.thefullmoonmorton.co.uk
Map ref: 8, SK75
Directions: Newark A617 to Mansfield. Past Kelham, turn left to Rolleston & follow signs to Morton
Open: 10–3 6–11 (Sun 12–3) ┖ L 12–2.30 D 6–9.30
┆☺┆ L 12–2.30 D 6–9.30 **Facilities:** Garden Parking
Notes: ⊕ Free House ┆┆ ┆┆ ♇ 8

This traditional country inn has a long history, and owners William and Rebecca White are assuring its future with their abundant enthusiasm, culinary skill and serious approach to their free-house status. Real ales include Bombardier and Black Sheep, alongside two local brews from, for instance, the Nottingham Brewery. Menus are changed daily, and include such dishes as roast monkfish wrapped in prosciutto with roast tomatoes, and wild venison with beetroot and squeak. Fish specialities are only decided upon after their fishmonger has selected for them the finest market-fresh seafood available that day. The lunchtime menu features baguettes and baked potatoes with interesting fillings, and such favourites as home-made pies, vegetable lasagne, and haddock in beer batter with minted pea purée and the Full Moon's famous hand-cut chips, made from locally grown potatoes (an attraction in themselves). There's an interesting wine list, with eight available by the glass. The interior of the inn is soon to get something of a make-over to enhance its cosy, traditional atmosphere with with wooden floors, antique pine furniture and eclectic touches to give a nice 'unplanned' feel.

Recommended in the area

Southwell Minster; Newark-on-Trent Aircraft Museum; Holme Pierrepont & National Watersports Centre

OXFORDSHIRE

All Souls College, Oxford

The Vines

Address: Burford Road, BAMPTON, Black Bourton,
OX18 2PF
Tel: 01993 843559
Fax: 01993 840080
Email: info@vineshotel.com
Website: www.vinesblackbourton.co.uk
Map ref: 3, SP20
Directions: From A40 Witney, A4095 to Faringdon,
1st right after Bampton
Open: 12–3 6–11 (Sun 7–11) ఉ L 12–2
D 6.30–9.30 ᴵⓄᴵ **L** 12–2 **D** 6.30–9.30 **Closed:** Mon lunch **Facilities:** Garden Parking
Notes: ⊕ Free House ♦♦ ♟ 7

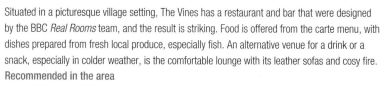

Situated in a picturesque village setting, The Vines has a restaurant and bar that were designed
by the BBC *Real Rooms* team, and the result is striking. Food is offered from the carte menu, with
dishes prepared from fresh local produce, especially fish. An alternative venue for a drink or a
snack, especially in colder weather, is the comfortable lounge with its leather sofas and cosy fire.
Recommended in the area
Cogges Manor Farm Museum; Cotswold Wildlife Park; Blenheim Palace

The Lord Nelson Inn

Address: BRIGHTWELL BALDWIN, nr Watlington,
OX49 5NP
Tel: 01491 612497
Website: www.lordnelson-inn.co.uk
Map ref: 3, SU69
Directions: Off B4009 between Watlington
& Benson
Open: 11–3 6–11 (Sun 7–11) ఉ L 12–2.30
D 6–10.30 ᴵⓄᴵ **L** 12–2.30 **D** 6–10.30
Facilities: Garden Parking
Notes: ⊕ Free House ♟ 20

This traditional 300-year-old inn, furnished with beautiful antiques, is set in an unspoilt village, opposite
the church, and its exterior will be familiar to *Midsomer Murders* fans. In 1905 it was forced to close by
the local lord who was trying to stop his workers from drinking, and did not reopen until 1971. There
is a comprehensive wine list, and all the dishes are freshly cooked to order by the inn's experienced
chefs. There are also some good hearty bar snacks and a varied Sunday lunch menu.
Recommended in the area
Stonor Park; The Rideway; Wallingford Museum

The Lamb Inn

★★★ 81% ◉◉ SMALL HOTEL

Address: Sheep Street, BURFORD, OX18 4LR
Tel: 01993 823155
Fax: 01993 822228
Email: info@lambinn-burford.co.uk
Website: www.cotswold-inns-hotels.co.uk/lamb
Map ref: 3, SP21
Directions: M40 junct 8, follow A40 & Burford signs, 1st turn down hill into Sheep St
Open: 11–11 ⓑ L 12–2.30 D 6.30–9.30
⑩ L 12–2.30 D 7–9.30 **Rooms:** 17 (4 GF) **S** £145 **D** £145–£255 **Facilities:** Garden
Notes: ⊕ Free House ♦♦ ♔ ♇ 9

This ancient inn dates back to 1420 and was originally built as weavers' cottages. In complete harmony with its lovely setting in the Cotswolds, it really does deserve the description of 'charming old inn'. From the wisteria-clad walls to the stone-flagged bar, from the delightful dining room to the beautifully refurbished bedrooms, the Lamb has been sympathetically restored to offer all the comfort of today while retaining the atmosphere of yesteryear. With its stone floor, log fire and fine selection of wines and traditional English real ales, the welcoming bar draws in guests and locals alike and is a favourite spot to exchange news and views. There is an extensive menu if you should wish to lunch or dine in these relaxed surroundings. The finest fresh ingredients, many produced locally, are used to create a cuisine that is contemporary English with strong traditional influences. A daily fish board is also available. Alternatively enjoy a drink or lunch in the walled patio garden, a veritable sun-trap which leads down to a beautiful traditional English cottage garden, a lovely area in which to relax, read or take and afternoon nap.

Recommended in the area

Blenheim Palace; Cotswold Wildlife Park; Burford Garden Company

The Bridge of Sighs, Oxford

The Sir Charles Napier

◎◎

Address: Spriggs Alley, CHINNOR, OX39 4BX
Tel: 01494 483011
Fax: 01494 485311
Website: www.sircharlesnapier.co.uk
Map ref: 3, SP70
Directions: M40 junct 6 to Chinnor. Turn right at rdbt, up hill to Spriggs Alley
Open: 12–3.30 6.30–12 ⓫ L 12–2.30 D 7–9.30 ⑩ L 12–2.30 D 7–10 **Closed:** 25–26 Dec (Mon, Sun eve) **Facilities:** Garden Parking **Notes:** ⊕ Free House ⅰⅼ ⏺ 15

The Sir Charles Napier is in the scenic Chiltern Hills surrounded by beech woods and fields. The furnishings are eclectic, and wonderful sculptures are exhibited throughout the year. In summer, lunch is served on the terrace beneath vines and wisteria, overlooking the herb gardens and lawns. The wine list complements blackboard dishes and imaginative seasonal menus that have earned this pub two AA Rosettes. Typical dishes are halibut with pea purée, and sea bream with saffron and crayfish tails.

Recommended in the area

The Chiltern Hills; West Wycombe Park; Garsington Opera

Coach & Horses Inn

★★★ ⬭ INN

Address: Watlington Road, CHISELHAMPTON, OX44 7UX
Tel: 01865 890255
Fax: 01865 891995
Email: enquiries@coachhorsesinn.co.uk
Website: www.coachhorsesinn.co.uk
Map ref: 3, SU59
Directions: On B480, 5m from Oxford
Open: 11.30–11 ⓫ L 12–2 D 7–10 ⑩ L 12–2 D 7–10 **Rooms:** 9 en suite **Facilities:** Garden Parking **Notes:** ⊕ Free House ⏺ 8

A charming, family-run 16th-century inn, just 200 yards from the River Thame. When it's chilly someone lights the huge log fire in the bar, while in the summer it's hard to beat the courtyard or lawn for a pleasant drink. You may eat outside, or in the oak-beamed, candlelit restaurant, from a seasonal menu featuring Angus steaks, game and fresh seafood, while at lunchtimes bar meals and snacks are available. The bedrooms are ranged around the courtyard, with most looking out over the countryside.

Recommended in the area

City of Oxford; Ridgeway Path; Hughenden Manor

The White Lion

Address: Goring Road, Goring Heath, CRAYS POND,
Reading, RG8 7SH
Tel: 01491 680471
Fax: 01491 684254
Email: reservations@thewhitelioncrayspond.com
Website: www.thewhitelioncrayspond.com
Map ref: 3, SU68
Directions: M4 junct 11 follow signs to Pangbourne,
through toll bridge to Whitchurch. N for 3m
Open: 10–3 6–11 ♿ **L** 12–1.30 **D** 6–9.30
🍴 **L** 12–2 **D** 6.30–9 **Closed:** 25–26 Dec, 1 Jan Sun eve, Mon **Facilities:** Garden Parking
Notes: 🌐 GREENE KING ♦♦ 🍴 ♟ 11

Up in the Chilterns' hamlet of Cray's Pond stands this popular, 250-year-old pub. Looking as though it was originally a cottage, it acts once a year as the unofficial headquarters of the Woodcote Rally, one of the country's largest veteran and vintage transport fairs, which is held in a nearby field. Photographs taken of steam engines during the last four decades line the deep red walls, while also worth a browse is the fascinating collection of old and new menus from famous restaurants around the world. The beamed ceilings are low, so watch your head; the dining room charms with its open fires, oak floors and candles; and the conservatory overlooks the garden through large bay windows. In the kitchen there is a real emphasis on quality, freshness and attention to detail before the frequently changing modern British menu sees the light of day. Usually offered are eight starters and main courses, among the latter possibly a whole Dover sole, grilled to perfection with a caper sauce, or dry aged beef from Macey's Organics in Cookham. Sticky toffee pudding, butterscotch sauce and Jersey clotted cream is but one of the tempting desserts. The wine list is compact, but well chosen.
Recommended in the area
Basildon House; Beale Park; Ridgeway Path

The White Hart

Address: Main Road, FYFIELD, Nr Abingdon, OX13 5LW
Tel: 01865 390585
Email: info@whitehart-fyfield.com
Website: www.whitehart-fyfield.com
Map ref: 3, SU49
Directions: 6m S of Oxford just off A420
Open: 12–3 5.30–11 (Tue–Fri) (Sat 12–11, Sun 12–10.30)
⓵ L 12–2.30 D 6.30–9.30 ⓘ⌯ L 12–2.30 D 6.30–9.30
Closed: Mon ex BHs **Facilities:** Garden Parking
Notes: ⊞ Free House ⑪ Ⓨ 14

An historic, 15th-century chantry house, the White Hart retains many original features, including a tunnel to Fyfield Manor (possibly used as an escape route for priests during the Dissolution of the Monasteries). The setting is breathtaking, from soaring eaves in the great hall and minstrels' gallery, to the terrace full of aromatic herb gardens. Given that owners, Mark and Kay Chandler, are self-confessed 'foodies' it is no surprise that the White Hart is renowned for superb locally-sourced food. Menus change daily depending on what is fresh and seasonal and everything is made in-house, including bread (using locally milled flour). Starters may include home-cured salmon gravadlax with marinated cucumber salad or ox tongue with potato and caper salad and salsa verde. For main courses there might be slow roasted pork belly with crackling, celeriac purée, potato and rosemary ravioli with wild mushrooms, tarragon and black truffle. Puddings are just as tempting, especially hot chocolate fondant with pistachio ice cream. Regular food and wine evenings are also popular. Although standards of food and service are high, the pub is still very much a village local, with a cosy bar and inglenook fireplace. Two beer festivals are held annually (May and August bank holiday weekends) with real ales, live jazz and hog roasts.

Recommended in the area

Ashmolean Museum, Oxford; White Horse, Uffington; Blenheim Palace, Woodstock

The Black Boy Inn

Address: MILTON, Banbury, OX15 4HH
Tel: 01295 722111
Email: info@blackboyinn.com
Website: www.blackboyinn.com
Map ref: 3, SP43
Directions: From Banbury take A4260 to Adderbury. After Adderbury turn right signed Bloxham. Onto Milton Road to Milton. Pub on right
Open: 12–11(Sun 12–10.30) ⓫ L 12–2.30
ⓘ L 12–2.30 D 6.30–9 **Facilities:** Garden Parking
Notes: ⊕ MERCHANT INNS PLC ⅰ ⅲ ⓟ 8

Although this 16th-century coaching inn has been completely refurbished, its stylish interior and solid pine furniture are entirely in keeping with such an old building. Located in picturesque Milton, the pub is thought to take its name from the dark-skinned Charles II, although other theories point to the slave trade. The long room has a real wood stove at one end and a comfortable dining room at the other; in between is the bar, with conservatory-style dining. Outside there is plenty of seating in the patio and garden, the latter providing a half-acre of space for children to run around. A rotating list of guest ales and a selection of wines by the glass ensure that drinkers can enjoy the informal atmosphere of this quintessentially English free house. Food is important here, with modern British dishes based on fresh seasonal ingredients at sensible prices the objective of executive chef Rob Clayton. There are plenty of pub classics, including beer-battered cod and home-made chips with crushed peas, as well as up-market mains such as roasted fillet of sea trout with crab tagliatelle and fennel. Excellent desserts, vegetarian options and a wide range of fresh salads and tasty sandwiches are also on offer.

Recommended in the area

Broughton Castle; Blenheim Palace; Cotswold villages

The Crown Inn

Address: PISHILL, Henley-on-Thames,
RG9 6HH
Tel: 01491 638364
Fax: 01491 638364
Email: lhdwood@hotmail.com
Website: www.crownpishill.co.uk
Map ref: 3, SU78
Directions: On B480 off A4130,
NW of Henley-on-Thames
Open: 11.30–2.30 6–11 (Sun 12–3, 7–10)
L 12–2.30 D 7–9.30 ꙮ L 12–2.30 D 7–9.30
Closed: 25–26 Dec
Facilities: Garden Parking **Notes:** Free House ♦ 8

A pretty 15th-century brick and flint former coaching inn, The Crown has enjoyed a colourful history. It began life in medieval times, serving ale to members of the thriving local monastic community, and in later years served as a refuge for Catholic priests escaping Henry VIII's draconian rule. It contains possibility the largest priest hole in the country, complete with a sad story about one Father Dominique, who met his end here. Moving forward to the 'swinging 60s', the barn housed a nightclub hosting the likes of George Harrison and Dusty Springfield. Today, the barn is licensed for civil ceremonies as well as serving as a function room. In the pub itself, the menu changes frequently and features local produce cooked fresh to order. Lunch and dinner are served every day and can be enjoyed in the picturesque garden or inside where there are three log fires lit when the weather is cooler. Bed and breakfast accommodation is available.

Recommended in the area

Stonor Park; Greys Court, (NT); River and Rowing Museum

Crooked Billet

Address: STOKE ROW, Henley-on-Thames, RG9 5PU
Tel: 01491 681048
Fax: 01491 682231
Website: www.thecrookedbillet.co.uk
Map ref: 3, SU68
Directions: From Henley towards Oxford on A4130. Left at Nettlebed for Stoke Row
Open: 12–10 🍺 L 12–2.30 D 7–10 🍽 L 12–2.30 D 7–10
Facilities: Garden Parking **Notes:** 🚾 BRAKSPEAR ♦♦ 🍷 12

The remote location of this charming pub was a boon to highwayman Dick Turpin, who avoided the law and courted the landlord's daughter here. Later, it became a favourite watering hole of George Harrison, who lived nearby. It was also the venue for Kate Winslet's first wedding reception. But you don't have to be a celebrity to appreciate its pretty farmland setting and its fascinating history, dating back to 1642. Award-winning chef/proprietor Paul Clerehugh is so keen to use local produce that he's even been known to swap meals for produce. Seafood is a speciality, with Sevruga caviar served with oysters, sour cream and smoked salmon blinis as a starter, and fillets of Dover sole with grilled king prawns and Puy lentils to follow. For game choices try hare braised with lardons, mushrooms, baby onions and thyme, served with herb dumplings. Other dishes include starters such as a selection of Italian salami, served with artichoke, mozzarella, olives and sun-blushed tomato; or crispy-fried salt and pepper squid with warm chick pea and roast vegetable salad; or main courses such as breast of chicken stuffed with goats' cheese and baked in pancetta, served with warm chorizo salad and Puy lentils. Vegetarians may find sage and pecorino polenta with asparagus and artichoke heart salad, or leek and Oxford Blue pancakes with roast winter roots and buttered spinach.

Recommended in the area

Mapledurham House; Greys Court (NT); Beale Park

The Mason's Arms

Address: Banbury Road, SWERFORD, Chipping
Norton, OX7 4AP
Tel: 01608 683212
Fax: 01608 683105
Email: themasonschef@hotmail.com
Website: www.masons-arms.co.uk
Map ref: 3, SP33
Directions: Between Banbury & Chipping Norton
on A361
Open: 10–3 6–11 (Jul–Aug all day) L 12–2.15 D 7–9.15 L 12–2.15 D 7–9.15 **Closed:** 25–26
Dec (Sun eve) **Facilities:** Garden Parking **Notes:** Free House 7

A former Masonic lodge built of local honey-coloured stone, this free house is situated in beautiful
surroundings just a stone's throw from the Hook Norton Brewery. Traditional charm is balanced by
plenty of modern comforts under the enthusiastic ownership of Bill and Charmaine Leadbeater. The
chef/proprietor trained with Gordon Ramsay and Marco Pierre White, so expect something special. All
the meat is from rare breeds; poultry is free range; fish is delivered daily. The menu, boldly entitled
Bill's Food, has a distinctly continental outlook, featuring unusual and frequently changing dishes.
Starters might include smoked halibut with avocado parfait and cider and apple dressing, while main
course options of chargrilled marlin loin; steamed vegetable pancake wrap; and Gloucester Old Spot
pork done three ways might feature. A treat for four to share, given 48 hours' notice, is whole roast leg
of Oxford Down lamb with rosemary and garlic, dauphinoise potatoes, haricot verts and rosemary jus.
Bar snacks take include a range of pub favourites, beers are well-kept, and there's also a good choice
of malt whiskies.

Recommended in the area

Burford Wildlife Park; Hook Norton Brewery and Pottery; Wiggington Waterfowl Sanctuary

Normanton church at Rutland Water

Kings Arms

★★★★ ❀ INN

Address: Top Street, WING, LE15 8SE
Tel: 01572 737634
Fax: 01572 737255
Email: info@thekingsarms-wing.co.uk
Website: www.thekingsarms-wing.co.uk
Map ref: 3, SK80
Directions: 1m off B6003 between Uppingham
& Oakham
Open: 12–3 6.30–11 ▥ L 12–2 D 6.30–8

▥ L 12–2 D 6.30–8 **Closed:** Sun eve, Mon (winter), Mon **lunch** (summer) **Rooms:** 8 en suite (4 GF)
S £85 D £75 Facilities: Garden Parking **Notes:** ⊕ Free House ♟ 20

Popular for its good food, beer and ambiance, the Kings Arms is a 17th-century, family-run pub in the quaint village of Wing. Eight en suite letting rooms are available, four on the ground floor, four on the first floor, with a separate entrance away from the pub. All are equipped with tea and coffee making facilities, trouser press, hairdryer, television and complimentary toiletries. The location is ideal for those participating in outdoor activities in and around Rutland Water: fishing, walking, cycling and sailing. The large car park is also convenient for light boats and motorised campers. The oldest part of the inn is the bar, dating from 1649, with flagstone floors and a beamed ceiling. Here traditional cask ales are served along with a good range of wines by the glass and an excellent choice of non-alcoholic drinks. All the food is freshly prepared and produced in-house, including smoked items like pancetta and bacon, as well as the stocks, sauces, chutneys, soups, dips, pestos, breads, pastries, desserts, ice creams and sorbets. Dishes range from traditional bar meals and sandwiches to confit duck leg, smokey bacon and bean cassoulet and pork chop with leek mash and black pudding in the restaurant.

Recommended in the area

Burleigh House; Barnsdale Gardens; Wing Maze Rutland

Shropshire Union Canal

The Boyne Arms

Address: Bridgnorth Road, BURWARTON,
WV16 6QH
Tel: 01746 787214
Email: theboynearms@btconnect.com
Website: www.theboynearms.co.uk
Map ref: 2, SO68
Directions: On B4364, between Ludlow & Bridgnorth
Open: 11–3.30 6–11.30 (Sat–Sun all day)
L 12–2.30 D 7–9.15 L 12–2.30 D 7–9.15
Facilities: Garden Parking
Notes: 8

Located in an Area of Outstanding Natural Beauty, the Boyne Arms is a striking example of a rural Georgian coaching inn. Boasting an impressive frontage and beautiful mature walled garden with a children's play area, the pub, which is part of the Boyne Estate and has been part of Lord Boyne's family for generations, has been drawing visitors and locals alike for some time. The food is a real draw, and husband and wife Jamie and Nere Yardley and their team offer a high quality dining experience either in one of the comfortable bars – where four real ales plus a real cider are always on the hand pumps – or in the elegant dining room, with its crisp white napery and attentive friendly service. Well-presented dishes combine fresh regional produce with classic French flavours, as in assiette of new season lamb with confit potatoes and vegetable jardinière or seared scallops with boudin noir, followed by simple lemon tart. More simple fare, such as an unbeatable pork pie ploughman's bar lunch, is also available. The extensive wine list to suit all tastes and pockets sits comfortably alongside a range of excellent local award-winning real ales from the likes of Hobsons and Wood's breweries.

Recommended in the area

Historic towns of Ludlow and Bridgnorth; Shropshire Hills; Ludlow Castle

The Countess's Arms

Address: WESTON HEATH, nr Shifnal, TF11 8RY
Tel: 01952 691123
Fax: 01952 691660
Email: countesssarms@countessarms.co.uk
Map ref: 2, SJ71
Directions: 1.5m from Weston Park. Turn off A5 onto A41 towards Newport
Open: 12–11(Sun 12–10.30) 🍺 L 12–6 D 6–9.30
🍴 L 12–6 D 6–9.30 **Facilities:** Garden Parking
Notes: 🌐 Free House 🍷 10

In the owners' own words, this is 'a large contemporary eatery in a refurbished traditional pub'. The owner in question is the Earl of Bradford, a well-known restaurateur and food critic, whose splendid family seat is Weston Park, just down the road. Formerly known as The Plough, The Countess's Arms (named for the earl's wife) has had a transformation, involving the removal of all the internal floors and walls and the addition of an extension. Customers in the spacious gallery bar able to look down on the blue glass mosaic-tiled bar below. Head chef Patrick Champion has brought the earl's concept of fun eating to fruition with his interesting menus. Bar snacks feature oriental dim sum, and chicken liver parfait with onion marmalade and French stick, alongside sausage with bubble and squeak. A stylish, modern approach to cooking results in main course dishes such as lamb chump, dauphinoise potatoes, roasted cherry tomatoes and redcurrant jus; roast duck breast with rösti potato, braised red cabbage and Kirsch sauce; and Cajun-spiced chicken salad. Seafood choices could include poached sea bass with shitake mushrooms, spring onions and jasmine rice; salmon fillet on crushed potatoes; and sautéed prawns, mussels and clams with gnocchi and basil dressing. There's an excellent wine list, and beer drinkers can savour Robinsons, St Austell Tribute and Woods Hopping Mad.
Recommended in the area
Weston Park; Lilleshall Abbey; Royal Air Force Museum

A figure woven from willow at Stoke St Gregory

The Hunters Rest

★ ★ ★ ★ INN

Address: King Lane, Clutton Hill, CLUTTON,
BS39 5QL

Tel: 01761 452303

Fax: 01761 453308

Email: info@huntersrest.co.uk

Website: www.huntersrest.co.uk

Map ref: 2, ST65

Directions: From Bristol on A37 follow signs for
Wells through Pensford, at large rdbt left towards
Bath, 100mtrs right into country lane, pub 1m up hill

Open: 11.30–3 6–11 (Fri–Sun all day) 🍴 **L** 12–2 **D** 6.30–9.45 🍴 **L** 12–2 **D** 6.30–9.45 **Rooms:** 5 en suite **S** £62.50–£79.50 **D** £87.50–£125 **Facilities:** Garden Parking **Notes:** 🍺 Free House 🚻 🐾 🍷 14

Originally a hunting lodge that was built for the Earl of Warwick in about 1750, the inn is situated amid beautiful countryside high on Clutton Hill overlooking the Cam Valley to the Mendips and the Chew Valley to Bristol. Historic character, including beams, exposed stonework and log fires, has been complemented by modern amenities, creating a cosy atmosphere inside. There's a landscaped garden outside, complete with a miniature railway to carry passengers around the grounds. The beers served here include Otter Ale, Sharps Own, Hidden Quest and Butcombe, and there is a reasonably priced wine list with a good choice by the glass. Home-made dishes from the menu range through bakehouse rolls and giant oggies (pasties) with a variety of fillings, to grills and other popular pub fare, while the list of daily specials might include rack of lamb with rosemary and garlic gravy, or salmon fishcakes with dill mayonnaise. The inn offers accommodation in individually designed bedrooms. These include four-poster suites, antique furniture, direct dial telephones, LCD televisions and Wi-fi.

Recommended in the area

Bath; Cheddar Caves; Wells Cathedral

Pulteney Bridge, Bath

The Queens Arms

Address: CORTON DENHAM, DT9 4LR
Tel: 01963 220317
Email: relax@thequeensarms.com
Website: www.thequeensarms.com
Map ref: 2, ST62
Directions: From A30 (take B3145 signed
Wincanton. Approx 1.5m left to Corton Denham. 1.5m
Open: 11–3 6–11 (Sat–Sun & BHs 11–11)
L 12–3 **D** 6–10 **Facilities:** Garden Parking
Notes: ⊞ Free House 👭 🐕 ♀ 16

Situated at the heart of an ancient village amidst beautiful rolling countryside, this welcoming pub has an informal bar, bustling dining room and garden in which to enjoy the exceptional choice of drinks that includes international beers, local ales and ciders, and an imaginative wine and whisky list. The changing menu of robust British cuisine is prepared with the freshest locally sourced ingredients and much innovative skill. With a warmth of hospitality that welcomes 'children, dogs and muddy boots', it's small wonder that The Queens Arms was selected as AA Pub of the Year 2008–9 for England.

Recommended in the area

Stourhead (NT); Yeovilton Air Museum; Sherborne Abbey

The Luttrell Arms

★★★ 73% ⚙ HOTEL

Address: High Street, DUNSTER, TA24 6SG
Tel: 01643 821555
Fax: 01643 821567
Email: info@luttrellarms.fsnet.co.uk
Map ref: 1, SS94
Directions: A39 Bridgewater to Minehead, A396
Dunster. 2m before Minehead
Open: 10–11 ⋒ L 12–3 D 7–10 ⏐⊙⏐ L 12–3 D 7–10
Rooms: 28 S £70–£102 D £104–£140
Facilities: Garden Notes: ⊕ Free House ⊨

Set in the only street in the medieval village of Dunster, within Exmoor National Park, this 15th-century hotel was once a guest house for the Abbots of Cleeve. Inside, it is certainly rich in atmosphere and history and is a good spot to escape the pace of modern life. The open fires and oak beams make the bar a welcoming place in winter, with locally brewed beers on offer, while the murmuring of ghostly monks is rumoured to cure even the most stubborn insomniacs, should you choose to stay the night in one of the stylish bedrooms. All of the rooms boast high ceilings and leather armchairs, and some have four-posters. The hotel has two eating places to choose from: the bar, which spills out onto the garden in summer months and serves such warming delights as rib-sticking wild venison casserole, or the more formal restaurant. Diners can enjoy meals such as smoked haddock fishcakes, followed by wild pigeon and mushroom parcels with cider jus in the latter. Desserts include sticky ginger parkin with vanilla-steeped pineapple and ginger ice cream in the restaurant, and clotted cream rice pudding in the bar. Locally brewed beers and a good-value wine list complete the picture.

Recommended in the area

Dunster Castle (NT); Exmoor National Park; Dunster Station Steam Railway

Glastonbury Tor at sunset

The Helyar Arms

★★★★ ⊛ INN

Address: Moor Lane, EAST COKER, BA22 9JR
Tel: 01935 862332
Fax: 01935 864129
Email: info@helyar-arms.co.uk
Website: www.helyar-arms.co.uk
Map ref: 2, ST51
Directions: A57 or A30, follow East Coker signs
Open: 11–3 6–11 (Sun 12–10.30) ⓑ L 12–2.30
D 6.30–9.30 ⓘⓞⓘ L 12–2.30 D 6.30–9.30
Rooms: 6 en suite **Facilities:** Garden Parking **Notes:** ⊕ PUNCH TAVERNS ⓘⓘ ⓘⓘ ⓘ 30

Parts of this traditional village inn date back to 1468. Forget the TV and games machines; instead enjoy the rustic charm of a beamed bar, open log fire, horse brasses, copper pots and a traditional skittle alley. Virtually all the food is prepared to order by whoever's name is on the notice board by the bar. Stocks, sauces, ice creams and chutneys are all home made, and what the pub can't grow or produce itself is sourced mostly from Somerset and Dorset. Character en suite rooms offer good amenities.

Recommended in the area

Glastonbury Tor; Barrington Court; Somerset Levels

The Crown Hotel

★★★ 75% ◉◉ HOTEL

Address: EXFORD, Exmoor National Park, TA24 7PP
Tel: 01643 831554
Fax: 01643 831665
Email: info@crownhotelexmoor.co.uk
Website: www.crownhotelexmoor.co.uk
Map ref: 2, SS83
Directions: From M5 junct 25 follow Taunton signs.
Take A358 then B3224 via Wheddon Cross to Exford
Open: 11–11 ⓑ L 12–5.50 D 6–9.30 ⓘ◎ D 7–9
Rooms: 17 S £70 D £110–£140 **Facilities:** Garden Parking **Notes:** ⊕ Free House ⚘ ♟ 12

A family-run, 17th-century coaching inn, the Crown Hotel is set in its own three acres of gardens at the heart of the Exmoor National Park. The surrounding countryside is renowned for its Exmoor ponies, red deer and birds of prey. In summer dine outside, in either the water garden or the terrace patio as an alternative to the elegant restaurant, you might prefer the cosy country bar, with its log fire and range of real ales. All meals are home made and freshly cooked to order using the freshest produce, locally sourced and organic where possible; the well-balanced menus have seasonal emphasis and a local twist. Smoked haddock, chilli and coriander fishcake with brie and cranberry wonton and roasted fillet of sea bass with basil crushed potatoes and vegetable Provençal can be found alongside organic pork loin with chorizo potatoes, apple compote and port sauce. Extensive vegetarian options are also available. Mouth-watering desserts include treacle tart with clotted cream ice cream and vanilla pavlova with crème Chantilly and summer fruits, or finish with the highly regarded Somerset and Devon cheese plate. Accommodation is available in 17 tastefully decorated, en suite bedrooms. Dogs and horses are also made most welcome.

Recommended in the area

Tarr Steps; Dunster Castle; Lynmouth

The Globe

★ ★ ★ 🍺 INN

Address: Fore Street, MILVERTON, TA4 1JX
Tel: 01823 400534
Email: info@theglobemilverton.co.uk
Website: www.theglobemilverton.co.uk
Map ref: 2, ST12
Directions: On B3187
Rooms: 3 en suite
Open: 12–3 6–11 (Fri –Sat 6–11.30, Sun 12–3,
Mon 6–11) 🍺 L 12–2 D 6.30–9 🍽 L 12–2
D 6.30–9 **Closed:** Mon lunch, Sun eve **Facilities:** Parking **Notes:** 🍷 👤 🍷 8

Originally a coaching inn, The Globe is a village free house with a difference. A Grade II listed building, it has been refurbished in a clean-looking, contemporary style that creates both its distinctive character, which follows through to the three en suite bedrooms, and its warm, friendly atmosphere. In addition, husband-and-wife team Mark and Adele Tarry are building an excellent reputation for their quality home-cooked food. As a result, the community has taken them to their hearts, and the walls of the restaurant and bar are adorned with the work of local artists. All of the food here is home made, including the bread, and the menus, which draw heavily on West Country sources, change frequently to offer attractions such as broccoli and gorgonzola soup; River Fowey mussels; traditional steak and kidney pie; grilled pollack with kale; slow-roasted Gloucester Old Spot belly pork; Mark's mum's faggots; and baked parsnip and onion tart with roasted root vegetables. The children's menu is also thoughtfully compiled, while a real taste of the west comes in the form of the cheese board. Local ales from Exmoor and Cotleigh sit alongside guest ales from brewers such as Otter and Quantock. Local cider and English wines are also available.

Recommended in the area

Exmoor National Park; Hestercombe Gardens; Dunster Castle (NT)

The Notley Arms

Address: MONKSILVER, Taunton, TA4 4JB
Tel: 01984 656217
Website: www.thenotleyarms.co.uk
Map ref: 2, ST03
Directions: Village on B3227 N of Wiveliscombe
Open: 12–2.30 6.30–11 (Fri 12–2,6.30–9)
L 12–2 D 7–9 Closed: Mon lunch in summer
Facilities: Garden Parking
Notes: ⊕ ENTERPRISE INNS 🐕 ♟ 10

This English country drinking and dining pub, built in the 1860s and named after a prominent local family, is located in a hamlet on the edge of Exmoor. The village name comes from the Latin word silva, meaning 'wooded area'. When monks from Monmouthshire arrived at nearby Cleeve Abbey, it became known as Silva Monachorum or Monksilver. The cuisine offers a distinct bias towards traditional but imaginative British food, using fresh produce from the south west of England. Look forward also, to southern African influences (the owners come from Zimbabwe), which show through in the form of ostrich steaks and bobotie. Menus change often so you may not always find pork and three mustard Stroganoff; Exmoor shin of beef and Seville orange casserole; Deerstalker venison pie; bacon-wrapped chicken breast stuffed with pepperoni and apricots; or Thai-style butternut and pineapple curry. Depending on catches landed at St Mawes in Cornwall, fresh fish on the plate may be lightly breaded whitebait with tartare sauce; chunky cod fillet with lemon sauce on parsley mash; or smoked Cornish haddock rarebit with sautééd spinach. Smaller portions are available for children. Puddings include Somerset apple and hazelnut cake with toffee sauce and clotted cream, and raspberry coulis and toasted almonds. The pretty garden is bordered by an Exmoor stream called the Silver, and there is also a selection of toys to keep children happy.

Recommended in the area

Exmoor National Park; Combe Sydenham Country Park; Cleeve Abbey

George Inn

Address: High St, NORTON ST PHILIP BA2 7LH
Tel: 01373 834224
Fax: 01373 834861
Email: georgeinnnsp@aol.com
Website: www.thegeorgeinn-nsp.co.uk
Map ref: 2, ST75
Directions: From Bath take A36 to Warminster, after
6m, right onto A366 to Radstock, village 1m
Open: 11–2.30 5.30–11 (Sat–Sun all day in
summer) ᕲ L 12–2 D 7–9.30 ᑢ L 12–2 D 7–9.30
Facilities: Garden Parking Notes: ⊕ WADWORTH ✦ ♟ 30

The George was originally built during the late 14th century as accommodation for travellers and merchants coming to medieval wool fairs, and it is one of the oldest inns in the country. It provided a meal for Samuel Pepys in 1668 and gave shelter to the Duke of Monmouth during his ill-fated 1685 uprising. The stone and timber-framed building has featured in movies and TV series including *Moll Flanders*, *The Remains of the Day*, *Tom Jones* (in which a young Albert Finney leapt from the gallery here) and Pasolini's 1972 *Canterbury Tales*. With its galleried courtyard, soaring timber roofs and 15th-century stair tower, the building alone merits a visit. The main bar contains a splendid inglenook fireplace and a 700-year-old writing desk once used by the monks. Well-kept Wadworth ales and a decent wine list complement the imaginative menus. Begin, perhaps, with New Zealand green lipped mussels in a garlic sauce; or deep-fried Somerset brie with cranberry dip; or one of the home-made soups. Follow this with an individual beef Wellington, with red wine gravy; or chicken breast stuffed with sun dried tomato, olive, garlic and mozzarella. Finish with one of the mouthwatering desserts on offer that make dining here a delight.

Recommended in the area

Westwood Manor; Brokerswood Country Park; Farleigh Hungerford Castle

The Carpenters Arms

Address: STANTON WICK, Nr Pensford, BS39 4BX
Tel: 01761 490202
Fax: 01761 490763
Email: carpenters@buccaneer.co.uk
Website: www.the-carpenters-arms.co.uk
Map ref: 2, ST66
Directions: A37 to Chelwood rdbt, then A368.
Pub 8m S of Bath
Open: 11–11 (Sun 12–10.30) ☕ L 12–2 D 7–10
🍴 L 12–2 D 7–10 (Sun 12–9) **Closed:** 25–26 Dec
Facilities: Garden Parking **Notes:** ⊕ BUCCANEER HOLDINGS ♦♦ 🍷 12

Just 20 minutes from either Bath or Bristol, this charming stone-built free house is set in the tranquil hamlet of Stanton Wick, overlooking the Chew Valley. It began life as a row of miners' cottages and retains its cottagey style, with a spacious terrace, perfect for summer drinks. Behind the pretty flower bedecked façade, you'll find a low-beamed bar with a convivial atmosphere and no intrusive music. A choice of real beers is served, including Butcombe, Wadworth 6X, and an extensive wine list. The menu changes regularly to offer the best seasonal produce, including fish from Cornwall, West Country beef and local game in season. Typical dishes include a starter of trio of smoked halibut, salmon and trout with light horseradish cream, and a main course of pork chop on mashed potato with braised savoy cabbage and an onion and thyme sauce. A function room is available for use by groups of 20–36. Twelve bedrooms, refurbished in contemporary style, provide en suite accommodation – nine king-size, double rooms and three twins. Each room is equipped with LCD flat-screen television (including Freeview and satellite), a hospitality tray, direct dial telephone and hairdryer.

Recommended in the area

Cheddar Gorge; Longleat; Wookey Hole Caves

Cheddar Gorge

Crossways Inn

Address: Withy Rd, WEST HUNTSPILL, Highbridge,
TA9 3RA
Tel: 01278 783756
Fax: 01278 781899
Email: crossways.inn@virgin.net
Website: www.crossways-inn.com
Map ref: 2, ST34
Directions: On A38, 3.5m from M5
Open: 12–3 5.30–11 (Sun 12–4.30, 7–10.30)
L 12–2.30 D 6.30–9 L 12–2 D 6.30–9
Closed: 25 Dec **Facilities:** Garden Parking **Notes:** Free House 8

The seasoned enthusiasm of Anna and Mike Ronca, who bought this 17th-century coaching inn more than 30 years ago, is nicely balanced by the youthful exuberance of their kitchen team. The result is an ever-changing menu of good home-cooked food, served with several real ales, and a small but interesting wine list. Look out for favourites like fiery chicken wings with chilli, sour cream and chive dip; venison sausage with chasseur sauce and cheesy spring onion mash; and cod and prawn mornay.

Recommended in the area

Local fishing; Cheddar Caves; Mid-Somerset Steam Railway

STAFFORDSHIRE

Thor's Cave, Manifold Valley, Peak District National Park

The George

Address: ALSTONEFIELD, Nr Ashbourne, DE6 2FX
Tel: 01335 310205
Email: emily@thegeorgeatalstonefield.com
Website: www.thegeorgeatalstonefield.com
Map ref: 7, SK15
Directions: 7m N of Ashbourne, signed Milldale/
Alstonefield to left
Open: 11.30–3 6–11 (Sat 11.30–11, Sun 12–11)
L 12–2.30 D 7–9 L 12–2.30 D 7–9
Facilities: Garden Parking
Notes: MARSTONS 8

No-one is certain exactly when this old coaching inn was built, but experts put it between 1710 and 1720. Situated in the centre of the village, it is run by landlady Emily Hammond, the third generation of her family since the 1960s to do so. Her sympathetic restoration has revealed many features, including a Georgian fireplace in the dining room, hidden for over a century. She runs The George as 'a proper pub', with decent real ales, wines by the glass, and an impressive local reputation for excellent home-made food. The menu changes daily, with an emphasis on seasonal, regional and traditional dishes. For lunch seek out Ashbourne mushroom and roast vegetable Wellington; or trio of Tissington sausages, mash and gravy. Dinner suggestions include warm salad of wood-pigeon breast with parsnip purée; followed by wild sea bass, roasted fennel, potatoes, tomatoes, lemon oil and celery leaf; rack of Derbyshire lamb, herb and grain mustard crust; or squash, goats' cheese and aubergine gratin with mushroom and leek topping. For dessert, maybe cinnamon rice pudding with autumn fruit compôte. The linked farm shop, formerly the coach house, sells a whole host of organic produce. Dogs are welcome in the pub.

Recommended in the area

Ilam Park; Alton Towers; Brindley Mill

The Holly Bush Inn

Address: Salt, STAFFORD, ST18 0BX
Tel: 01889 508234
Fax: 01889 508058
Email: geoff@hollybushinn.co.uk
Website: www.hollybushinn.co.uk
Map ref: 7, SJ92
Directions: Telephone for directions
Open: 12–11 ⬛ **L** 12–9.30 **D** 12–9.30
Facilities: Garden Parking
Notes: ⊞ Free House ♦♦ ♀ 12

In an area cut through by several major trunk roads, it's good to find such a peaceful spot, and then take time to discover the glorious Staffordshire countryside that lies hidden away from the highways. The Holly Bush Inn was licensed during the reign of Charles II (1660–85), although the building itself dates from around 1190, and heavy carved beams, open fires and cosy alcoves still characterise the comfortably old-fashioned interior. Like most other landlords, owner Geoff Holland aims to serve good quality real ales and wines. What helps to differentiate Geoff, though, is his insistence on providing non-processed, mostly organic, fully traceable food, and on minimising his hostelry's impact on the environment by setting up a worm farm. Traditional British dishes on the main menu include grilled pork chops with a honey and whole-grain mustard glaze; braised lamb and apples flavoured with nutmeg and allspice; and breaded wholetail scampi. Daily specials might be butternut squash and goats' cheese lasagne; fillet of beef Wellington; chargrilled red snapper with Jamaican spiced chutney; and baked perch with watercress sauce. Holly Bush mixed grill is a favourite plateful. At lunchtime tripledecker sandwiches, jacket potatoes and toasties are available. Beers include Adnams, Pedigree and guest ales.

Recommended in the area

Shugborough Hall (NT); Weston Park; Cannock Chase

The Crown Inn

Address: Den Lane, WRINEHILL, Crewe, CW3 9BT
Tel: 01270 820472
Fax: 01270 820547
Email: mark_condliffe@hotmail.com
Map ref: 6, SJ64
Directions: Village on A531, 1m S of Betley. 6m S of Crewe; 6m N of Newcastle-under-Lyme
Open: 12–3 6–11 (Sun 6–10.30, closed Mon lunch)
L 12–2 **D** 6.30–9.30 **Closed:** 26 Dec
Facilities: Garden Parking **Notes:** ⊕ Free House ♀ 9

A former coaching inn with a village setting, The Crown stands six miles equidistant from Crewe and Newcastle-under-Lyme. The interior is largely open plan but retains its oak beams and large inglenook fireplace, and the renovated garden has an attractive patio area for dining. A family-run free house for some 30 years, the pub has a great reputation for its real ales. There is always a choice of six traditional cask ales, including Marstons Pedigree, Adnams Bitter and Timothy Taylor Landlord, and there are two regularly changing guest beers. Wine is an integral part of the inn's drinks portfolio, including nine by the glass. Food also plays a significant part in this establishment's success, and it is renowned in the area for its generous portions and consistent good quality. The menu changes on a monthly basis with dishes reflecting the time of year and the fresh produce available locally. The team here is well established – Charles and Sue Davenhill run the business with their daughter and son-in-law, Anna and Mark Condliffe. Mother and daughter are both vegetarians, so the food on offer always includes meat-free choices and a vegan dish. Meat-eaters are spoilt for choice, with such dishes as piri-piri chicken; Cumberland grill; and plaice roulade with a hazelnut and gruyère crust, and desserts include sticky toffee pudding, ice cream sundaes and home-made jam sponge and custard.

Recommended in the area

The Potteries; Bridgemere Garden World; Trentham Gardens and Monkey Forest

River Stour, Dedham

The Swan Inn

Address: Swan Lane, BARNBY, NR34 7QF
Tel: 01502 476646
Fax: 01502 562513
Map ref: 4, TM49
Directions: off A146 between Lowestoft & Beccles
Open: 11–3 6–12 ⓛ L 12–2 D 7–9.30
🍽 L 12–2 D 7–9.30 Facilities: Garden Parking
Notes: ⊕ Free House ♦♦

Two windows upstairs, two down and a central
door – the classic front elevation of buildings everywhere. Behind the distinctive pink-painted façade of this warm and friendly gem in the Suffolk countryside is one of the county's foremost fish restaurants – it is, after all, owned by Donald and Michael Cole, whose family have been fish wholesalers in Lowestoft since grandfather set up the business in 1936. With deep-sea trawling in deep decline by the mid-1980s, Donald thought it prudent to diversify and bought the run-down Swan. It was during the refurbishment that he had a dinghy installed up in the rafters (although he might try and kid you there's just been a particularly high tide!). The property dates from 1690, and in the rustic Fisherman's Cove restaurant you'll find the original low beams and a collection of nautical memorabilia, including trawlers' bells, wheels and a binnacle, all placed on show as 'a tribute to the brave people who bring ashore the fruits of the sea'. The menu, which lists some 80 different seafood dishes, is very much aimed at fish-lovers, with starters including smoked sprats, smoked trout pâté and Italian seafood salad, and main dishes such as whole grilled wild sea bass; whole grilled turbot; whole grilled Dover sole; monkfish tails in garlic butter; and crab gratin. The Swan has its own smokehouse, one of just three remaining out of 200 in what was once one of Britain's busiest fishing ports. Anyone preferring meat to fish has a choice of fillet, rump and gammon steaks.

Recommended in the area

Lowestoft; Suffolk Heritage Coast; Great Yarmouth

Anchor Inn

Address: 26 Court Street, NAYLAND, Colchester,
CO6 4JL
Tel: 01206 262313
Fax: 01206 264166
Email: enquiries@anchornayland.co.uk
Website: www.anchornayland.co.uk
Map ref: 4, TL93
Directions: 3.5m N of Colchester, 300mtrs off A134
at River Stour bridge
Open: 11–11 (Sun 10–10.30, Mon–Fri (winter)11–3,
5–11) ♿ L 12–2 D 6.30–9 🍽 L 12–2 D 6.30–9 **Facilities:** Garden Parking **Notes:** ⊕ Free House ♟

Nestling on the banks of the River Stour, the Anchor Inn is a haven for food-lovers and provides a
perfect setting for a great culinary experience. Nearly all of the meat and vegetables on the menu are
sourced from the Inn's own Heritage Farm, extending to 100 acres and right behind the Anchor. The
Heritage Farm has restored traditional non-intensive farming to the landscape of the Stour Valley. The
day-to-day relationship between the farm and kitchen is crucial to the Anchor's quality of food. Menus
change regularly and are shaped by seasonal ingredients available from the Heritage Farm and the
'kitchen garden' right on the doorstep. Customers are welcome to wander around the 'kitchen garden'
to have a close look at the herb and vegetable production as well as the farm to see the animals at
various times of the year; often including the Suffolk Trinity – Red Poll cattle, Suffolk sheep and Suffolk
Punch heavy horses. Visitors can see the Suffolk Punches working the land using traditional farming
methods at scheduled times during the week, and livestock happy and thriving in their free-range
environment.

Recommended in the area

Carter's Vineyards; Colchester Zoo

The Crown Inn

Address: Bridge Road, SNAPE, Nr Saxmundham,
IP17 1SL
Tel: 01728 688324
Email: snapecrown@tiscali.co.uk
Map ref: 4, TM35
Directions: A12 N to Lowestoft, right to Aldeburgh,
right in Snape at x-rds, pub at hill bottom
Open: 12–3 6–11 ⓑ **L** 12–2.30 **D** 6–9.30
🍴 **L** 12–2.30 **D** 6–9.30 **Facilities:** Garden Parking
Notes: ⊕ ADNAMS ♦♦ ⚲ ⚲ 18

Within walking distance of Snape Maltings, this atmospheric pub is the perfect place for a pre- or post-show meal. Inside, it is not too difficult to imagine its 15th-century incarnation as a haunt of smugglers. The old beams and brick floors are still in place, but these days it's far more salubrious, with a warm welcome from landlord/chef Garry Cook and his partner Teresa Golder, top quality Adnams ales, and superb food. Garry offers modern British cuisine using local ingredients such as rare-breed pork, Suffolk lamb and quails, and the fresh vegetables come from their own allotment in nearby Orford.

Recommended in the area

Suffolk Coast National Nature Reserve; RSPB Mismere and Orford Ness reserves; Framlingham Castle

The Crown Hotel

★★ 85% ◉ HOTEL
Address: The High Street, SOUTHWOLD, IP18 6DP
Tel: 01502 722275
Fax: 01502 727263
Email: crown.hotel@adnams.co.uk
Website: www.adnamshotels.co.uk
Map ref: 4, TM57
Directions: In town centre
Open: 8–3 6–11 (all day during peak times)
ⓑ **L** 12–2.30 **D** 6.30–9.30 **Rooms:** 14 S £86–£96
D £132–£212 **Facilities:** Parking **Notes:** ⊕ ADNAMS ♦♦ ⚲ 20

Combining the appeal of a pub, wine bar and restaurant, this small hotel is always buzzing with lively informality. The Crown is one of two Adnams-owned hotels in the home of their renowned brewery, and has an excellent reputation for it food, wine and, of course, beer. Originally a posting inn, the building dates from 1750 and its central location is just two minutes from the beach. Visit the cellar and kitchen store in the hotel's yard for a full selection of wines and bottled beers.

Recommended in the area

Minsmere RSPB Reserve; Suffolk Wildlife Park; Suffolk Heritage Coast

The Westleton Crown

★★★ 78%  HOTEL

Address: The Street, WESTLETON, Nr Southwold, IP17 3AD
Tel: 01728 648777
Fax: 01728 648239
Email: reception@westletoncrown.co.uk
Website: www.westletoncrown.co.uk
Map ref: 4, TM46
Directions: Turn off A12 just past Yoxford N'bound, follow signs for Westleton for 2m
Open: 7–11 (Sun 7.30–10.30) ⬚ **L** 12–2.30 **D** 7–9.30
⬚ **L** 12–2.30 **D** 7–9.30 **Closed:** 25 Dec **Rooms:** 25 (8 GF)
S £95–£115 **D** £120–£180 **Facilities:** Garden Parking
Notes: ⬚ Free House ⬚⬚ ⬚ ⬚ 9

Nestled in a quiet village close to Suffolk's wild salt marshes, the coast and RSPB bird reserves, is this atmospheric and hospitable inn. Its origins go back to the 12th century, but the building itself dates from the 17th. The original buildings belonged to nearby Sibton Abbey, and the Crown has succeeded in combining the rustic charm of its heritage with the comforts of contemporary living. Inside you will find crackling log fires, real ales, good wines and an enticing menu. The team at the Crown are passionate about cooking. Meals are made from fresh, locally-sourced ingredients, and can be taken in the parlour, the dining room or the conservatory. Start with baked goats' cheese with red onion crumble, or spicy pumpkin tart, before moving on to roast loin of venison with griottine cherries and root vegetable creamed potatoes; or the Crown's own cod and chips. Leave some space for dessert, which may take the form of pear tarte Tatin with blackberry ice cream, home-made Arctic roll, or marmalade and orange steamed sponge pudding with English egg custard sauce.

Recommended in the area

Ipswich; Aldeburgh; Suffolk Heritage Coast; Southwold; Minsmere RSPB; Dunwich

SURREY

Gothic tower on Leith Hill

The Stephan Langton

Address: Friday Street, ABINGER COMMON, Dorking, RH5 6JR
Tel: 01306 730775
Email: info@stephan-langton.co.uk
Website: www.stephan-langton.co.uk
Map ref: 3, TQ14
Directions: Exit A25 at Hollow Lane, W of Wootton. 1.5m left into Friday St. At end of hill right at pond
Open: 11–3 5–11 (Sat–Sun 11–11) ⓑ L 12.30–2.30 D 7–9
🍽 L 12.30–2.30 D 7–9 **Facilities:** Garden Parking
Notes: 🛢 Free House ⫯ ⫯ 🍷 14

The historic Stephan Langton is an unspoilt and independently run country pub and restaurant on the Wotton Estate, in the heart of an Area of Outstanding Natural Beauty. It can be rather difficult to find, but give up on the search and you will be missing a very satisfying pub experience. Chris and Rosie Robinson have maintained its traditional atmosphere of the brick and timber building with their sympathetic decor, relaxed ambience and friendly staff, and are continuing its long-held reputation for good food. Chef Simon Adams has created a pleasing menu of freshly prepared dishes – even the granary bread and after-dinner fudge are home made – and local produce is used wherever possible. Items on offer might include Abinger watercress soup, char-grilled English asparagus, Tillingbourne trout fillets and home-made pork pie with the pub's own piquant piccalilli. A daily blackboard menu lists such choices as liver and bacon with Clonakilty black pudding mash and gravy; pan-fried sea trout with crushed potatoes and leaf salad; and Aberdeen Angus rib-eye steak with horseradish potatoes and vegetables. The comprehensively stocked bar includes 18 wines by the glass, fine Scottish and Irish malt whiskies and three cask ales, of which the Surrey Hills' Shere Drop and Hog's Back TEA are from local breweries.

Recommended in the area

North Downs Way; Polesden Lacy; Guildford

Hare and Hounds

Address: Common Road, LINGFIELD, RH7 6BZ
Tel: 01342 832351
Fax: 01342 832351
Email: hare.hounds@tiscali.co.uk
Website: www.hareandhoundslingfield.co.uk/index.htm
Map ref: 3, TQ34
Directions: From A22 follow signs for Lingfield Racecourse into Common Rd
Open: 11.30–11 ⓑ L 12–2.30 D 7–9.30
ⓘ L 12–2.30 D 7–9.30 **Closed:** 1 Jan, Sun Eve
Facilities: Garden Parking **Notes:** ⊕ PUNCH TAVERNS ⚑ ♟ 8

The promise of this friendly establishment is that, despite a commitment to providing food of unusual excellence, it remains at heart a proper pub. This means there are plenty of real ales, including Greene King IPA, Flowers Original and Old Speckled Hen, and a friendly bunch of locals who enjoy nothing more than a convivial conversation at the bar. There's a peaceful atmosphere throughout because the pub is entirely free of the electronic interference that has ruined many good places, and the walls are decked with a changing display of original art works, all of which are for sale. There's also a lovely split level garden to enjoy when the weather is sunny. The food really is a highlight. The menu is eclectic, and everything – bread, pasta, ice cream – is made on the premises. You might begin with a dish of linguini, spinach, parmesan, poached egg and truffle oil, before choosing between enticing main courses that might include slow-roasted belly of pork with chorizo mash and Granny Smith, tomato and basil salsa; or baked stuffed aubergine, with crostini and basil dressing, rocket, pink grapefruit and parmesan salad. The equally unusual desserts take some classic ideas and give them a startling twist, resulting in mouthwatering delights.

Recommended in the area

Standen (NT); Godstone Farm; Hever Castle

Waterfall, Virginia Water

Bryce's at The Old School House

Address: OCKLEY, Dorking, RH5 5TH
Tel: 01306 627430
Fax: 01306 628274
Email: bryces.fish@virgin.net
Website: www.bryces.co.uk
Map ref: 3, TQ14
Directions: 8m S of Dorking on A29
Open: 11–3 6–11 ⅃ L 12–2.30 D 6.30–9.30
⅃ L 12–2.30 D 7–9.30 **Closed:** 25–26 Dec, 1 Jan,
Sun pm Nov, Jan–Feb **Facilities:** Parking **Notes:** ⊕ Free House ⅃ 15

Formerly a boarding school, this Grade II listed building dates from 1750 and has been established for 16 years as Bryce's. The village is set amid lovely countryside offering some great downland walking. Its distance from the sea may come as a surprise, as Bill Bryce is passionate about fresh fish and offers seven starters and seven main courses of exclusively fish dishes in the restaurant, with non-fish daily specials and a vegetarian selection. The bar has its own interesting menu.

Recommended in the area

High Beeches Garden, Handcross; Horsham Museum; Leonardslee Lakes and Gardens

The Inn @ West End

Address: 42 Guildford Road, WEST END, GU24 9PW
Tel: 01276 858652
Email: greatfood@the-inn.co.uk
Website: www.the-inn.co.uk
Map ref: 3, SU96
Directions: On A322 towards Guildford. 3m from M3 junct 3, just beyond Gordon Boys rdbt
Open: 12–3 5–11 ⓑ L 12–2.30 D 6–9.30
🍴 L 12–2.30 D 6–9.30
Facilities: Garden Parking
Notes: ⊕ Free House 🐾 🍷 12

The name gives a hint that the refurbished Inn @ West End is a modern place. It is a restaurant pub run for the last eight years by owners (Gerry and Ann Price) who pride themselves on the great food, wine and atmosphere here. Indeed, its role as a focus for local social life has seen it being described as more of a community centre than a pub or restaurant, with special events such as quiz nights and wine tastings, and involvement in a variety of clubs and societies. In addition to the dining room, the bar and the garden room, there is a private gastronomic cellar, available for private hire, and the garden offers further facilities in the shape of a lovely dining patio and a boules terrain. An interesting wine list takes in wines from all over the world, but with a leaning towards Portugal and Spain; there is also an impressive Champagne section. Real ales include Fuller's London Pride and a changing selection of guests. Food is fresh and local, with fish and game dishes as a speciality on the modern British menu. Fish is acquired on weekly buying trips to Portsmouth Harbour and game comes directly from the farm for processing – they even have their own plucking machine here.

Recommended in the area

Windsor Great Park; Airborne Forces Museum; Thorpe Park; National Shooting Centre, Bisley

The King William IV

Address: 83 The Street, WEST HORSLEY, KT24 6BG
Tel: 01483 282318
Fax: 01483 282318
Email: kingbilly4th@aol.com
Map ref: 3, TQ05
Directions: On The Street off A246 (Epsom to Guildford)
Open: 11.30–11 (Fri 11.30–12)
🍽 L 12–3 D 6.30–9.30 🍴 L 12–3 D 6.30–9.30
Facilities: Garden Parking
Notes: 🛢 ENTERPRISE INNS ⚭ 🐕 🍷 12

There's plenty of character in this fine old pub, and much of its interesting history is portrayed in dated photographs that adorn the walls. Ale was at one time brewed on the premises and sold to passers by through the windows, and though the brewery is long defunct, local beers are available on tap, including Surrey Hills' Shere Drop. The building retains many of its original Georgian features, and the warm and welcoming atmosphere is enhanced by roaring log fires in winter. Summer sees the pleasant garden full, with plenty of walkers taking a well-earned rest and perhaps partaking of the Saturday lunchtime barbecues (weather permitting). All year round the bar and conservatory restaurant draw a loyal clientele for the top quality 'pub grub', with daily specials and a menu that includes a Tex-Mex selection, a choice of platters, and traditional favourites such as steak and local ale pie, honey-glazed ham with eggs and chips, and curry, chilli and lasagne. There's also a good range of filled ciabatta, baguettes and jacket potatoes. All of the meat is sourced locally, and cheese, eggs and milk come from the local West Horsley Dairy. Children are welcomed with their own menu and plenty of toys and board games, and water bowls are provided for dogs.

Recommended in the area

Hatchlands Park; Clandon Park; Guildford

Bodiam Castle, East Sussex

Distant view of the white cliffs of the Seven Sisters

The Coach and Horses

Address: DANEHILL, RH17 7JF
Tel/Fax: 01825 740369
Map ref: 3, TQ42
Directions: From East Grinstead, S through Forest Row on A22. Onto A275, 2m to Danehill, left onto School Lane, 0.5m
Open: 11.30–3 6–11 ⓛ L 12–2 D 7–9
🍽 L 12–2 D 7–9 **Facilities:** Garden Parking
Notes: ⊕ Free House ♁ ♞ ♟ 10

Built in 1847 of local sandstone, the Coach and Horses is ideal for walkers and lovers of stunning scenery. Homely winter fires and neatly tended gardens add plenty of character, and half-panelled walls, highly polished wooden floorboards and vaulted beamed ceilings give the place a charming, timeless feel. Food plays a key role in the pub's success, locally-sourced venison and woodpigeon are often on the menu along with organic vegetables from local market gardens. Fresh fish caught off the Sussex coast features regularly, with dishes like pan-fried skate wing or roasted fillet of halibut on Jerusalem artichoke and butter bean bonne femme.

Recommended in the area

Sheffield Park (NT); Bluebell Railway; Wakehurst Place (NT)

The Bull

★★★★ ⇔ INN

Address: 2 High Street, DITCHLING, BN6 8TA
Tel: 01273 843147
Fax: 01273 843147
Email: info@thebullditchling.com
Website: www.thebullditchling.com
Map ref: 3, TQ31
Directions: S on M23/A23 5m. N of Brighton, follow signs to Pyecombe/Hassocks then signed to Ditchling 3m
Open: 11–11 (Sun 12–10.30) 🍴 L 12–2.30 D 7–9.30
Facilities: Garden Parking **Notes:** ⊕ Free House ♦♦ 🐾 ♈ 13

The Bull, a 16th-century former coaching inn, is the place to head for following a day on the South Downs. It's been restored with passion (and a contemporary touch), by Dominic Worrall, yet still exudes historic charm and character. In the bar you'll find feature fireplaces with glowing log fires, sagging ceiling timbers, bare boards and a mixture of simple benches, carved settles and farmhouse chairs at big scrubbed wooden tables. Quirky objets d'art, modern art and vases of lilies on the bar add a touch of class. There are four individually decorated bedrooms, each named after their principle colour. Ruby, for example, has bright red walls, white-painted wall timbers, Thai silk curtains, a plasma TV/DVD player, digital radio, a sleigh bed with Egyptian cotton sheets and a claw-foot bath in the tiled bathroom. Local is the watchword when it comes to food and drink, with top notch ales from Harvey's (Lewes) and Welton's (Horsham) breweries on hand pump and a quaffable fizz from Ridge View Vineyard up the road. Menus change daily and make good use of lamb from Foxhole Farm on the edge of the village, seasonal game, including venison from the Balcombe Estate and south coast fish.

Recommended in the area

Booth Museum of Natural History; Royal Pavilion, Brighton; Borde Hill Garden

The Royal Pavilion, Brighton

The Griffin Inn

Address: FLETCHING, Uckfield, TN22 3SS
Tel: 01825 722890
Fax: 01825 722810
Email: info@thegriffininn.co.uk
Website: www.thegriffininn.co.uk
Map ref: 3, TQ42
Directions: M23 junct 10 to East Grinstead, then A22, then A275. Village signed on left
Open: 12–3 6–11 (Sat–Sun all day summer)
🍴 L 12–2.30 D 7–9.30 🍽 L 12.15–2.30
D 7.15–9.30 **Closed:** 25 Dec **Facilities:** Garden Parking **Notes:** 🍺 Free House ♦♦ 🍷 15

Having steered clear of the sanded-floor and stripped-pine look, the owners stick closely to the original concept of an inn – which basically means you can enter the bar with muddy boots! Good food, good wine and local ales are all-important at the Griffin. Food miles are kept to a minimum – for example, rump of Romney Marsh lamb with roasted winter vegetables, and Rye Bay roasted cod, cockle and mussel stew, and local game. Bedrooms are in the main house, the old coach house and next door.

Recommended in the area

Bodiam Castle; Bentley Wildfowl and Motor Museum; Bluebell Railway

The Hatch Inn

Address: Coleman's Hatch, HARTFIELD, TN7 4EJ
Tel/Fax: 01342 822363
Email: nickad@bigfoot.com
Website: www.hatchinn.co.uk
Map ref: 3, TQ43
Directions: From A22 take B2110 at Forest Row.
3m. Right by church. Straight on at next junct
Open: 11.30–3 5.30–11 (Sat–Sun all day in summer
& BHs) ☕ L 12–2.30 D 7–9.15 🍴 L 12–2.30
D 7–9.15 **Closed:** 25 Dec **Facilities:** Garden
Notes: ⊕ Free House 🐾 🍷 10

Reputedly dating back to 1430, The Hatch Inn was converted from three cottages thought to have housed workers at the local water-driven hammer mill and it may also have been a smugglers' haunt. It is named after the coalmen's gate at the nearby entrance to Ashdown Forest. The pub is well placed for country walking, and features in a number of 'top ten pubs' lists, as well as serving as a filming location for television dramas and advertisements. There are two large beer gardens for al fresco summer dining, one of which enjoys views out over the forest, and is only minutes away from the restored Poohsticks Bridge, immortalised in A.A. Milne's *Winnie the Pooh* stories. Cooking by owner Nicholas Drillsma, who trained as a chef in both the UK and the US, combined with the customer service background of his partner Sandra, have created a recipe for success. Quality ingredients and imaginative techniques make for an exciting menu, which includes a good selection of light bites and home-cooked traditional dishes. These might include starters such as hot duck salad with fresh mango and field mushrooms and main courses like pork tenderloin on crushed celeriac, with a sweet mustard seed cream sauce. No reservations are available at lunchtime and evening booking is essential.

Recommended in the area

Ashdown Forest; Standen (NT); Royal Tunbridge Wells

The Middle House

Address: High Street, MAYFIELD, TN20 6AB
Tel: 01435 872146
Fax: 01435 873423
Email: kirsty@middle-house.com
Map ref: 4, TQ52
Directions: E of A267, S of Tunbridge Wells
Open: 11–11 (Sun 12–10.30)
 L 12–2 D 7–9.30 L 12–2 D 7–9
Facilities: Garden Parking
Notes: Free House   9

Built in 1575 for Sir Thomas Gresham, Elizabeth I's Keeper of the Privy Purse and founder of the London Stock Exchange, The Middle House is one of the finest timber-framed buildings in Sussex, with a wonderfully ornate wooden façade. Inside, the house retains many of its original features, including a Grinling Gibbons' fireplace and a splendid oak-panelled restaurant. This is a family-run business specialising in a very wide variety of food using all local, fresh produce. On offer are over 40 dishes, including a large fish selection and vegetarian options on an ever-changing menu. Among the choices that may be enjoyed in the cosy bar or the more formal restaurant, are chicken breast filled with leeks and gruyère cheese wrapped in filo pastry with a parsley, cream and white wine sauce; seared tuna loin steak on a bed of pak choi with a sweet and sour sauce; pan-fried local venison steak served with game crisps and a rich bacon lardon, port and prune sauce. An extensive wine list offers wines and champagne by the glass, and the pub's bar offers real ales including Harveys, the local brew and several guest beers. A great high street pub whether you're nipping in for a pint or stopping a little longer to enjoy both the food and the atmosphere. Ample parking is available.

Recommended in the area

Bateman's (NT); Spa Valley Railway; Royal Tunbridge Wells

The Ypres Castle Inn

Address: Gun Garden, RYE, TN31 7HH
Tel: 01797 223248
Email: info@yprescastleinn.co.uk
Website: www.yprescastleinn.co.uk
Map ref: 4, TQ92
Directions: Behind church & adjacent to Ypres Tower
Open: 11.30–11 (Fri 11–1am) ⓑ L 12–3 D 6–9
▮◎▯ L 12–3 D 6–9 **Facilities:** Garden
Notes: ⊞ Free House ▯▯ ⚲ 11

'The Wipers', as locals call it, was once the haunt of smugglers. Built in 1640 in weather-boarded style, and added to by the Victorians, it's the only pub in the citadel area of the old Cinque Port of Rye with a garden. The garden, with roses, shrubs, a boules pitch and views of the 13th-century Ypres Tower, once defensive, then became a prison before becoming a museum, and of the River Rother with its working fishing fleet. Colourful art and furnishings help make the interior warm and friendly. The seasonally changing menu is largely sourced locally, providing a good range of lunchtime snacks, including ploughman's, and sandwiches, backed by half a dozen daily specials. The evening menu may propose starters like moules marinière, cracked Dungeness crab, grilled Rye Bay plaice and turbot, and meaty options of grilled rack of Romney salt marsh lamb, organic Winchelsea beef and pork, and home-made prime beefburger. There are usually four cask-conditioned ales and an extensive wine list. On Friday nights the atmosphere hots up with live jazz, rock and blues. The pub has no accommodation facilities, but there are plenty of possibilities nearby, including Rye Windmill, one of the town's most famous landmarks.

Recommended in the area

Smallhythe Place; Romney, Hythe & Dymchurch Railway; Port Lympne Wild Animal Park

The Lamb Inn

Address: WARTLING, Herstmonceux, BN27 1RY
Tel: 01323 832116
Website: www.lambinnwartling.co.uk
Map ref: 4, TQ60
Directions: A259 from Polegate to Pevensey rdbt.
Take 1st left to Wartling & Herstmonceux Castle.
Pub 3m on right
Open: 11–3 6–11 ⊯ L 11.45–2.15 D 6.45–9
⦿ L 11.45–2.15 D 6.45–9
Facilities: Garden Parking
Notes: ⊞ ☻ 8

A family-run inn with a long history, this white-painted building
is a popular watering hole for locals and walkers enjoying the tiny hamlet and stunning East Sussex
countryside. Inside, it provides comfortable cream sofas, which can be drawn up to the fire on chilly
days, and a good selection of real ales and wines by the glass. The pub is well known for the quality
of its food, and the ethos is to source the best of local produce, from meat and fish through to locally
grown vegetables. Everything is home made including the bread. The inn makes good use of meat from
nearby Chilley Farm, which specialises in raising stock without additives in unhurried fashion, and rears
animals such as Gloucester Old Spot pigs and Kent Cross lamb. Fish from Hastings and Newhaven is a
house speciality, offered daily on the specials board. As well as a comprehensive dinner menu, which
might include braised shank of lamb on roasted smoked garlic mash and thoughtful vegetarian options
such as Wellington of mushrooms with goats' cheese, lighter dishes, baps and ploughman's are served
at lunchtime. Traditional desserts along the lines of lemon and sultana bread-and-butter pudding are
not to be missed.

Recommended in the area

Rye; De La Warr Pavilion, Bexhill; Herstmonceux Castle

The Dorset Arms

Address: WITHYHAM, Nr Hartfield, TN7 4BD
Tel: 01892 770278
Fax: 01892 770195
Email: pete@dorset-arms.co.uk
Website: www.dorset-arms.co.uk
Map ref: 3, TQ43
Directions: 4m W of Tunbridge Wells on B2110 between Groombridge & Hartfield
Open: 11–3 6–11 (Sun 12–3, 7–10.30) 🍴 L 12–2 D 7–9 🍽 L 12–2 D 7–9 **Facilities:** Garden Parking
Notes: ⊕ HARVEYS OF LEWES 🐾 🍷 8

Local records suggest that this tile-hung, family-run pub and restaurant at the edge of the Ashdown Forest has been an inn since the 18th century. Its origins go much further back – to the 15th century when it was an open-halled farmhouse. Today it retains its original flagstone floors, and among the many interesting features that remain are the ice-house buried in the hillside behind the building, the oak-floored bar, a magnificent open log fireplace, and the massive wall and ceiling beams in the restaurant. There's seating on the lawn outside for fine summer days. As a focus of village life, the Dorset Arms hosts periodic quiz nights and occasional live music. When it comes to the food on offer, wherever possible owner Peter Randell sources ingredients locally, including what some say is the best fillet steak in the area. Starters might include oak-smoked salmon with brown bread; deep-fried tempura battered king prawns with chilli dip; or crispy whitebait. Continue with a fillet steak, wrapped in bacon and in a port and redcurrant sauce; a halibut steak, poached in white wine; medallions of pork fillet with mushrooms in a stilton, white wine and cream sauce; or perhaps seared scallops with bacon and onions. For dessert, one of the favourites is warm chocolate fudge brownies with ice cream.

Recommended in the area

Tunbridge Wells; Groombridge Place; Spa Valley Railway

Chichester Cathedral

George & Dragon

Address: BURPHAM, Arundel, BN18 9RR
Tel: 01903 883131
Email: sara.cheney@btinternet.com
Website: www.burphamgeorgeanddragoninn.com
Map ref: 3, TQ00
Directions: Off A27, 1m E of Arundel, signed
Burpham, 2.5m pub on left
Open: 11–2.30 6–12 ⓑ L 12–2 D 7–9
Ⓘ L 12–2 D 7–9 **Facilities:** Parking
Notes: ⓑ Free House ♙ ♞

In a tranquil village at the end of a long no-through road, this lovely old pub has the church and cricket pitch as its close neighbours. The interior is full of old-world character, with beams and worn flagstone floors providing a setting for the modern prints on the walls. Smaller rooms have been opened out to create space, but there are still some nooks and crannies for that quiet meal or drink. Real ales come from nearby Arundel Breweries, with guests from surrounding counties. The owners acknowledge that during the last 30 years the pub has developed from a village local serving mostly beer, into not so much a gastro-pub, but a 'traditional pub that serves excellent food'. It offers a seasonal, largely locally-sourced menu of British rustic cooking, but with clear international influences as seen in honey-roasted Scottish salmon on citrus couscous, pan-roasted vegetables and soy sauce dressing. From nearer home might come wild mushroom, garlic, leek and thyme crumble topped with Sussex Cheddar. Diners don't risk breaking the bank with the compact wine list. The area is well endowed with walks, especially over the South Downs and along the River Arun (dogs are welcome in the bar area).

Recommended in the area

Arundel Castle; Amberley Working Museum; Goodwood

The Foresters Arms

Address: The Street, GRAFFHAM, GU28 0QA
Tel: 01798 867202
Email: info@forestersgraffham.co.uk
Website: www.forestersgraffham.co.uk
Map ref: 3, SU91
Open: 12–3 6–11 (Sun 12–4, Summer all day)
🍽 L 12–2.30 D 6.30–9.30 🍴 L 12–2.30
D 6.30–9.30 Closed: Mon Facilities: Garden
Parking Notes: 🌐 Free House 🐾 🍷 16

This cosy and inviting village-centre free house offers a good selection of quality microbrewery English ales, stout and lager on the hand pumps. Owner-chef Robert Pearce offers a daily-changing menu using ingredients that are all sourced within 50 miles of the pub. Chunky home-made focaccia bread is served as an opener to a meal that might include pan-fried skate wing; mushroom and leek frittata; or rib-eye of veal with mustard cream sauce, rounded off, perhaps, with one of the interestingly flavoured home-made ice creams. The tastefully decorated bedrooms are in an adjacent building, to which a Continental breakfast can be delivered in a hamper.

Recommended in the area

South Downs; Goodwood; Petworth House

Black Horse Inn

Address: Nuthurst Street, NUTHURST, Horsham,
         RH13 6LH
Tel: 01403 891272
Email: clive.henwood@btinternet.com
Website: www.theblackhorseinn.com
Map ref: 3, TQ12
Directions: 4m S of Horsham, off A281, A24 & A272
Open: 12–3 6–11 (Sat–Sun & BH all day)
🍽 L 12–2.30 D 6–9.30 🍴 L 12–2.30 D 6–9.30
Facilities: Garden Parking
Notes: 🌐 Free House 👫 🐾 🍷 7

Once on the main route from Brighton to Horsham, this used to be a smugglers' hideout, with a secret passage from the pub to the church which can still be seen. Quietly hidden away, it retains plenty of original features: stone-flagged floors, an inglenook fireplace and an exposed wattle and daub wall. The pub has a reputation for good ales and home-made, freshly prepared food, with universal appeal and menus that specify gluten-free and vegetarian options. There are also some very tempting desserts.

Recommended in the area

Four local pub walks; Wakehurst Place; Pulborough Brooks Nature Reserve; Leonardslee Gardens

The Grove Inn

Address: Grove Lane, PETWORTH, GU28 0HY
Tel: 01798 343659
Email: steveandvaleria@tiscali.co.uk
Website: www.groveinnpetworth.co.uk
Map ref: 3, SU92
Directions: On outskirts of town, 0.5m from Petworth Park
Open: 12–3 6–11.30 ⓑ L 12–2 D 6–9
🍽 L 12–2 D 6–9 **Closed:** 2nd & 3rd wk Jan
Sun eve & Mon **Facilities:** Garden Parking
Notes: ⊕ Free House

The Grove Inn is a 17th-century free house in the heart of the South Downs. It sits on the outskirts of historic Petworth, a town much visited for its many and varied antique shops. Inside, the inn provides a cosy bar with oak-beamed ceilings and a large stone inglenook fireplace, as well as the Conservatory Restaurant, where diners can look out over the garden and enjoy good views of the South Downs. There is also a patio area with a pergola. Dishes are chosen from a seasonal menu, which is completely rewritten every six to eight weeks, with some daily changes for good measure. Typical starters include smoked salmon, chive and cream cheese roulade; home-made parsnip soup; and duck liver and mushroom terrine. Among the main courses are natural smoked haddock topped with Welsh rarebit; well-matured chargrilled fillet steak with truffle mash and cracked black peppercorn sauce; and wild mushroom risotto with parmesan and truffle oil. To follow there could be banana pancake with honey rum toffee sauce or lemon posset, as well as a choice of cheeseboards. Three whites, three reds and a rosé are available by the glass, with many more available on the main wine list.

Recommended in the area

Cowdray Park; Lurgashall Winery; Petworth House and Park

Devil's Dyke

Royal Oak Inn

Address: The Street, POYNINGS, BN45 7AQ
Tel: 01273 857389
Fax: 01273 857202
Email: ropoynings@aol.com
Website: www.royaloakpoynings.biz
Map ref: 3, TQ21
Directions: on A23 from Brighton, take A281 (signed for Henfield & Poynings)
Open: 11–11 (Sun 12–10.30) ♿ L 12–9.30 D 12–9.30 **Facilities:** Garden Parking
Notes: ⊕ Free House ♥ ♟ 12

Built as a small hotel and tea gardens during the 1880s, the inn has undergone a comprehensive refurbishment. It has a smart cream-painted exterior, and inside you'll find solid oak floors, old beams and crackling log fires along with more contemporary decor and comfy sofas. For summer enjoyment there is a large garden with splendid views of the Downs. This popular free house, has, for more than a decade, maintained a commitment to good quality pub food featuring locally sourced produce.

Recommended in the area

Brighton; South Downs Way; Bramber Castle (NT)

The Countryman Inn

Address: Countryman Lane, SHIPLEY, RH13 8PZ
Tel: 01403 741383
Fax: 01403 741115
Email: countrymaninn@btopenworld.com
Website: www.countrymanshipley.co.uk
Map ref: 3, TQ21
Directions: From A272 at Coolham into Smithers Hill Lane.
1m to junct with Countryman Lane
Open: 11–3 6.30–11 🍴 L 12–3 D 7–9.30 🍽 L 12–2.30
D 7–9.30 **Facilities:** Garden Parking **Notes:** 🍺 🍷 20

A rural hostelry in the traditional style, The Countryman is
set in open countryside close to the small village of Shipley,
surrounded by 3,500 acres of farmland owned by the Knepp Castle Estate. The area is in the process of
being turned back to a more natural state, with the introduction of fallow deer, free-roaming Tamworth
pigs, Exmoor ponies and English longhorn cattle. Many wild birds have also been encouraged to return
to the area, as the new growth of wild grasses and plant life provide a welcoming habitat. You can even
do a bit of bird watching from the inn's garden in fine weather. During the winter you'll find warming
log fires, Harvey's and organic Horsham ales in the cosy bar, together with over 30 wines from around
the world, and freshly ground coffee. Free-range meat and vegetables from local farms make their
appearance on the restaurant menu alongside fresh fish from Shoreham and Newhaven and local game
in season. Menus change frequently, and as well as the carte there is also a range of ploughman's
lunches, bar snacks and daily specials. Shipley's historic eight-sided smock mill (so-called because of
its likeness to a traditional farm labourer's smock) is worth a visit.

Recommended in the area

Leonardslee Lakes & Gardens; Parham House & Gardens; Amberley Working Museum

Warwick Castle

Kenilworth Castle

The Fox & Hounds Inn

★★★★ ⇔ INN

Address: GREAT WOLFORD CV36 5NQ
Tel: 01608 674220
Fax: 01608 674160
Email: enquiries@thefoxandhoundsinn.com
Website: www.thefoxandhoundsinn.com
Map ref: 3, SP23
Directions: Off A44 NE of Moreton-in-Marsh
Open: 12–2.30 6–11 ⓑ L 12–2 D 6.30–9
⍟ L 12–2 D 7–9 **Closed:** 1st 2wks Jan, Mon

Rooms: 3 S £50 D £80 **Facilities:** Garden Parking **Notes:** ⊕ Free House ♦ ♞

Landlords have been welcoming travellers to this fine, stone-built country inn since 1540. It stands in the heart of a pretty village where Gloucestershire, Warwickshire and Oxfordshire meet. Local brews in the welcoming (particularly so when the inglenook is blazing) bar include Hook Norton and Purity Brewery's Ubu, while wines are chosen predominantly from single-estate vineyards worldwide. Chef Jamie's balanced menu features traditional English dishes, as well as others inspired by his travels.

Recommended in the area

Rollright Stones; Stratford-upon-Avon; Cotswold Falconry Centre

The Duck on the Pond

Address: The Green, LONG ITCHINGTON, CV47 9QJ
Tel: 01926 815876
Fax: 01926 815766
Email: duckonthepond@aol.com
Website: www.duckonthepond.co.uk
Map ref: 3, SP46
Directions: On A423 in village centre, 1m N of Southam
Open: 12–3 5–11 (Sat 12–11, Sun 12–10.30)
🛏 L 12–2 D 6.30–10 ⒪ L 12–2.30 D 6.30–10
Closed: Mon (ex BH) **Facilities:** Garden Parking **Notes:** ⊕ CHARLES WELLS ♉ 10

Children will be delighted to discover that the name of this attractive village inn does indeed indicate the presence of a pond replete with drakes and mallards. Adults, meanwhile, will be comforted to learn that the inn's appearance, which is reminiscent of a French bistro, is entirely substantiated by the food. Winter fires light an entirely intriguing interior, crammed with French artwork, road signs and bottles, not to mention an unusual willow baton ceiling. Service is friendly and attentive, so you'll never be left without a drink for long. Drinks of choice are Wells Bombardier plus guest ales and a good list of wines from around the world, including 12 different vintage Dom Perignons. Owners Andrew and Wendy Parry's passion for food is evident in their appealing menu, which mixes traditional dishes with more innovative selections, with a selection of sandwiches also available at lunchtime. 'Food miles' are kept to a minimum as the vast majority of the produce is sourced from within walking distance. Try the fresh mussels steamed with chorizo, garlic and tomato sauce, followed by roast pork with nettle stuffing on apple mash with cider cream. Regular cabaret nights are a feature, but booking for these is essential.

Recommended in the area

Warwick Castle; Heritage Motor Centre; Kenilworth Castle

Town Hall, Leamington Spa

Golden Lion Inn and Hotel

★★★ 72% HOTEL

Address: Easenhall, RUGBY, CV23 0JA
Tel: 01788 832265
Fax: 01788 832878
Email: reception@goldenlionhotel.org
Website: www.goldenlionhotel.org
Map ref: 3, SP57
Directions: From Rugby take A426, follow signs for Nuneaton. Through Newbold, follow brown sign, turn left, pub in 1m

Open: 11–11 ♿ L 12–3 D 6–9.30 ⊙ L 12–2 D 6–9.30 **Rooms:** 20 en suite (6 GF) **S** £50–£85 **D** £60–£95 **Facilities:** Garden Parking **Notes:** ⊕ Free House ♦ ♟ 7

Set amidst idyllic countryside in one of Warwickshire's best-kept villages, this charming 16th-century free house has low oak-beamed ceilings and narrow doorways. James and Claudia are the third generation of the Austin family at the Golden Lion, where you'll find traditional ales, roaring winter fires and an extensive wine list. Choose between home-cooked bar food or more formal dining in the restaurant.

Recommended in the area

Webb Ellis Rugby Football Museum; Garden Organic Ryton; Stanford Hall

The Red Lion

★★★★ INN

Address: Main Street, Long Compton, SHIPSTON ON STOUR,
CV37 5JS
Tel: 01608 684221
Fax: 01608 684968
Email: info@redlion-longcompton.co.uk
Website: www.redlion-longcompton.co.uk
Map ref: 3, SP24
Directions: On A3400, N of Chipping Norton
Open: 11–2.30 6–11 (Fri–Sun 11–11) ♿ **L** 12–2.30 **D** 6–9.30
Rooms: 5 en suite **S** £45–£55 **D** £75–£110 **Facilities:** Garden
Parking **Notes:** ⊕ Free House ♦♦ ♂ ♀ 7

Built as a coaching inn in 1748, this Grade II listed stone free house is located in an Area of
Outstanding Natural Beauty, with many attractions in the locality. Though with tales of witches in the
village and a nearby prehistoric stone circle, there is as a much to interest the historian as there is the
tourist. If you're tempted to stay, five elegant en suite bedrooms offer tea- and coffee-making facilities
and flat-screen televisions. The inn's interior retains its old world atmosphere with oak beams, log fires
and gleaming wood, but has a contemporary vibe with comfy leather armchairs. Eat in the character
bar, with its settles and inglenook fireplace, or the smart restaurant area, choosing from one long menu
or daily blackboard specials. Options range from a sandwich of crayfish, rocket and lemon mayonnaise
on ciabatta to rack of lamb with crushed black olive and herb crust, grilled aubergine and provençale
sauce. Favourites include cod and chips served on the Red Lion Times and a steak and Hook Norton
pie, washed down with real ale or your choice from a carefully selected wine list. Live acoustic music is
featured on the first Wednesday of the month.
Recommended in the area
Shakespeare's Birthplace; Warwick Castle; Cotswold Wildlife Park

The Fox & Goose Inn

⚊ INN

Address: Armscote, STRATFORD-UPON-AVON,
CV37 8DD
Tel: 01608 682293
Fax: 01608 682293
Email: mail@foxandgoosecountryinn.co.uk
Website: www.foxandgoosearmscote.co.uk
Map ref: 3, SP25
Directions: 1m off A3400
Open: 12–3 6–11 ♿ L 12–2.30 D 7–9.30

🍴 L 12–2.30 D 7–9.30 **Rooms:** 4 en suite S £55–£85 D £85–£120 **Facilities:** Garden Parking
Notes: ⊕ Free House ♟ 8

This privately owned inn, originally two cottages and a blacksmith's forge, is located in a beautiful village eight miles south of Stratford-upon-Avon, set amid lovely countryside within easy reach of Warwick and several Cotswold villages. Its distinctively decorated interior comprises a smart dining room, cosy bar and four en suite bedrooms. The bar, with its walls painted 'Eating Room Red', has masses of velvet cushions, an open fire, flagstone floors and reading matter to enjoy while supping a pint of Old Hooky or Shepherd Neame Spitfire. If you prefer wine (or even champagne) there is a selection by the glass or bottle, and for further refreshment there is a menu of light meals and nibbles. The dining room offers an imaginative seasonal menu with the likes of parsnip and English mustard soup; lamb shank glazed with honey and cinnamon with a rosemary jus; and woodland berry frangipane with clotted cream. Out in the garden there's a large grassy area, a decked space and 20 seats for dining under the vines. At the time of going to press the inn had not had its AA rating confirmed under the Guest Accommodation Scheme. Please see the AA website for up-to-date information.

Recommended in the area

Hill Close Gardens; Warwick Castle; Stow Toy Museum

The Bulls Head

Address: Stratford Road, WOOTTON WAWEN,
B95 6BD
Tel: 01564 792511
Map ref: 3, SP16
Directions: On B3400, 4m N of
Stratford-upon-Avon, 1m S of Henley-in-Arden
Open: 12–3 5–11 (Sun 12–10.30)
🛏 L 12–9 D 2–9 🍽 L 12–2.30 D 6–9.30
Closed: Mon (exc BH)
Facilities: Garden Parking
Notes: ⊕ WOLVERHAMPTON & DUDLEY BREWERIES PLC ♦♦ 🍷 10

A picturesque pub and serious dining destination, the extensively refurbished Bulls Head was originally two separate cottages dating from the 16th-century. Set in the ancient village of Wootton Wawen, it is ideally placed for the discerning diner exploring the lovely landscapes of Warwickshire and the Cotswolds. A decent pint is served, too, including Marston's Pedigree, Banks Bitter, Banks Original, and guest ales. Low beams, leather sofas, open fires and old church pews set the scene in the bar and snug areas, and the same tone and style are maintained in the magnificent 'great hall' restaurant, with its vaulted ceiling and exposed beams. Outside you'll find a lawned garden and paved patio surrounded by mature trees. Owners Andrew and Wendy Parry describe their cooking style quite simply as 'food we love to eat and food we love to cook'. Local suppliers are visited personally in order to ensure that the very best of the county's produce finds its way into the kitchen. Typical dishes from a very wide range include home-cured Sambuca and lemongrass salmon with citrus potato salad, and Lighthorne shoulder of lamb stuffed with apricot, prune, pistachio and mint. Keep an eye out for daily specials such as grilled mahi mahi with niçoise salad and poached egg. Booking ahead is recommended.

Recommended in the area

Stratford-upon-Avon; Shakespeare's Birthplace; Warwick Castle

WEST MIDLANDS

Gas Street Basin, Birmingham

Walsall Arboretum

The Orange Tree

Address: Warwick Road, CHADWICK END, B93 0BN
Tel: 01564 785364
Fax: 01564 782988
Email: theorangetree@lovelypubs.co.uk
Website: www.theorangetreepub.co.uk
Map ref: 3, SP27
Directions: 3m from Knowle towards Warwick
Open: 11–11 ♿ L 12–2.30 D 6–9.30
🍴 L 12–2.30 D 6.30–9.30 **Closed:** 25 Dec
Facilities: Garden Parking **Notes:** 🍺 👬 🐕 🍷 8

Despite its peaceful countryside setting, this pub/restaurant is just minutes from the National Exhibition Centre, Solihull and Warwick. A relaxed Italian influence is reflected in the furnishings and the food. The bar with its comfortable seating and ambient music is a great place to meet, and the sunny lounge area, all sumptuous leather sofas and rustic decor, opens out onto the patio. The deli counter dispenses breads, cheeses and olive oils, and there are several pasta dishes, fired pizzas, and a choice of stove-cooked, grilled or spit-roasted meats and fish.

Recommended in the area

Baddesley Clinton Hall; Kenilworth Castle; National Motorcycle Museum

Walking Madonna statue by Dame Elisabeth Frink, Salisbury Cathedral

White Horse at Westbury

The Tollgate Inn

★★★★ @ @ INN

Address: Holt, BRADFORD-ON-AVON, BA14 6PX
Tel: 01225 782326
Fax: 01225 782805
Email: alison@tollgateholt.co.uk
Website: www.tollgateholt.co.uk
Map ref: 2, ST86
Directions: From A4 (E of Bath) take A363 to
Bradford-on-Avon. B3107 to Holt
Open: 11–2.30 5.30–11 ᴸ L 12–2 D 7–9.30

❍I L 12–2 D 7–9.30 **Closed:** Mon **Rooms:** 4 en suite **S** £50–£100 **D** £80–£100
Facilities: Garden Parking **Notes:** ⊕ Free House 🐾 ♟ 9

A handsome country inn offering en suite accommodation in attractively presented bedrooms, with oak
beams and antiques. There is a dining terrace, gardens and a paddock with goats and sheep. Modern
English and Mediterranean food is prepared from fresh local produce and served in two restaurant areas
– a cosy downstairs room and the first-floor former chapel. Daily changing guest beers are sourced.
Recommended in the area

Lacock National Trust Village; Georgian town of Bradford-on-Avon; Bath

The Three Crowns

Address: BRINKWORTH, Chippenham,
SN15 5AF
Tel: 01666 510366
Website: www.threecrowns.co.uk
Map ref: 3, SU08
Directions: From Swindon take A3102 to Wootton
Bassett, then B4042, 5m to Brinkworth
Open: 11–3 6–11 🍺 **L** 12–2 **D** 6–9.30
🍽 **L** 12–2 **D** 6–9.30 **Closed:** 25–26 Dec
Facilities: Garden Parking
Notes: ⊕ ENTERPRISE INNS 👬 🛏 🍷 20

The current licensees, Anthony and Allyson Windle, have been here over 20 years and are now well into researching this quiet little pub's history. They know that it opened with its current name in 1801, but suspect that in the 18th century it traded under a different name. In 1927 Kelly's directory lists it as a hotel, serving teas and light refreshments; today it is one of the area's most popular eating venues. Menus are written on large blackboards, which make it easy to keep up with the daily, market-driven changes. Everything is home made using top quality ingredients, main dishes being typified by Somerset wild boar, lamb and mint pie, and supreme of halibut and vegetarian tagliatelle, all cooked to order and served with a generous selection of fresh vegetables. Lighter lunches range from filled double-decker rolls to slow-roast belly pork and beef chilli. The bar stocks a wide range of well-kept cask ales, keg beers and lagers, and Anthony and his wine merchant have carefully chosen (and tasted, over a period, naturally!) an 80-bin wine list. In winter there is an open log fire, while in summer the doors are flung open to the peaceful patio and garden.

Recommended in the area

Westonbirt Arboretum; Cotswold Water Park; Lydiard Park

The Fox and Hounds

Address: The Green, EAST KNOYLE, Salisbury,
SP3 6BN
Tel: 01747 830573
Fax: 01747 830865
Email: pub@foxandhounds-eastknoyle.co.uk
Website: www.foxandhounds-eastknoyle.co.uk
Map ref: 2, ST83
Directions: 1.5m off A303 at the A350 turn off,
follow brown signs
Open: 12–2.30 6–11 🍺 L 12–2.30 D 6.30–9.30
🍽 L 12–2.30 D 6.30–9.30 Facilities: Garden Parking Notes: 🛢 Free House ♦♦ 🐾 🍷 10

Surrounded by excellent walking and with stunning views of the Blackmore Vale, the Fox and Hounds is a picturesque 15th-century thatched free house that was built originally as three cottages. Here, guests can enjoy an imaginative menu and a range of traditional ales and ciders from West Country brewers as well as over 20 wines by the glass. The village, which is situated on a greensand ridge, was once home to the family of Jane Seymour, Henry VIII's third wife, as well as Christopher Wren, whose father was the local vicar. Inside the pub, all is comfortable and cosy, with flagstone flooring, natural stone walls and sofas positioned next to wood-burning fires in winter. Diners can enjoy a meal in the light, airy conservatory or in the patio area. A varied menu, based on local produce, contains a range of snacks and main meals. These might include ploughman's or pizzas (from the clay oven), as well as lamb chump on mash, venison, 21-day-old fillet or sirloin steak with a choice of sauces, Thai green curry or Moroccan vegetable tagine. For those with room to spare, pavlova with passion fruit coulis and warm chocolate fudge cake are among the desserts.

Recommended in the area

Stonehenge (EH); Stourhead House and Gardens (NT); Longleat House and Safari Park

Wilton House gardens

The Angel Coaching Inn

Address: High Street, HEYTESBURY, BA12 0ED
Tel: 01985 840330
Fax: 01985 840931
Email: admin@theangelheytesbury.co.uk
Website: www.theangelheytesbury.co.uk
Map ref: 2, ST94
Directions: A303, A36 towards Bath, 8m
Open: 12–12 🍽 **L** 12–2.30 **D** 7–9.30
🍽 **L** 12–2.30 **D** 7–9.30 **Facilities:** Garden Parking
Notes: ⊕ GREENE KING ♦ ⊷ ⚐ 10

Surrounded by stunning countryside, The Angel Coaching Inn is located in the quiet, picturesque village of Heytesbury and is an enjoyable place for a drink, a superb meal or a relaxing weekend away. A complete refurbishment has transformed the 16th-century inn into a stunning mix of original features and contemporary comfort. With its beamed ceilings and open fires, The Angel Coaching Inn welcomes you into its cosy and informal atmosphere. Whether you're looking for a fabulous venue for dinner or lunch, a countryside retreat or a welcome haven for a drink, this is the perfect choice.

Recommended in the area

Stourhead; Longleat House and Safari Park; Stonehenge

The Lamb at Hindon

★★★★ ◉ INN

Address: High Street, HINDON, Salisbury, SP3 6DP
Tel: 01747 820573
Fax: 01747 820605
Email: info@lambathindon.co.uk
Website: www.lambathindon.co.uk
Map ref: 2, ST93
Directions: A303, follow signs to Hindon. At Fonthill Bishop right, B3089 to Hindon. Pub on left
Open: all day, incl breakfast ♿ L 12–2.30
D 6.30–9.30 ⭐ L 12–2.30 D 6.30–9.30 **Rooms:** 14 en suite **S** £70 **D** £99–£135
Facilities: Garden Parking **Notes:** ⊞ 🐕 🍷

The Lamb is set in the centre of a charming village just 20 minutes from Salisbury. It began trading as a public house as long ago as the 12th century and by 1870 it supplied 300 horses to pull coaches on the London–West Country route. The inn is part of the Boisdale group, with two other establishments in London (Belgravia and Bishopsgate), and this is reflected in the distinctive interior design and in the quality of the food and wine. The building still has plenty of historic character, with beams, inglenook fireplaces, and wood and flagstone floors, all set off by fine antique furniture, old paintings and open fires. Food is served from breakfast to dinner in the dining room or the intimate Whisky and Cigar Bar. Dishes are prepared from carefully sourced ingredients, including fresh fish and game in season. A recent dinner menu featured main courses such as Macsween haggis; Gloucester Old Spot sausages with Beaune mustard mash and gravy; and the 'famous Boisdale' burger, plus a fish of the day and pie of the day. The Meeting Room, in a sunken area just off the main dining room, is available for private dining or meetings. Each bedroom is richly decorated and has LCD screens and Sky television.

Recommended in the area

Longleat; Stonehenge; Stourhead House & Gardens

Compasses Inn

★★★★ ⑳ INN

Address: Langpond Lane, LOWER CHICKSGROVE,
Nr Tisbury, SP3 6NB
Tel: 01722 714318
Email: thecompasses@aol.com
Website: www.thecompassesinn.com
Map ref: 2, ST92
Directions: On A30 (1.5m W of Fovant) 3rd right to
Lower Chicksgrove. 1.5m left
Open: 12–3 6–11 (Sun 7–10.30) 🍴 **L** 12–2

D 6.30–9 🍽 **L** 12–2 **D** 6.30–9 **Closed:** 25–26 Dec **Rooms:** 5 en suite **S** £65–£90 **D** £85–£90
Facilities: Garden Parking **Notes:** ⊕ Free House 👶 🐕 🍷 24

You'll find this thatched inn tucked away down a single track lane in a tiny hamlet amid beautiful
rolling countryside, which in turn forms part of a designated Area of Outstanding Natural Beauty. The
Compasses is a 14th-century building of great character, and beyond the latched door there's a long,
low beamed bar with high-backed stools, stone walls, worn flagstone floors and a large inglenook
fireplace. Here, a wood-burning stove is lit in the colder months. Adjacent to the bar is a dining room,
ideal for private parties. There is a regularly changing blackboard menu of dishes freshly prepared from
seasonal produce, and a choice of ales including Keystone Solar Brew, Hidden Potential, Bass and
Keystone Large One. Extra seating is set out in the big garden, which has a grassed area and some
wonderful views. If you want to make the most of the lovely location and stay over, there are lovely
double bedrooms and a detached cottage accessed separately from the inn. All the bedrooms have
hospitality trays and remote control TVs, one room is perfect for families, with an additional single bed,
and z-beds for children.

Recommended in the area

Longleat Safari Park; Stonehenge; Farmer Giles Farmstead

Horse & Groom

Address: The Street, Charlton, MALMESBURY,
SN16 9DL
Tel: 01666 823904
Email: info@horseandgroominn.com
Website: www.horseandgroominn.com
Map ref: 2, ST98
Directions: M4 junct 17, A429 follow Cirencester
signs. Through Corston & Malmesbury. Straight on
at Priory rdbt, at next rdbt to Cricklade & Charlton
Open: 12–11 ⓑ **L** 12–2.30 **D** 6.30–9.30

⦿ **L** 12–2.30 **D** 6.30–9.30 **Facilities:** Garden Parking **Notes:** ⊕ MERCHANT INNS PLC ⍾ ⌁ ♈ 8

The Horse & Groom is a proper English country inn offering great food, drink and accommodation in glorious surroundings. Situated in the small village of Charlton, just east of Malmesbury, this solidly elegant 16th-century Cotswold stone house boasts a stunning interior full of roaring log fires and classic country inn charm. Outside, extensive grounds include a gorgeous walled garden, a separate children's play area and Wiltshire's only outside bar. The inn is renowned for good quality, sensibly priced food, presented in relaxed, informal surroundings making it equally suitable for a casual lunch or a special occasion meal. Local produce sourced from within a 40-mile radius is a priority for the kitchen. Aside from the carte, there is a bar menu and a selection of classic pub dishes. Showcase dishes include home-made crab cakes with dill mayonnaise and baby salad leaves; double cooked Cotswold shoulder of lamb with whole grain mustard mash, sautéed curly kale and red wine sauce; and warm chocolate fondant with stem ginger ice cream. There are five spacious bedrooms with flat-screen TV, complimentary toiletries, tea- and coffee-making facilities and free Wi-fi.

Recommended in the area

Malmesbury Abbey; The Abbey House Gardens; The Cotswold Water Park

Castle Coombe

The Bridge Inn

Address: 26 Church Street, WEST LAVINGTON,
Devizes, SN10 4LD
Tel/Fax: 01380 813213
Email: portier@btopenworld.com
Website: www.the-bridge-inn.co.uk
Map ref: 3, SU05
Directions: Approx 7m S of Devizes on A360
towards Salisbury
Open: 12–3 6.30–11 ⓛ L 12–2 D 6.30–9
ⓘ L 12–2 D 6.30–9 **Closed:** 2wks Feb, Sun eve &
Mon **Facilities:** Garden Parking **Notes:** ⊕ ENTERPRISE INNS ♦ 12

Located on the outskirts of a village on the edge of Salisbury Plain, the Bridge Inn is a small but perfectly formed pub and restaurant with a beamed bar and log fire, and local paintings adorning the walls. The food-led establishment caters for all appetites, with light lunches, a regular carte and a specials board, and the kitchen produces English food with a French twist. It is a well-known place frequented both by locals and those from further afield. In the large garden there is a boules pitch.

Recommended in the area

Longleat; Stonehenge; Lacock Abbey, Fox Talbot Museum & Village

The Pear Tree Inn

★★★★★ ⑱ ⑱ RESTAURANT WITH ROOMS
Address: Top Lane, WHITLEY, SN12 8QX
Tel: 01225 709131
Fax: 01225 702276
Email: enquiries@thepeartreeinn.com
Website: www.maypolehotels.com
Map ref: 2, ST86
Directions: A365 from Melksham towards Bath, at
Shaw right onto B3353 into Whitley, 1st left
Open: 11–3 6–11 ⓛ **L** 12–2.30 **D** 6.30–9.30

❤️ **L** 12–2.30 **D** 6.30–9.30 **Closed:** 25–26 Dec, 1 Jan **Rooms:** 8 en suite (4 GF) **S** £75 **D** £110
Facilities: Garden Parking **Notes:** ⊕ Free House 👫 🐾 🍷 12

Here you'll find a delightful, stone-built country pub and restaurant that also offers cosy accommodation
in beautifully designed bedrooms. Flagstone floors and two log fires help to give it a comfortable,
lived-in feel, with pitchforks, old scythes and other agricultural antiques reminding one of its past as a
farm. Indeed, the surrounding acres of wooded farmland prepare you for the possible imminent arrival
of Farmer Giles for his pint of Henry's Original IPA from Wadworth, or one of the six regularly changing
guest beers. Twenty-five wines are available by the glass. The food, prepared from locally supplied
produce, has been much praised and awarded two AA Rosettes. The menu, served throughout the
pub, including in the terracotta and mustard barn-conversion restaurant, offers an updated approach
to traditional British food, with a typical three-course meal comprising Middle White pork and liver
pâté with bacon and red onion marmalade; breaded cutlets of salt marsh lamb with orange and mint
couscous; and lemon tart made with lemons from the Amalfi coast. There is a healthy menu for
children. Outside, in addition to the lovely cottage garden, there is also a patio area and a boules pitch.
Recommended in the area
Lacock Abbey; Avebury; Silbury Hill

Broadway Tower

Worcestershire Beacon

The Fleece Inn

Address: The Cross, BRETFORTON, WR11 7JE
Tel: 01386 831173
Email: nigel@thefleeceinn.co.uk
Website: www.thefleeceinn.co.uk
Map ref: 3, SP04
Directions: From Evesham follow signs for B4035 towards Chipping Campden. Through Badsey into Bretforton. Right at village hall, past church
Open: 11–11 (Sun 12–10.30, winter Mon–Thu 11–3, 6–11) ⓑ L 12–2.30 D 6.30–9
Facilities: Garden Notes: ⊕ Free House ⦁ ♀ 12

The Fleece was built as a longhouse 600 years ago and its last private owner, Lola Taplin, – who died in the snug in 1977, bequeathing it to the National Trust, – was a direct descendant of the man who built it. Restorations after a fire in 2004 ensured that the Fleece looks as good as ever. Home-made dishes include local sausage of the day with mash, pork belly marinated in plum cider brewed on the premises and a fresh fish dish of the day. Look out for Morris dancers, folk singing and asparagus!

Recommended in the area

Chipping Campden; Hidcote Manor (NT); Cotswold Way; Abbey Park, Evesham

Robin Hood's Bay

The Black Bull Inn

Address: 6 St James Square, BOROUGHBRIDGE,
YO51 9AR
Tel: 01423 322413
Fax: 01423 323915
Map ref: 8, SE36
Directions: A1(M) junct 48 take B6265 E for 1m
Open: 11–11 (Sun 12–10.30) ♿ L 12–2 D 6–9
🍽 L 12–2 D 6–9 **Facilities:** Parking
Notes: ⊕ Free House ♦ 🍴 🍷 10

Built in 1258, The Black Bull was one of the main watering holes for coaches travelling what is now the A1. Back then it had stables and a blacksmith's shop attached; and these days, it still retains plenty of original features, including old beams, low ceilings and roaring open fires, not to mention the supposed ghost of a monk. Traditional pub fare is the order of the day here, with extensive menus covering all the options. Starters such as chicken liver pâté with Cumberland sauce; king prawn tails and queen scallops; and Scottish smoked salmon are sure to whet the appetite. The main courses that follow might include rump of English lamb with rosemary and olive mashed potato; chicken breast wrapped in Parma ham with pan-fried wild mushroom; and a selection of very substantial steak dishes. Several fish options are also available, including the likes of salmon, halibut, sea bass, tuna and Dover sole. Desserts include banoffee meringue roulade with toffee sauce; dark chocolate truffle torte; apple pie with custard; and mixed ice creams encased in brandy snap with fruit purées. Sizeable bar snacks range from pork and chive sausage with onion gravy, and deep-fried prawns, to Thai beef strips with egg noodles and stir fry vegetables. Among the array of sandwiches are hot roast pork and apple sauce; and cold smoked salmon with dill mayonnaise. Yorkshire beers are available, and there is a selection of 17 malts.

Recommended in the area

Knaresborough Castle and Museum; Newby Hall and Gardens; Fountains Abbey and Studley Royal

Malt Shovel Inn

Address: BREARTON, Harrogate, HG3 3BX
Tel: 01423 862929
Email: bleikers@themaltshovelbrearton.co.uk
Map ref: 8, SE36
Directions: From A61 (Ripon/Harrogate) onto B6165 towards Knaresborough. Left & follow Brearton signs. In 1m right into village
Open: 12–3 6–11 (Sun 12–7) ⓑ L 12–2 D 6–9
⦿ L 12–2 D 6.30–9 **Closed:** Mon & Sun eve
Facilities: Garden Parking
Notes: ⊕ Free House ♦♦ ♟ 18

At the heart of the picturesque village of Brearton lies the Malt Shovel, a fine family-run 16th-century inn. Although the pub is surrounded by rolling farmland, it is just 15 minutes from Harrogate and within easy reach of both Knaresborough and Ripon. One of the oldest buildings in an ancient village, it was taken over by the Bleiker family in 2006 and has been transformed into an atmospheric venue for eating and drinking, with open fires in winter, flagstoned floors and pianos in the bar and conservatory. Swiss-born Jürg's innovative cooking specialises in fresh fish – there's an on-site smoking kiln – classic sauces and well-sourced local produce, and diners can choose from the lunchtime and early-evening bistro menu or opt to eat à la carte. He and wife Jane bring their wealth of experience in food, hospitality and entertainment to create an ambience that combines elegance and theatricality – his son and daughter-in-law are international opera soloists, and it's not unheard of for the odd aria to be served up at dinner. However it's their commitment to great food, fine wine (nearly twenty are served by the glass), impeccable cask ales and the warmest of welcomes that bring customers back again and again.

Recommended in the area

Ripley Castle; Fountains Abbey (NT); Yorkshire Dales

The Abbey Inn

Address: BYLAND ABBEY, Coxwold, York YO61 4BD
Tel: 01347 868204
Fax: 01347 868678
Email: abbeyinn@english-heritage.org.uk
Website: www.bylandabbeyinn.com
Map ref: 8, SE57
Directions: From A19 follow signs to Byland Abbey
Open: Wed–Sat 12–2.30 6–11 (Sun 12–3 Sunday lunch) ⃝ **L** 12–2.30 **D** 6–8.30 (last orders)
Closed: 25–26 Dec, 24 & 31 Dec eve, 1 Jan, Sun eve, Mon–Tue **Facilities:** Garden Parking **Notes:** Free House ⃝ ⃝ 8

The Abbey Inn sits nestled at the foot of the Hambleton Hills, together with Byland Abbey. Imaginatively restored, with an eclectic mix of old style architecture and modern amenities and facilities. Guests can choose between intimate dining rooms – Wass and Coxwold – with vistas of Byland Abbey, or the Piggery and Patio Gardens for larger groups. The modern English menu changes seasonally using the finest and freshest local produce. In addition, real ales and an extensive wine list are available.

Recommended in the area

Hambleton Hills; Rievaulx Abbey, Terrace and Temples; Helmsley Castle; Byland Abbey; Shandy Hall

The Fox & Hounds

Address: CARTHORPE, Bedale, DL8 2LG
Tel: 01845 567433
Fax: 01845 567155
Website: www.foxandhoundscarthorpe.co.uk
Map ref: 7, SE38
Directions: Carthorpe signed from A1
Open: 12–3 7–11 ⃝ **L** 12–2 **D** 7–9.30 ⃝ **L** 12–2 **D** 7–9.30 **Closed:** 25–26 Dec eve & 1st wk Jan, Mon **Facilities:** Parking **Notes:** Free House ⃝

Near the Great North Road, but in rural surrounds, The Fox and Hounds has been serving travellers for the past 200 years, and for the last 25, the same family have been making a thoroughly good job of continuing the tradition. The restaurant, once the village smithy, serves up imaginative dishes, and the midweek set-price menu is particularly good value, with dishes such as pan-fried lambs' liver with bacon and onion gravy; or, from the specials board, grilled whole Dover sole with parsley butter. Home-made desserts might include chocolate fondue; or almond raspberry tart with vanilla ice cream.

Recommended in the area

Ariel Extreme; Snape Arboretum; Black Sheep Brewery Visitor Centre

The Durham Ox

★★★★ RESTAURANT WITH ROOMS

Address: Westway, CRAYKE, York, YO61 4TE
Tel: 01347 821506
Fax: 01347 823326
Email: enquiries@thedurhamox.com
Website: www.thedurhamox.com
Map ref: 8, SE57
Directions: Off A19 (York to Thirsk) to Easingwold.
Then Crayke, left up hill
Open: 12–3 6–11 (Sat–Sun 12–11) ⓑ L 12–3

D 6–9.30 ⓘ L 12–2.30 D 6–9.30 **Closed:** 25 Dec **Rooms:** 4 en suite (2 GF) **S** £80 **D** £100–£140
Facilities: Garden Parking **Notes:** ⊕ Free House ♂ ♀ 9

Three hundred years old, and family-owned for the last nine, the Durham Ox is an award-winning traditional pub with flagstone floors, exposed beams, oak panelling and roaring fires. Situated in historic Crayke, with breathtaking views over the Vale of York on three sides, and a charming view up the hill (reputedly the one the Grand Old Duke of York's men marched up and down) to the church. A print of the eponymous ox – and a hefty beast it was too – hangs in the bottom bar. The Ox prides itself on serving good pub food, using the best locally sourced ingredients when possible for seasonal menus, complemented by blackboard specials. Dishes likely to be found are braised lamb shank and clapshot mash; grilled plaice, new potatoes, spinach and brown shrimp butter sauce; and root vegetable casserole with 'wartime' herb dumplings. On Sundays, traditional rib of beef and Yorkshire puddings, fresh fish and other dishes are complemented by delicious desserts. Snacks include eggs Benedict, or Florentine, with cured bacon; chargrilled Ox burger with cheese, bacon, chips and onion rings; and a variety of open sandwiches. Four converted farm cottages provide overnight accommodation.

Recommended in the area

Castle Howard; Scampston; Byland Abbey

The Wheatsheaf Inn

Address: EGTON, YO21 1TZ
Tel: 01947 895271
Fax: 01947 895391
Map ref: 8, NZ80
Directions: Off A169, NW of Grosmont
Open: 11.30–3 5.30–11.30
🍴 L 12–2 D 6–9
🍽 L 12–2 D 6–9
Facilities: Garden Parking
Notes: ⊕ Free House 👫 🐴

The Wheatsheaf stands in the centre of Egton, a village with wonderful views of the surrounding North Yorks Moors National Park. It dates from the 19th century, when it was the centre of village life; it still is today, with features including real fires, comfortable seating and a collection of pictures, fishing rods, gun cases, sports equipment and antique model boats acquired by the owner at local auctions. The restaurant is furnished with traditional tables and chairs and is warmed by an open fire. It offers a varied and seasonal menu and daily specials using fresh fish and game (when in season), together with locally grown vegetables. Breakfast on pork sausage, black pudding, smoked bacon, tomato and mushrooms; for lunch maybe a sandwich, hot focaccia, Finnan haddock kedgeree with toast, poached egg and side salad, or forest mushroom risotto; and for dinner try beef Stroganoff or wholetail Whitby scampi, accompanied by one of the Wheatsheaf's good wines or local ales. The accommodation consists of three comfortably furnished double rooms, two with Victorian-style en suite bathrooms and one with an en suite power shower. They all have a TV and tea- and coffee-making facilities.

Recommended in the area

Robin Hood's Bay; North Yorkshire Moors Railway; Cleveland Way

The Plough Inn

Address: Main Street, FADMOOR, York, YO62 7HY
Tel: 01751 431515
Fax: 01751 432492
Map ref: 8, SE68
Directions: 1m N of Kirkbymoorside on A170
Open: 12–2.30 6.30–11 ⓑ **L** 12–1.45
D 6.30–8.45 ⓘ **D** 6.30–8.45 **Closed:** 25–26 Dec,
1 Jan **Facilities:** Garden Parking
Notes: ⊕ Free House ⏺⏺ ⏺ 8

Ramblers sampling the delights of the North Yorkshire Moors National Park will be pleased to find this stylishly well-appointed country pub and restaurant in the pretty village of Fadmoor. The setting overlooking the village green could not be more idyllic, and the inn boasts dramatic views over the Vale of Pickering and the Wolds. Inside it is cosy, snug and welcoming, with log fires, beams and brasses in the bar: the ideal spot to enjoy a pint of Black Sheep Best. The food is an undoubted attraction, with meals available in the bar or in the attractively furnished rustic-style restaurant. A good value, two-course meal is available at lunchtime and early evening. Options include smoked salmon and asparagus terrine, followed by medallions of pork tenderloin with blue Stilton and white wine sauce; or home-made steak and ale pie. The carte menu features such dishes as deep-fried duck and mango spring rolls; seafood paella with Italian sausage; and pan-seared king scallops with a fricassée of spring onion, garlic and bacon as starters, followed by, for example, basil and parmesan crusted cod; slow roasted boneless half Gressingham duckling with orange and brandy sauce; or fillet of beef Wellington topped with liver paté and Madeira sauce. A dedicated menu for vegetarians has a thoughtful range of options, including pear and Stilton puff pastry parcels; and wild mushroom Stroganoff. If you've room, round off with a decadent smooth dark chocolate and Malibu terrine, or peach and raspberry tiramisu.

Recommended in the area

North Yorkshire Moors National Park; Rievaulx Terrace and Temples

The Bridge Inn

Address: GRINTON, Richmond, DL11 6HH
Tel: 01748 884224
Email: atkinbridge@btinternet.com
Website: www.bridgeinngrinton.co.uk
Map ref: 7, SE09
Directions: Exit A1 at Scotch Corner & towards Richmond. At Richmond take A6108 towards Reeth, 10m to inn
Open: 12–11 🍴 L 12–3 D 12–9 🍽 L 12–5 D 5–9
Facilities: Garden Parking
Notes: ⊕ JENNINGS BROTHERS PLC 🐾 ♟ 7

With a host of activities such as walking, fishing, horse riding and mountain biking all on the doorstep, and a range of en suite rooms available to stay in, The Bridge Inn makes a good base for those in search of country pursuits. Situated on the banks of the River Swale in the heart of the Yorkshire Dales National Park this fine former coaching inn dates from the 13th century. Now with its beamed ceilings and open fires tastefully restored, the inn is fast becoming known for its great food and ales. Customers are invited to sample Jennings award-winning cask ales, or try something a little different from a micro-brewery; there is also an extensive wine cellar. Menus are based on seasonal local produce under the experienced eye of resident chef John Scott, and flavoured with herbs from the pub's own garden. Light snacks such as hot or cold baguettes and jacket potatoes are served in the bar, while in the à la carte restaurant, typical main courses range from lamb shank in red wine and rosemary to spiced parsnip pie with herby pastry. For those with room to spare, the dessert menu includes a daily choice of old-fashioned traditional puddings.

Recommended in the area

Yorkshire Dales; Reeth; St Andrew's Church

Fields near Pateley Bridge

Sandpiper Inn

Address: Market Place, LEYBURN, DL8 5AT
Tel: 01969 622206
Fax: 01969 625367
Email: hsandpiper99@aol.com
Website: www.sandpiperinn.co.uk
Map ref: 7, SE19
Directions: From A1 take A684 to Leyburn
Open: 11.30–3 6.30–11 (Sun 12–3, 6.30–10.30)
🍺 L 12–2.30 D 6.30–9 🍽 L 12–2.30 D 6.30–9
Closed: Mon & occasionally Tue Facilities: Garden
Notes: ⊕ Free House ♦ ♦ ♀ 8

Although the Sandpiper Inn has been a pub for only 30 years, the building is the oldest in Leyburn, dating back to around 1640. It has a beautiful terrace, a bar, snug and dining room, and the menu offers a varied mix of traditional (fish in real ale batter and chips; steaks) and more unusual dishes, which might include apple-smoked black pudding on a garlic mash with a port wine jus; warm goats' cheese on rocket and beetroot salad; and crispy duck leg with fried potatoes and oriental dressing.

Recommended in the area

Wensleydale Railway; Forbidden Corner; Leyburn Model Village

The Golden Lion

Address: 6 West End, OSMOTHERLEY, DL6 3AA
Tel: 01609 883526
Map ref: 8, SE49
Open: 12–3 6–11 (Sat–Sun all day)
▟ **L** 12–2.30 **D** 6–9.15
⚍ **L** 12–2.30 **D** 6–9.15
Closed: 25 Dec
Facilities: Garden
Notes: ⊕ ⫯ ⇴ 4

A 250-year-old sandstone pub in an unspoilt and picturesque village on the edge of North Yorks Moors National Park. The atmosphere is warm and welcoming, with open fires, wooden flooring, simple furnishings, whitewashed walls, mirrors and fresh flowers. The bar serves Timothy Taylor Landlord, Hambleton Bitter, Jennings Bitter Beck's and Leffe, and an extensive range of quality wines from France, Italy, Spain and elsewhere. The menu runs from basic pub grub to more refined dishes, with starters of deep-fried squid and tartare sauce; spicy pork ribs; bresaola (cured beef) with rocket and fresh Parmesan; and avocado and king prawn salad. Mains are along the lines of grilled sea bass, new potatoes and peas; home-made chicken Kiev, chips and green salad; pan-fried pork and Parma ham, and sage and Marsala wine sauce; home-made lamb burger with mint jelly and balsamic vinegar dip; and, for vegetarians, spicy chilladas (lentil burgers) with fresh tomato sauce, jacket potato and peas. Specials such as pork Stroganoff and rice, or lamb and feta lasagne might appear. Popular desserts include bread and butter pudding; Middle Eastern orange cake with marmalade cream; and home-made vanilla ice cream and raspberry purée. Three double/twin bedrooms have en suite wetrooms.

Recommended in the area

Mount Grace Priory; Rievaulx Abbey; Cleveland Way

St Hilda's Abbey ruins

The Sportsmans Arms Hotel

Address: Wath-in-Nidderdale, PATELEY BRIDGE,
Harrogate, HG3 5PP
Tel: 01423 711306
Fax: 01423 712524
Map ref: 7, SE16
Directions: A59/B6451, hotel 2m N of
Pateley Bridge
Open: 12–2 7–11 (Sun 7–10.30) ⌂ L 12–2
D 7–9 ◎ L 12–2 D 7–9 Closed: 25 Dec Facilities:
Garden Parking Notes: ⊕ Free House ♦ 12

This very special pub is in one of the loveliest areas of the Yorkshire Dales. A custom-built kitchen, run by chef/patron Ray Carter for nearly 25 years (now assisted by his son), is the heart of the operation. True to the best pub traditions, real ales and wines accompany dishes served in an informal bar, while daily restaurant menus tempt all comers. Delights include loin of pork with mustard and mushroom sauce; and roast Scottish salmon with spring onions and stem ginger. Round off the meal in style with double chocolate roulade or the ever-popular Sportsmans summer pudding.

Recommended in the area

Fountains Abbey and Studley Royal; Stump Cross Caverns; Brimham Rocks

---

Fox & Hounds Country Inn

★★ 78% ◉ HOTEL
Address: Sinnington, PICKERING, YO62 6SQ
Tel: 01751 431577
Fax: 01751 432791
Email: foxhoundsinn@easynet.co.uk
Website: www.thefoxandhoundsinn.co.uk
Map ref: 8, SE78
Directions: 3m W of town, off A170
Open: 12–2 6–11 (Sun 6–10.30) ⌂ L 12–2
D 6.30–9 ◎ L 12–2 D 6.30–9 Rooms: 10 (4 GF)
S £49–£69 D £70–£130 Facilities: Garden Parking Notes: ⊕ Free House ♦♦ ✂ ♦ 7

Set in a pretty village with a river running by, and a large green with a small pack-horse bridge, this 18th-century inn offers good drinking, imaginative modern cooking, and well-designed rooms. In the bar, oak beams, wood panelling and an open fire make ideal surroundings for a pint of Black Sheep Special or a glass of wine. The menus range from sandwiches and light lunches to dishes like pan-fried calves' liver with spring onion mashed potato. The rooms are equipped with TV and drinks trays.

Recommended in the area

North Yorkshire Moors Railway; Rievaulx Abbey; Nunnington Hall

Nags Head Country Inn

★★ 75% 🏵 HOTEL

Address: PICKHILL, nr Thirsk, YO7 4JG
Tel: 01845 567391
Fax: 01845 567212
Email: enquiries@nagsheadpickhill.co.uk
Website: www.nagsheadpickhill.co.uk
Map ref: 8, SE38
Directions: 1m E of A1(4m N of A1/A61 junct)
Open: 11–11 🍽 L 12–2 D 6–9.30 🍽 L 12–2
D 7–9.30 **Closed:** 25 Dec **Rooms:** 14 S £60–£70
D £80–£95 **Facilities:** Garden Parking **Notes:** ⊕ Free House ♦♦ ⌒ ♆ 8

This 200-year-old establishment, with beamed ceilings and stone-flagged floors, stands in Pickhill (mentioned in the Domesday Book) and a perfect spot for exploring 'Herriot Country'. Under the same ownership for over 35 years, the inn offers superb hospitality and a relaxed atmosphere. The same wide ranging menu, with hand picked wines, is available throughout – in the restaurant, lounge bar or tap room. There are modern, well equipped bedrooms and a two-bedroom cottage available.

Recommended in the area

Yorkshire Dales; Lightwater Valley Theme Park; Falconry Centre

The Buck Inn

★★★ INN

Address: THORNTON WATLASS, Ripon, HG4 4AH
Tel: 01677 422461
Fax: 01677 422447
Email: innwatlass1@btconnect.com
Website: www.buckwatlass.co.uk
Map ref: 7, SE28
Directions: From A1 at Leeming Bar take A684 to Bedale, then B6268 towards Masham. Village 2m on right, hotel by cricket green
Open: 11–11 🍽 L 12–2 D 6.30–9.30 🍽 L 12–2 D 6.30–9.30 **Closed:** 25 Dec eve
Rooms: 7 (5 en suite) (1 GF) S £65 D £90 **Facilities:** Garden Parking **Notes:** ⊕ Free House ♦♦ ⌒ ♆ 7

Margaret and Michael Fox have to refit the occasional tile on the inn, but this is a small price to pay for its idyllic situation on the boundary of the village cricket pitch. Five real ales are served, most from local independent breweries, and the bar menu offers such specialities as Masham rarebit (Wensleydale cheese with local ale on toast, topped with bacon); and classics such as fish and chips and lasagne.

Recommended in the area

Lightwater Valley Theme Park; Theakson Brewery Visitor Centre; Yorkshire Dales National Park

The Star Country Inn

Address: WEAVERTHORPE, Malton, YO17 8EY
Tel: 01944 738273
Fax: 01944 738273
Email: starinn.malton@btconnect.com
Map ref: 8, SE97
Directions: From Malton take A64 towards Scarborough. 12m, at Sherborn right at lights. Weaverthorpe 4m, inn opposite junct
Open: 12–11 (Fri–Sat 12–12)
L 12–9 L 12–9 D 7–9
Facilities: Garden Parking **Notes:** Free House

This traditional 18th-century country inn has expanded over the years to incorporate adjoining cottages, which now house overnight accommodation. Its location makes it a handy base for exploring the Yorkshire Wolds, or a day out in Bridlington. The rustic nature of the two bar areas and dining room, where large fires blaze away in winter, creates a welcoming, convivial atmosphere. The food is cooked to traditional recipes using fresh local produce. Bar meals may include chicken breast wrapped in bacon with mozzarella; and king prawn balti served with rice, poppadoms, and home-made mango chutney. Typical dishes from either the main menu or the specials board include pigeon in horseradish sauce; pheasant in red wine sauce; and chicken and ribs, while there's also a good number of fresh fish dishes, ranging from fish pie, trout in lemon butter, and trio of fish in white wine, through to more exotic offerings. To finish, home-made desserts, such as apple and blackberry crumble, spiced roast rhubarb with creamy rice pudding, and rich chocolate tart ensure that no-one should leave wanting more. There is a beer garden and a large car park.

Recommended in the area

Nunnington Hall; Sledmere House; Castle Howard

The Bruce Arms

Address: Main Street, WEST TANFIELD, HG4 5JJ
Tel: 01677 470325
Fax: 01677 470925
Email: info@bruce-arms.co.uk
Website: www.bruce-arms.co.uk
Map ref: 7, SE27
Directions: On A6108 Ripon/Masham Rd
Open: 12–11 ⬥ L 12–9.30 D 12–9.30
🍴 L 12–2 D 6.30–9.30 **Closed:** Mon
Facilities: Garden Parking
Notes: ⊕ Free House ⫯ ⌁ ♟ 10

A traditional Yorkshire pub in a pretty village setting, The Bruce Arms welcomes you with cosy log fires in winter and an attractive garden for whiling away the warmer summer days. There are three en suite bedrooms, if you are looking to extend your stay and visit the area's many attractions, which include Ripon Racecourse and the Lightwater Valley Theme Park and Country Shopping Village. The full English breakfast, or healthier alternative, will certainly set you up for the day. Home-made food is freshly prepared in the kitchens from fresh, local, seasonal produce, with dishes such as warm salad of wood pigeon, braised ox tongue and Cumberland sauce to start, and roast rump of 'Binsoe' lamb as a main. The restaurant comprises two rooms, one more formal – ideal for private dining or functions – and the other more relaxed with an open fire. Alternatively, old favourites like steak and kidney pie are served in the bar. There's a large selection of reasonably priced beers, such as Black Sheep Best, and fine wines, and you might finish your evening with an Irish coffee or liqueur in the leather chairs around the fire.

Recommended in the area

Bolton Castle; Fountains Abbey & Studley Royal Water Garden; RHS Garden Harlow Carr

The Hole of Horcum

Conisbrough Castle ruins

Cubley Hall

Address: Mortimer Road, Cubley, PENISTONE, S36 9DF
Tel: 01226 766086
Fax: 01226 767335
Email: info@cubleyhall.co.uk
Website: www.cubleyhall.co.uk
Map ref: 7, SE20
Directions: M1 junct 37, A628 towards Manchester, or M1 junct 35a, A616. Hall just south of Penistone
Open: 11–11 L 12–9.30 **D** 12–9.30
L 12–9.30 **Facilities:** Garden Parking **Notes:** Free House 7

Steeped in history, Cubley Hall started out in the 1700s as a farm on a Pennine packhorse route, was later transformed into a gentleman's residence, and then became a children's home. Many original features survive, including the oak-beamed restaurant that was tastefully converted from a barn. The menu offers a choice of pizzas, pastas, chargrills and blackboard specials. Favourites include 'posh fish and chips' and English brisket beef with fondant mash, tarragon carrots and caramelised shallots.

Recommended in the area

Yorkshire Sculpture Park; Millennium Galleries; Peak District National Park

Roseberry Topping, North Yorkshire Moors National Park

The Fat Cat

Address: 23 Alma Street, SHEFFIELD, S3 8SA
Tel: 0114 249 4801
Fax: 0114 249 4803
Email: info@thefatcat.co.uk
Website: www.thefatcat.co.uk
Map ref: 8, SK38
Directions: Telephone for directions
Open: 12–12 🍽 **L** 12–2.30 **D** 6–7.30
Closed: 25 Dec **Facilities:** Garden Parking
Notes: 🌐 Free House 👫 🐕

A smart Grade II listed, back street city pub, the Fat Cat dates from 1852 and is reputed to be haunted. Ale afficionados will delight in the constantly changing list of guest beers, especially from micro-breweries. Traditional scrumpy and unusual bottled beers are also sold, while the Kelham Island Brewery, owned by the pub, accounts for at least four of the ten traditional draught real ales. There are open fires inside, and an attractive walled garden outside. Home-cooked food – steak pie; spinach and red bean casserole – includes vegetarian and vegan options.

Recommended in the area

Kelham Island Museum; Winter Gardens; Millennium Galleries

Falling Foss, North Yorkshire
Moors National Park

THe Bronte Way, South Dean Beck

The Three Acres Inn

Address: SHELLEY, Huddersfield, HD8 8LR
Tel: 01484 602606
Fax: 01484 608411
Email: 3acres@globalnet.co.uk
Website: www.3acres.com
Map ref: 7, SE21
Directions: From Huddersfield take A629 then B6116, turn left for village
Open: 12–3 7–11 ⓛ L 12–2 D 7–9.45
🍽 L 12–2 D 7–9.45 **Closed:** 25–26 Dec, 1–2 Jan
Facilities: Garden Parking **Notes:** ⊕ Free House ♦ ♥ 16

The Three Acres Inn has been co-owned for well over 30 years by Brian Orme and Neil Truelove, and it has been in Neil's family since his father, Derrick, acquired the business in 1969. The Krug Room offers a private dining facility for up to 20 guests incorporating a Champagne bar listing an extensive range of premier marque Champagnes. In the bar, you can enjoy the Three Acres Bitter, Tetley's and Black Sheep ales and there's a good selection of wines by the glass. Running your eyes down the menu reveals starters such as 'Bobby Baxter's' famous potted shrimps on toasted home-made granary bread with watercress and lemon; and main courses might include steak, kidney and mushroom pie under a grain mustard shortcrust; venison, pigeon and mallard pasty; Lunesdale duck; braised lamb shank and lamb faggots, and fillet of Eyemouth plaice with a gravadlax dressing, mustard and dill mash and garden peas, just one of several fish dishes available. The seafood bar offers a fruits de mer platter and whole fresh lobster among its selections. The Three Acres also has facilities for private parties, conferences and meetings as well as wedding receptions.

Recommended in the area

National Mining Museum for England; Last of the Summer Wine country; Yorkshire Sculpture Park

Kaye Arms, Public House & Dining Room

Address: 29 Wakefield Road, Grange Moor, WAKEFIELD,
WF4 4BG
Tel: 01924 848385
Fax: 01924 848977
Email: kayearms@hotmail.co.uk
Website: www.thekayearms.com
Map ref: 8, SE32
Directions: On A642 between Huddersfield & Wakefield
Open: 11.30–3 7–11 ⓜ L 12–2.30 ⓘ L 12–2.30
D 5.30–9.30 (Sat & Sun 12–9.30) **Closed:** 25 Dec–2 Jan, Mon
Facilities: Parking Disabled Access **Notes:** ⓦ Free House ⓖ 15

The Kayes has stood overlooking the landscape of Grange Moor for over 500 years and has, over the last 40, become a popular dining destination. As a pub it provides the comfort of the old world and mixes it with the tradition of the area, and serves quality local produce dishes. The mixture of the old and the new, from pickled herrings to pressed game terrine with handmade bread and chutney to the famous signature dish of twice baked farmhouse cheese soufflé, the choice makes deciding a rather difficult affair. Main course range from hand reared venison to beer battered scampi, Anglaise chicken to 4-hour roasted belly pork, and are priced for all pockets. New owners Paul and Helen Andrews Garth have brought years of experience in catering back to their roots in Yorkshire and strive to give all their customers an experience of hospitality and welcome. Families are encouraged and children's meals are taken from the main menu. There is also an extensive wine by the glass list and wine menu.

Recommended in the area

National Coal Mining Museum; Temple Newsam; Yorkshire Sculpture Park

The Rochdale Canal at Hebden Bridge

SCOTLAND

Princes Street Gardens, Edinburgh

Glenfinnan Viaduct, Highlands

The Lairhillock Inn

Address: NETHERLEY, By Stonehaven, AB39 3QS
Tel: 01569 730001
Fax: 01569 731175
Email: info@lairhillock.co.uk
Website: www.lairhillock.co.uk
Map ref: 10, NO89
Directions: From Aberdeen take A90. Right at Durris
Open: 11–11 (Fri–Sat 11–12, Sun 11–11)
 L 12–2 D 6–9.30 L 12–1.45 D 7–9.30
Closed: 25–26 Dec, 1–2 Jan
Facilities: Garden Parking **Notes:** Free House 7

Only 15 minutes from Aberdeen, this 200-year-old inn offers real ales like Cairngorm Trade Winds in the bar and real fires in the comfortable lounge. The bar and restaurant offer robust dishes, using fresh, quality local produce. Try the locally smoked salmon with quails' eggs and horseradish crème fraîche to start, followed by a main course of venison layered with peppered potatoes, wild mushrooms and a port and thyme jus.

Recommended in the area

Dunnottar Castle; Crathes Castle and Garden; Storybook Glen

The Pierhouse Hotel & Seafood Restaurant

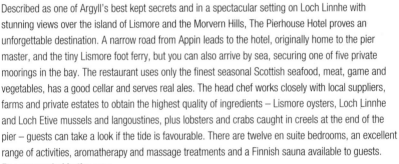

★★★ 74% SMALL HOTEL
Address: PORT APPIN, PA38 4DE
Tel: 01631 730302
Fax: 01631 730400
Email: marketingandpr@pierhousehotel.co.uk
Website: www.pierhousehotel.co.uk
Map ref: 9, NM94
Directions: A828 from Ballachulish to Oban. In Appin right at Port Appin & Lismore ferry sign. After 2.5m left after post office, hotel at end of road by pier
Open: 8–11.30 **L** 12.30–2.30 **D** 6.30–9.30 **L** 12.30–2.30 **D** 6.30–9.30 **Closed:** 25 Dec
Rooms: 12 en suite **D** £95–£160 **Facilities:** Garden Parking **Notes:** Free House

Described as one of Argyll's best kept secrets and in a spectacular setting on Loch Linnhe with stunning views over the island of Lismore and the Morvern Hills, The Pierhouse Hotel proves an unforgettable destination. A narrow road from Appin leads to the hotel, originally home to the pier master, and the tiny Lismore foot ferry, but you can also arrive by sea, securing one of five private moorings in the bay. The restaurant uses only the finest seasonal Scottish seafood, meat, game and vegetables, has a good cellar and serves real ales. The head chef works closely with local suppliers, farms and private estates to obtain the highest quality of ingredients – Lismore oysters, Loch Linnhe and Loch Etive mussels and langoustines, plus lobsters and crabs caught in creels at the end of the pier – guests can take a look if the tide is favourable. There are twelve en suite bedrooms, an excellent range of activities, aromatherapy and massage treatments and a Finnish sauna available to guests.

Recommended in the area

Scottish Sea Life Sanctuary; Castle Stalker; Sutherland Grove Forestry Park

The Steam Packet Inn

Address: Harbour Row, ISLE OF WHITHORN
DG8 8LL
Tel: 01988 500334
Fax: 01988 500627
Email: steampacketinn@btconnect.com
Website: www.steampacketinn.com
Map ref: 5, NX43
Directions: From Newton Stewart take A714,
then A746 to Whithorn, then Isle of Whithorn
Open: 11–11 ㅂ **L** 12–2 **D** 6.30–9 ⵏ⃝ **L** 12–2
D 6.30–9 **Closed:** 25 Dec, Winter Tue–Thu 2.30–6
Facilities: Garden Parking **Notes:** ⊞ Free House ⁑ ⼂ ⵏ 9

The Steam Packet is a family-run, quayside pub with a picturesque village setting at the southern tip of the Machars peninsula. The inn offers a window on the local fishermen at work, while the menu features the fruits of their labours. Food is served in the two bars, the dining room and conservatory. Seven en suite bedrooms, including deluxe rooms, are available.

Recommended in the area

Whithorn Story Visitor Centre; Creetown Gem and Rock Museum; The Tollbooth Arts Centre

Cawdor Tavern

Address: The Lane, CAWDOR, Nairn, IV12 5XP
Tel: 01667 404777
Fax: 01667 404777
Email: enquiries@cawdortavern.info
Map ref: 12, NH85
Directions: From A96 (Inverness-Aberdeen) take
B9006 & follow Cawdor Castle signs. Tavern in
village centre
Open: 11–3 5–11 (May–Oct 11–11) ㅂ **L** 12–2
D 5.30–9 ⵏ⃝ **L** 12–2 **D** 6.30–9 **Closed:** 25 Dec,
1 Jan **Facilities:** Garden Parking **Notes:** ⊞ Free House ⁑ ⼂ ⵏ 8

The Tavern is at the heart of a beautiful conservation village, close to the famous castle, and was formerly a joinery workshop for the Cawdor Estate. The handsome oak panelling in the lounge bar came from the castle and was a gift from the former laird. Roaring log fires keep the place cosy on long winter nights, while in the summer guests can sit on the patio. The menu options include prime meats, fresh local seafood, game and vegetarian dishes, complemented by a hand-picked wine list.

Recommended in the area

Cawdor Castle; Fort George; Culloden Battlefield

The Plockton Hotel

★★★ 75% SMALL HOTEL
Address: Harbour Street, PLOCKTON, IV52 8TN
Tel: 01599 544274
Fax: 01599 544475
Email: info@plocktonhotel.co.uk
Website: www.plocktonhotel.co.uk
Map ref: 11, NG83
Directions: On A87 to Kyle of Lochalsh take turn at Balmacara. Plockton 7m N
Open: 11–11.45 (Sun 12.30–11) ⓑ L 12–2.15
D 6–9 ⓘⓞⓘ L 12–2.15 D 6–9 **Rooms:** 15 en suite (1 GF) **S** £55–£80 **D** £80–£100 **Facilities:** Garden
Notes: ⓦ Free House ⓘⓧ ⓟ 6

The award-winning Plockton Hotel sits right next to the gently lapping waters of Loch Carron, a sheltered sea loch warmed by the Gulf Stream and fringed with palm trees. It is the only waterfront hostelry in this lovely National Trust village, the location for the cult film *The Wicker Man*. The breathtaking view, across the bay to the Applecross Hills, is enjoyed by many of the hotel's comfortable en suite bedrooms. Converted from a ship's chandlery in 1913, this establishment has been run by the Pearson family and their staff for nearly 20 years. Menus are based on the very best of Highland produce, with seafood a major strength: expect to find locally caught langoustines, shellfish from Skye, fresh fish landed at Gairloch and Kinlochbervie, and smoked fish from Aultbea. Products from the smokehouse feature in one of the hotel's specialities – cream of smoked fish soup. Other starters may include Talisker whisky pâté and fresh Plockton prawns. Top quality Highland beef appears in flamed peppered whisky steaks from the charcoal grill. Other main courses include casserole of Highland venison, Argyle chicken, and wild boar burger with salad and fries. A fine range of malts is offered.

Recommended in the area

Isle of Skye; Eilean Donan Castle; Applecross Peninsula

Younger Botanic Gardens

Plockton Inn & Seafood Restaurant

Address: Innes Street, PLOCKTON, IV52 8TW
Tel: 01599 544222
Fax: 01599 544487
Email: info@plocktoninn.co.uk
Website: www.plocktoninn.co.uk
Map ref: 11, NG83
Directions: On A87 to Kyle of Lochalsh take turn at
Balmacara. Plockton 7m N
Open: 11–1am (Sun 12.30–11) ₤ **L** 12–2.30
D 6–9.30 ⏶ **D** 6–9.30 **Facilities:** Garden Parking
Notes: ⊕ Free House ⵏ⛵

Situated in one of Scotland's most beautiful fishing villages, near the harbour, this inn is a great base
to explore the Isle of Skye and the Torridon Mountains. The inn has regular music nights in the bar,
making for a lively atmosphere. A good choice of real ales is offered, plus more than 50 malt whiskies.
There are two eating areas inside, the Dining Room and Lounge Bar, plus an area laid with decking
outside. Fresh West Coast fish and shellfish are a speciality, plus West Highland beef, game and lamb.

Recommended in the area

Eilean Donan Castle; Lochalsh Woodlands (NTS); Strome Castle (NTS)

Killiecrankie House Hotel

◎◎

Address: KILLIECRANKIE, Nr Pitlochry, PH16 5LG
Tel: 01796 473220
Fax: 01796 472451
Email: enquiries@killiecrankiehotel.co.uk
Website: www.killiecrankiehotel.co.uk
Map ref: 10, NN96
Directions: Take B8079 N from Pitlochry. Hotel in
3m after NT Visitor Centre
Open: 12–2.30 6–11 ㄥ L 12.30–2 D 6.30–9
⭘ D 6.15–8.30 **Closed:** Jan & Feb
Facilities: Garden Parking **Notes:** ⊕ Free House ⅰ ⚞ ⚈ 8

This long-established hotel is set in four acres of neat grounds overlooking Killiecrankie Pass, a deep river gorge formed by the River Garry cutting its way through the surrounding granite hills, and there are fabulous views. Delightful gardens include lawns, a rose garden, herbaceous border and a woodland. Built as a private residence in 1840, the house was converted in 1939 and stands near the site of the Battle of Killiecrankie and the intriguingly named Soldier's Leap. A National Trust for Scotland Visitor Centre nearby is dedicated to the area's interesting history and rich wildlife. Locals and visitors alike frequent the panelled bar and the snug to enjoy a great range of Scottish malts and fine wines available by the glass. The menu draws on the finest of local produce, including vegetables, fruits and herbs from the garden, and the restaurant has two AA Rosettes. Food is served in the bar, the elegant dining room and the conservatory, and might include game casserole with mashed potato and fresh vegetables, or roast fillet of monkfish wrapped in Parma ham. The wine list is also a notable feature.

Recommended in the area

Queen's View Visitor Centre; Blair Castle; Scottish Hydro Electric Visitor Centre

Loch Lubhair

The Black Bull

★★★★ INN

Address: Market Place, LAUDER, TD2 6SR
Tel: 01578 722208
Fax: 01578 722419
Email: enquiries@blackbull-lauder.com
Website: www.blackbull-lauder.com
Map ref: 10, NT54
Directions: In centre of Lauder on A68
Open: 12–2.30 5–9 (Winter 12–2, 5.30–9)
 L 12–2.30 D 5–9 L 12–2.30 D 5–9
Closed: Feb **Rooms:** 8 en suite **S** £60–£75 **D** £80–£100 **Facilities:** Parking
Notes: Free House 16

A handsome white-painted former coaching inn, the Black Bull stands three storeys high and dates from 1750. The building has been restored to create a cosy haven in the heart of the Borders, just 20 minutes' drive from Edinburgh. The interior is full of character with lots of interesting pictures and artefacts. The large dining room used to be a chapel and the church spire remains in the roof. Food is also served in the Harness Room Bar or the cosy lounge. The same seasonal menu is served throughout, specialising in quality country fare prepared from locally grown produce where possible. Aberdeen Angus beef and Texel lamb from Wedderlie Farm features regularly. Additional dishes are also offered from the specials board, and there's an interesting choice of wines and Broughton Ales. The accommodation is beautiful, and includes three bedrooms that are suitable for family occupation. All have hairdryers, TV, telephone, internet access, luxurious Penhaligon's toiletries, and tea- and coffee-making facilities. Decorated in period style, the rooms have modern baths and/or showers.

Recommended in the area

Thirlstone Castle; Mellerstain House; Melrose Abbey

WALES

Ruins of Laugharne Castle

Caesars Arms

Address: Cardiff Road, CREIGIAU, CF15 9NN
Tel: 029 2089 0486
Fax: 029 2089 2176
Email: caesarsarms@btconnect.com
Map ref: 2, ST08
Directions: 1m from M4 junct 34
Open: 12–2.30 6–10.30 (Sun 12–4) ♨ L 12–2.30
D 6–10.30 ⒪ L 12–2.30 D 6–10.30
Closed: 25 Dec **Facilities:** Garden Parking
Notes: ⊕ Free House ⛺ ♉ 8

Just ten miles outside Cardiff, Caesars Arms sits tucked away down winding lanes. With fine views of the surrounding countryside from its heated patio and terrace, it attracts a well-heeled clientele. And it is little wonder, as its restaurant has a vast selection of fresh fish, seafood, meat and game taking pride of place. The emphasis here is on locally sourced food, displayed on shaven ice. Starters might include imaginative choices such as Bajan fishcakes, scallops with leek julienne or cherry-smoked duck breast with organic beetroot. Main courses take in hake, halibut, Dover sole and lobster, as well as a show-stopping Pembrokeshire sea bass baked in rock salt, which is cracked open and filleted at your table. But it's not all about fish – other choices include steak from slow-reared, dry-aged pedigree Welsh Blacks plus lamb and venison from the Brecon Beacons and free-range chickens from the Vale of Glamorgan. Home-grown organic herbs, salads and vegetables are all used as much as possible, and the inn has its own smokery. Another attraction is the farm shop, which provides a range of home-produced honey, free-range eggs, Welsh cheeses, home-baked bread and chef's ready-prepared meals to take away.

Recommended in the area

Castell Coch; Llandaff Cathedral; St Fagans: National History Museum

The Groes Inn

★★★★★ ⊛ INN
Address: CONWY, LL32 8TN
Tel: 01492 650545
Fax: 01492 650855
Email: reception@groesinn.com
Website: www.groesinn.com
Map ref: 5, SH77
Directions: Off A55 to Conwy, left at mini rdbt by
Conwy Castle onto B5106, 2.5m inn on right
Open: 12–3 6.30–11 ⓑ L 12–2.15 D 6.30–9
⑩ L 12–2.15 D 6.30–9 **Rooms:** 14 en suite (6 GF) **S** £85–£157 **D** £103–£189
Facilities: Garden Parking **Notes:** ⊕ Free House ⌾ 10

Built in the 15th century, this was the first licensed house in Wales, established as an inn in 1573. The location is stunning, with a panorama over the River Conwy from the front, and slopes rising towards Snowdonia at the rear. Traditional British and Welsh dishes, prepared from quality ingredients – salt marsh lamb, Conwy crab and local game – are served in the bar, restaurant, conservatory or garden.
Recommended in the area
Snowdonia; Bodnant Gardens; Conwy Castle

Clytha Arms

Address: Clytha, ABERGAVENNY, NP7 9BW
Tel/Fax: 01873 840209
Email: theclythaarms@tiscali.co.uk
Website: www.clytha-arms.com
Map ref: 9, SO21
Directions: From A449/A40 junction follow signs for
'Old Road Abergavenny/Clytha'
Open: 12–3 6–12 (Fri–Sat 12–12, Sun 12–10.30)
ⓑ L 12.30–2.15 D 7–9.30 ⑩ L 12.30–2.15
D 7–9.30 **Closed:** 25 Dec, Mon lunch
Facilities: Garden Parking **Notes:** ⊕ Free House ⬥ ⌾ 10

Andrew and Beverley Canning have been running this free house for 17 years. Once a dower house, it is surrounded by lawns and interesting gardens, and is not far from the River Usk. Happily informal in character, it offers six different real ales a week (that's 300-plus a year), a good choice of wines by the glass, and snacks and tapas. In the restaurant, try leek and laver rissoles with beetroot chutney, fillet of Hereford beef with pink peppercorns, or faggots and peas with Rhymney gravy.
Recommended in the area
Brecon Beacons National Park; Blaenafon World Heritage Site; Castell Dinas

The White Hart Village Inn

Address: LLANGYBI, Usk, NP15 1NP
Tel: 01633 450258
Email: info@whitehartvillageinn.com
Website: www.whitehartvillageinn.com
Map ref: 2, ST39
Directions: M4 junct 25 onto B4596 Caerleon road, through town centre on High St, straight over rdbt onto Usk Rd continue to Llangybi
Open: 11.30–3 5.30–11 (Sun 11.30–6) 🍴 L 12–2 D 6–9.30 🍽️ L 12–2 D 6–9.30 **Closed:** Mon
Facilities: Garden Parking **Notes:** ⊕

Located in the beautiful Usk Vale, this historic inn was originally built in the 12th century for Cistercian monks. In the early 1500s it became the property of Henry VIII as part of Jane Seymour's wedding dowry, and a century later Oliver Cromwell is reputed to have used it as his Gwent headquarters. The interior still retains original 12th-century fireplaces, eleven more fireplaces from the 1600s, a wealth of exposed beams, original Tudor plasterwork and even a priest hole. Rooms are in The Hay Loft, which were built as stables in Victorian times, and are thus rich in character, with exposed beams set into sloping ceilings. Facilities include en suite bedrooms with shower, hairdryer, Freeview TV, Wi-fi access, alarm clock, complimentary tea and coffee tray and Continental breakfast. The restaurant menu provides a selection of 'traditional rustic', such as Welsh faggots, peas, mash and onion gravy, and 'gastro-fare', such as freshwater crayfish in a rich garlic and tomato provençal sauce. Tapas and seafood evenings are held from time to time and occasional barbecues, hog roasts and live jazz take place on the extensive flagstone seating area to the rear, from which there are far-reaching views to the Wentwood Hills.

Recommended in the area

Gwent Rural Life Museum; Tintern Abbey; Brecon Beacons National Park

Horseshoe Inn

Address: MAMHILAD, NP4 8QZ
Tel: 01873 880542
Email: horseshoe@artizanleisure.com
Website: www.artizanleisure.com
Map ref: 2, SO30
Directions: A4042 Pontypool to Abergavenny road, at Mamhilad estate rdbt take 1st exit onto Old Abergavenny Rd. 2m over canal bridge on right
Open: 12–3 5.30–11 (Fri–Sun all day) ⓑ L 12–2.30 D 6.30–9.30 ⏀ L 12.30–2.30 D 6.30–9.30
Facilities: Garden Parking **Notes:** ⊕ Free House ⅰ↑ ♐ 10

The Horseshoe kitchen team is led by Kurt Flemming, a member of the Wales Culinary Olympic team, whose weekly changing, sensibly priced menus feature roasted escalope of cod with Welsh rarebit crust, tomato and red onion confit, baked breast of chicken with butter bean and chorizo sausage cassoulet, and goat's cheese, pepper and leek strudel.

Recommended in the area

Cwmcarn Forest Drive; Parc Cwm Darran; Usk Rural Life Museum

The Newbridge Inn

Address: TREDUNNOCK, NP15 1LY
Tel: 01633 451000
Fax: 01633 451001
Email: thenewbridge@tinyonline.co.uk
Website: newbridge@evanspubs.co.uk
Map ref: 2, ST39
Directions: M4 junct 24/26 from Usk take road towards Llangybi. 0.5m, turn left for Tredunnock. Pub in 800yds
Open: 12–2.30 6.30–9.30 (Sun 12–3, 6.30–8.30)
ⓑ L 12–2.30 ⏀ L 12–2.30 D 6–9.30 **Facilities:** Garden Parking **Notes:** ⊕ Free House ♐ 12

The Newbridge has commanded this River Usk crossing since 1800. Its decor and furnishings are warm and welcoming, with works by famous Irish painter Graham Knuttel hanging in the Gallery. Head Chef Iain Sampson is responsible for consistently high quality modern British and Mediterranean-influenced food. For lunch try baked portobello mushroom, locally cured bacon and Gorwydd Caerphilly cheese; while for dinner, fillet of Usk Valley beef with mushroom jus, or catch of the day, might feature.

Recommended in the area

Cwmcarn Forest Drive; Usk Rural Life Museum; Brecon Beacons National Park

Whitesands Bay, Pembrokeshire Coast National Park

The Lion Inn

Address: TRELLECH, Monmouth, NP25 4PA
Tel: 01600 860322
Fax: 01600 860060
Email: debs@globalnet.co.uk
Website: www.lioninn.co.uk
Map ref: 2, SO50
Directions: From A40 S of Monmouth take B4293,
follow signs for Trellech. From M8 junct 2, straight
across rdbt, 2nd left at 2nd rdbt, B4293 to Trellech
Open: 12–3 6–11 (Mon 7–11,Thu–Sat 6–12, Sat all
day summer) ⅃ **L** 12–2 **D** 6–9.30 ⅃⊙⅃ **L** 12–2 **D** 6–9.30 **Closed:** Sun eve
Facilities: Garden Parking **Notes:** ⊕ Free House ⅃⅃ ⅃

This popular and well-established free house is opposite St Nicholas's Church. Guests are greeted by welcoming real fires in the winter months, while in the summer drinks and meals can be served in the garden, which overlooks fields and features a stream and large aviary. The former brew house has won many accolades for its food and hospitality over the years, and its reputation is growing. Visitors aiming to explore the nearby walking trails and notable historic buildings, or visit Trelleck's own archaeological dig, will find it a useful staging post. The extensive pub menu caters for all tastes, from bar snacks and basket meals to blackboard specials, including fresh fish dishes. There is also an adventurous menu featuring wild and hedgerow ingredients, such as nettles and wild mushrooms. Real ales include Bath Ales, Wye Valley Butty Bach, Rhymney Best, Cottage Brewery and many more regularly changing brews. Anyone who wants to extend their visit to the Lion can stay overnight in the pub's one-bedroom cottage, which is suitable for up to three guests. It features an en suite bathroom and kitchenette. Dogs are allowed at the pub, and water and biscuits are provided for them.

Recommended in the area

Tintern Abbey; Chepstow Castle; Wye Valley Forest Park

The Georges Restaurant/Café Bar

Address: 24 Market Street, HAVERFORDWEST,
SA61 1NH
Tel: 01437 766683
Fax: 01437 760345
Email: llewis6140@aol.com
Map ref: 1, SM91
Directions: Drive through town centre, continue up
hill, then follow signs to St Thomas Green, park free
and walk down Hill Street or Upper Market Street to
Market Street

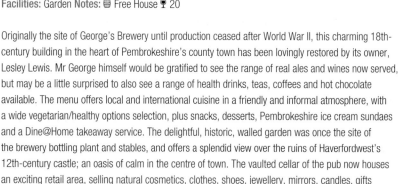

Open: Tues–Thurs 10–5.30, Fri–Sat 10am–11pm 🍴 L 11.45–4.50 D 6–9.30
🍽 L 11.45–4.50 D 6–9.30 **Closed:** 25 Dec, 1 Jan, Sun, Mon
Facilities: Garden **Notes:** ⊞ Free House ♟ 20

Originally the site of George's Brewery until production ceased after World War II, this charming 18th-century building in the heart of Pembrokeshire's county town has been lovingly restored by its owner, Lesley Lewis. Mr George himself would be gratified to see the range of real ales and wines now served, but may be a little surprised to also see a range of health drinks, teas, coffees and hot chocolate available. The menu offers local and international cuisine in a friendly and informal atmosphere, with a wide vegetarian/healthy options selection, plus snacks, desserts, Pembrokeshire ice cream sundaes and a Dine@Home takeaway service. The delightful, historic, walled garden was once the site of the brewery bottling plant and stables, and offers a splendid view over the ruins of Haverfordwest's 12th-century castle; an oasis of calm in the centre of town. The vaulted cellar of the pub now houses an exciting retail area, selling natural cosmetics, clothes, shoes, jewellery, mirrors, candles, gifts and crystals.

Recommended in the area

Pembrokeshire Coast National Park and footpath; Pembroke Castle; St David's Cathedral

The Swan Inn

Address: Point Road, LITTLE HAVEN, Haverfordwest,
SA62 3UL
Tel: 01437 781880
Fax: 04137 781880
Email: enquiries@theswanlittlehaven.co.uk
Website: www.theswanlittlehaven.co.uk
Map ref: 1, SM81
Directions: From Haverfordwest take B4341 (Broad
Haven road). In Broad Haven follow seafront and
signs for Little Haven, 0.75m

Open: 11–3 5–11 (Sat–Sun all day) ⓑ **L** 12.30–2 **D** 7–9 ⚊ **L** 12.30–2 **D** 7–9 **Closed:** Mon (Jan)
Facilities: Garden **Notes:** ⊕ ⛌ ⏇ 8

This historic seaside inn has been impeccably renovated but retains its rustic charm thanks to the
beams, blazing log fires, old settles and exposed stone walls. It was built by a fisherman and is literally
just a stone's throw from the beach, offering great Pembrokeshire views from some tables. Cooking,
with the emphasis on seasonal, local produce, is modern British in style, and is very accomplished,
though informal. Diners can eat in the elegant contemporary upstairs dining room, or in the intimate
restaurant below. The menu might include honey and parsnip soup; local diver-caught scallops; corn-
fed chicken and foie gras terrine; dressed St Brides Bay crab; roast belly pork with black pudding and
cider sauce; or Welsh rib-eye steak with béarnaise sauce, red onion confit and chips. There are also
vegetarian options, such as wild mushroom and butternut squash risotto. To follow, you may be offered
vanilla pannacotta with Kirsch-soaked cherries, Welsh cheeses or locally made ice cream. The busy bar
serves a range of bar snacks and well-kept real ales, and there are many wines available by the glass,
all to be enjoyed in one of the leather armchairs.

Recommended in the area

Pembrokeshire Coast National Park; West Wales Divers; Skomer Island

River Afon Glaslyn, Snowdonia National Park

The White Swan Inn

Address: Llanfrynach, BRECON, LD3 7BZ
Tel: 01874 665276
Fax: 01874 665362
Website: www.the-white-swan.com
Map ref: 2, SO02
Directions: A40, B4558, follow Llanfrynach signs
Open: 12–2 6.30–11 ▨ L 12–2 D 7–9.30
🍽 L 12–2 D 7–9.30 **Closed:** 25–26 Dec,
1 Jan (Mon ex Summer, Dec & BH)
Facilities: Garden Parking **Notes:** ⊕ Free House ⦚ ⚑ 8

A 17th-century coaching inn, completely restored, The White Swan is set in the village of Llanfrynach, by the foothills of the Brecon Beacons, an Area of Outstanding Natural Beauty. The bar has oak flooring, old beams and leather sofas by an open fire, providing the perfect setting for traditional local ales. There is also a spacious restaurant with a coal burner, flagstone floors and beams; in summer you can sit outside. A seasonal menu of innovative dishes is based on produce sourced from local farms.

Recommended in the area

Brecon Beacons National Park; South Wales Borderers Museum; Hay-on-Wye book shops

Stack Rocks, Pembrokeshire Coast National Park

The Castle Coaching Inn

Address: TRECASTLE, nr Brecon LD3 8UH
Tel: 01874 636354
Fax: 01874 636457
Email: guest@castle-coaching-inn.co.uk
Website: www.castle-coaching-inn.co.uk
Map ref: 2, SN82
Directions: On A40 W of Brecon
Open: 12–3 6–11 L 12–2 **D** 6.30–9
L 12–2 **D** 6.30–9 **Facilities:** Garden Parking
Notes: Free House

Once a Georgian coaching inn on the old London to Carmarthen coaching route, The Castle sits right on the northern edge of the Brecon Beacons/Black Mountain area, with myriad streams flowing down to join the River Usk nearby. The inn has been carefully restored in recent years, and retains lovely old fireplaces, a remarkable bow-fronted bar window and has a peaceful terrace and garden. A good selection of real ales is on offer, including Fuller's London Pride, Breconshire Brewery Red Dragon and Timothy Taylor Landlord. Food can be eaten in the bar or more formally in the restaurant, and bar lunches feature tasty, freshly-cut sandwiches (maybe roast beef, turkey or Stilton), a ploughman's with cheese or perhaps duck and port pâté, and hot crusty baguettes with fillings such as steak with melted Stilton or bacon with mushrooms and melted mature cheddar. Of the more substantial offerings, specialities include mature Welsh 12oz sirloin steak served with mushrooms and onion rings; home-made lasagne with parmesan cheese; and supreme of chicken with a Marsala and mascarpone sauce. The tasty desserts are worth saving room for, and might include strawberry crush cake, hot jaffa puddle pudding; and Dutch chunky apple flan. Or perhaps sample the fine selection of Welsh farmhouse cheeses. There is a separate children's menu with the usual favourites.

Recommended in the area

Dan-yr-Ogof The National Showcaves Centre; Brecon Beacons National Park; Usk Reservoir

Mount Snowdon from Llynnau Mymbyr, Snowdonia National Park

The Bush Inn

Address: ST HILARY, nr Cowbridge, CF71 7DP
Tel: 01446 772745
Website: www.artizanleisure.com
Map ref: 2, ST07
Directions: S of A48, E of Cowbridge
Open: 11.30–11 (Sun 12–10.30) 🍴 L 12–2.30
D 6.45–9.30 🍴 L 12–2.30 D 6.45–9.30
Facilities: Garden Parking
Notes: ⊕ PUNCH TAVERNS 🛏 🐾 ♟ 10

In the beautiful Vale of Glamorgan is the picturesque village of St Hilary. The cosy interior of this low thatched inn features a huge inglenook fireplace, flagstone floors and a stone spiral staircase. Among those who have quenched their thirst here during the last 400 years was Ianto Ffranc, a highwayman who turned up in the village, got caught and was hanged nearby. His presence lingers on in the form of the pub's resident ghost. Despite this, the Bush is a warm, happy and friendly pub. Quality real ales are on tap, together with a varied wine list. The weekly changing menu might offer roasted rump of Welsh lamb with kohlrabi purée, parsnip and potato mash, while the bar menu offers lighter fare.

Recommended in the area

Glamorgan Heritage Coast; Old Beaupré Castle; Rhondda Heritage Park

The Bishop's Palace, Brecon Beacons National Park

MAPS

KEY TO ATLAS PAGES

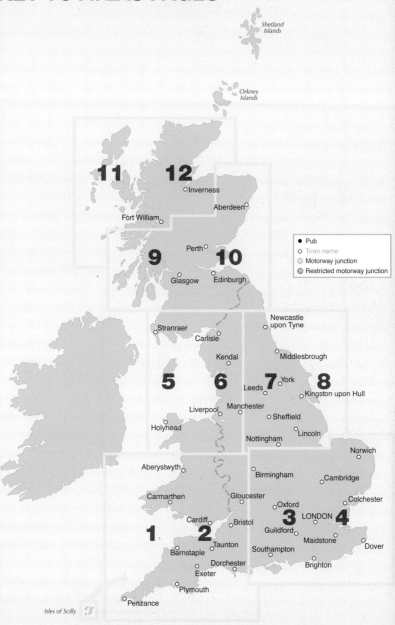

Shetland Islands

Orkney Islands

11 12
○Inverness
Aberdeen○
Fort William○
9 Perth○ 10
○Glasgow ○Edinburgh

● Pub
○ Town name
Ⓜ Motorway junction
🅡 Restricted motorway junction

Newcastle upon Tyne○
○Stranraer
Carlisle○
Kendal○
Middlesbrough○
5 6 7○York 8
Leeds○ Kingston upon Hull○
Liverpool○ Manchester○
Holyhead○ Sheffield○
Nottingham○ Lincoln○
Norwich○
Aberystwyth○
Birmingham○ Cambridge○
Carmarthen○ Gloucester○ Colchester○
Cardiff○ ○Oxford LONDON 4
1 2 Bristol○ 3 Guildford○ Maidstone○ Dover○
Taunton○ Southampton○ Brighton○
Barnstaple○ Dorchester○
Exeter○
Plymouth○
Isles of Scilly
Penzance○

© Automobile Association Developments Limited 2009

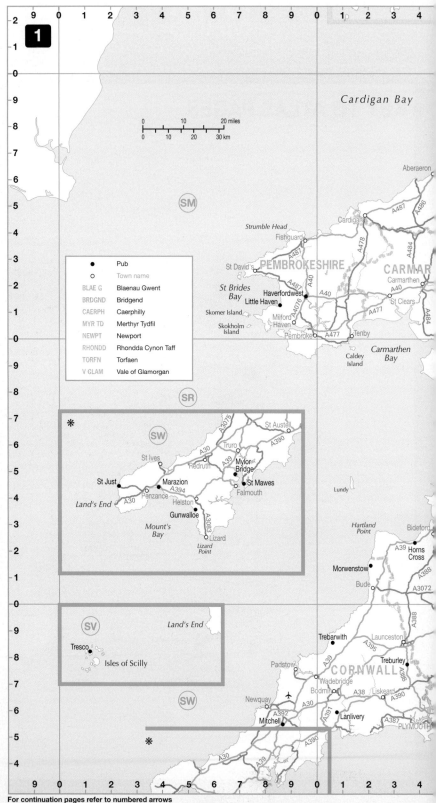

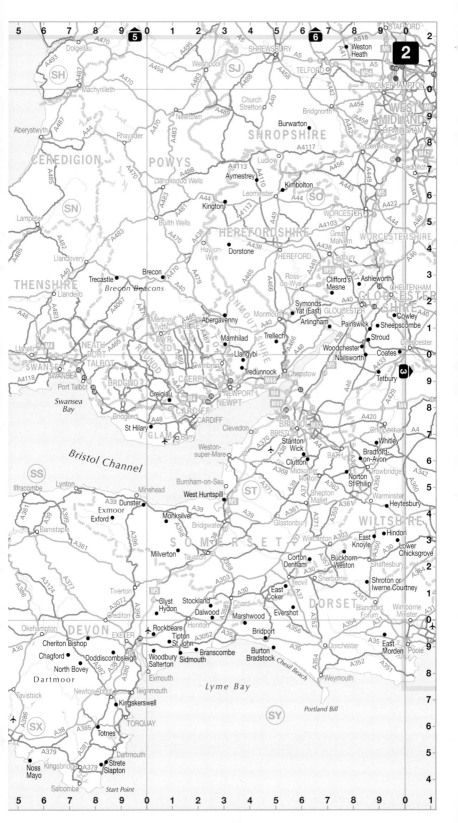

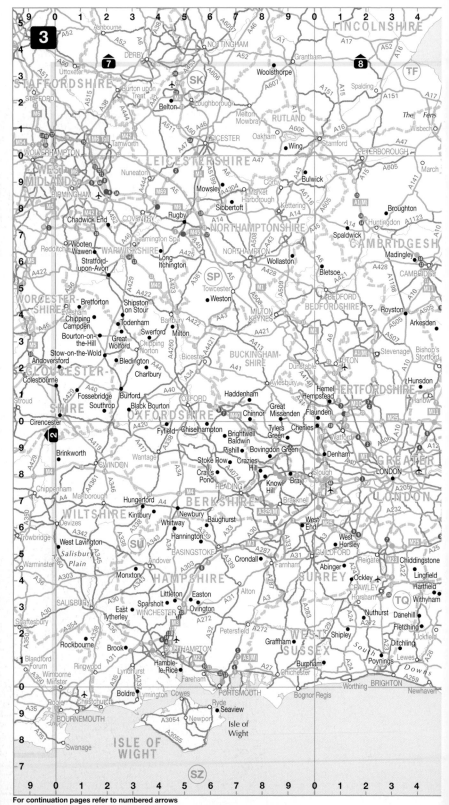

For continuation pages refer to numbered arrows

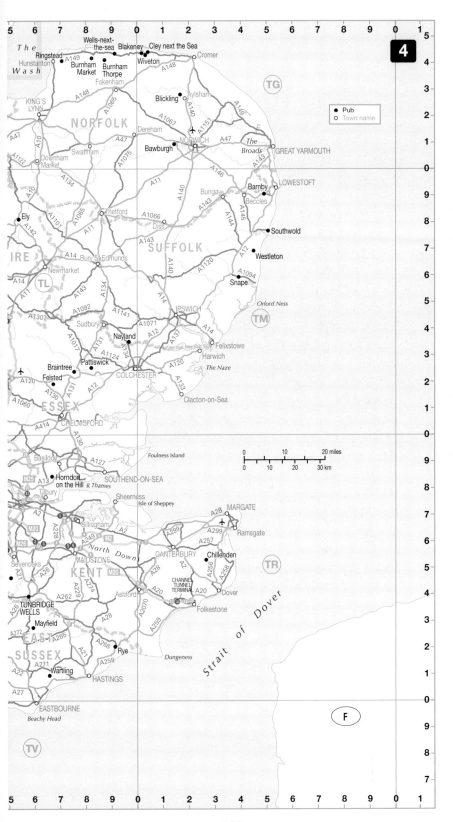

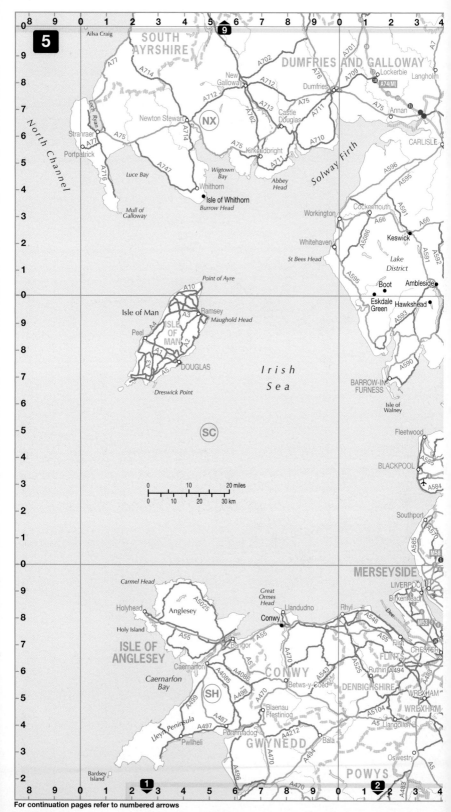

North Channel

SOUTH AYRSHIRE

Ailsa Craig

A77

A714

New Galloway

A712

A712

A713

A762

DUMFRIES AND GALLOWAY

A702

A76

Dumfries

A709

Lockerbie

Langholm

A7

A701

A74(M)

A75

Annan

CARLISLE

Newton Stewart

A714

NX

Castle Douglas

A75

A711

A710

A75

A747

Kirkcudbright

A711

Solway Firth

A596

A595

Stranraer

A77

Portpatrick

A716

A75

Luce Bay

Wigtown Bay

Whithorn

Isle of Whithorn

Burrow Head

Abbey Head

Cockermouth

A591

A66

Workington

A66

A5086

Keswick

A592

Mull of Galloway

Whitehaven

St Bees Head

A595

Lake District

Boot

Eskdale Green

Ambleside

Hawkshead

A593

Point of Ayre

A10

Isle of Man

Peel

A4

A3

Ramsey

Maughold Head

ISLE OF MAN

A1

A3

A5

DOUGLAS

Dreswick Point

Irish Sea

SC

BARROW-IN-FURNESS

A590

Isle of Walney

Fleetwood

A585

BLACKPOOL

A584

| 0 | 10 | 20 miles |
| 0 | 10 | 20 | 30 km |

Southport

A565

M58

MERSEYSIDE

LIVERPOOL

Carmel Head

Great Ormes Head

Llandudno

Rhyl

Birkenhead

M53

Dee

Holyhead

A5025

Anglesey

Conwy

A548

A55

Flint

CHESTER

Holy Island

A55

Bangor

A55

A470

A5

FLINTS

ISLE OF ANGLESEY

Caernarfon

A4085

CONWY

A543

A525

Ruthin

A494

Caernarfon Bay

SH

A4086

A5

Betws-y-Coed

A498

A470

DENBIGHSHIRE

WREXHAM

Lleyn Peninsula

A499

Blaenau Ffestiniog

A470

A5104

Llangollen

A5

Oswestry

A497

A487

Porthmadog

A4212

Bala

A494

WREXHAM

Pwllheli

GWYNEDD

Bardsey Island

A496

A470

A483

POWYS

For continuation pages refer to numbered arrows

314

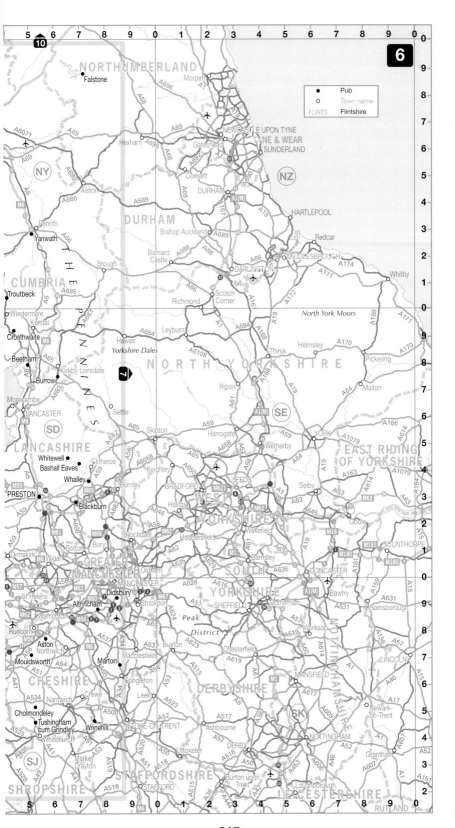

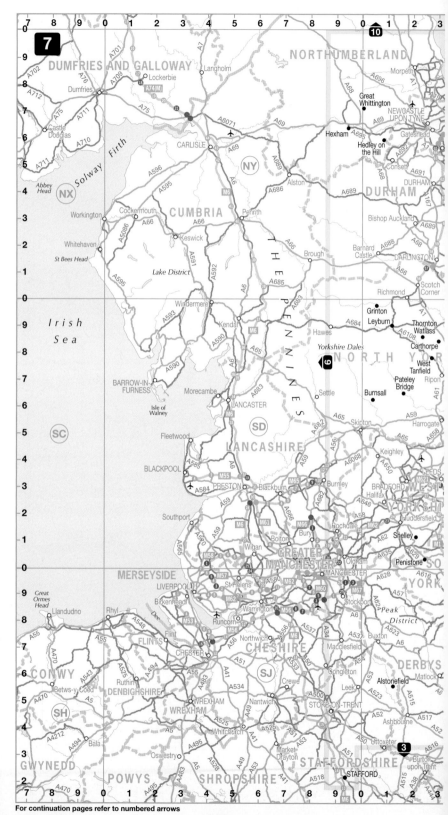

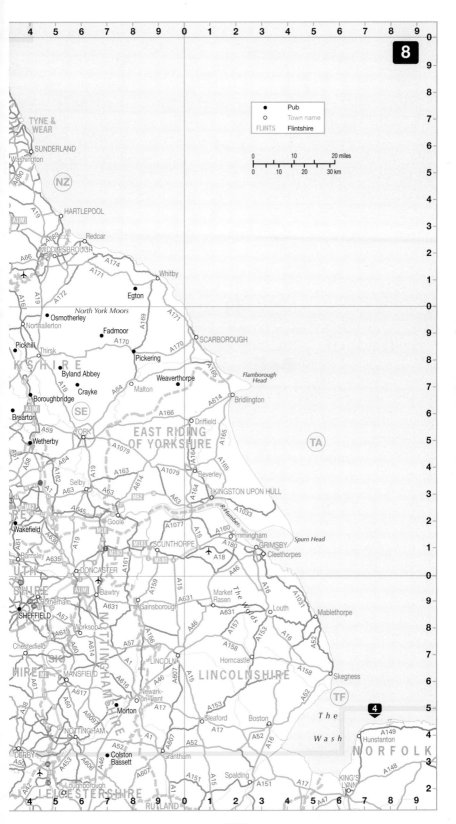

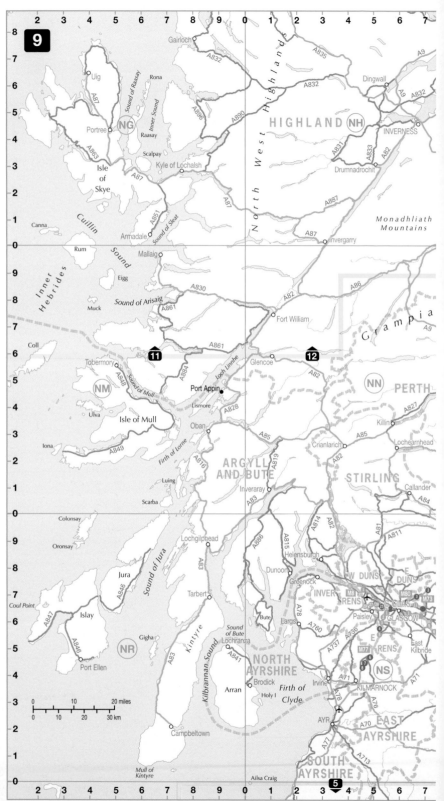

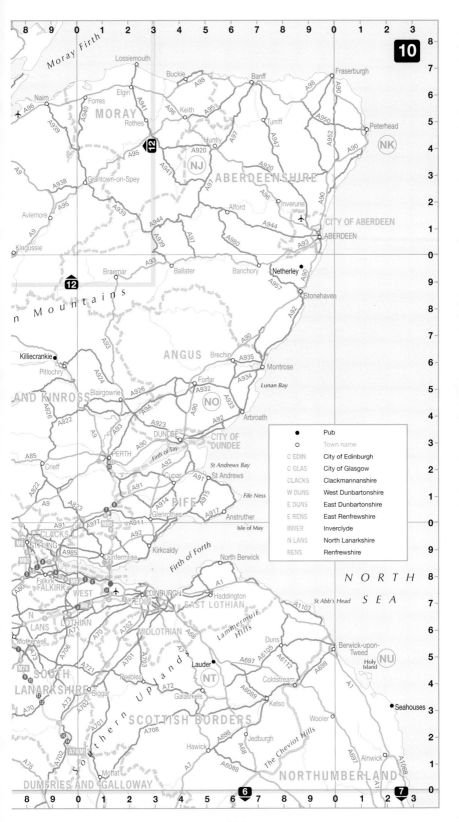

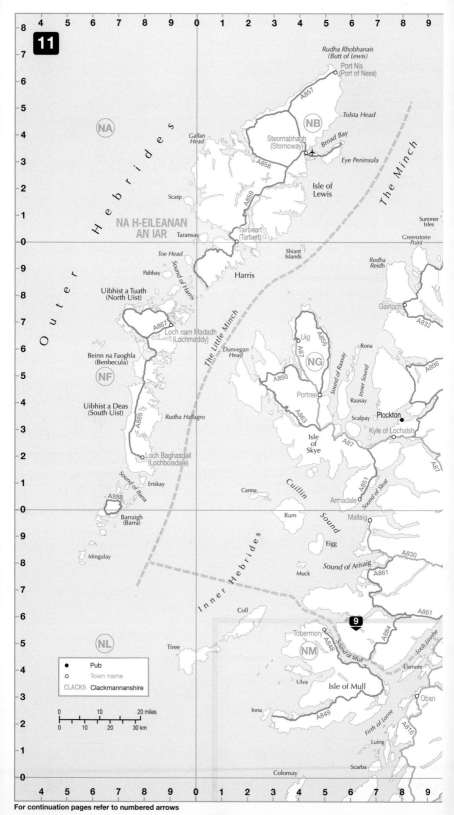

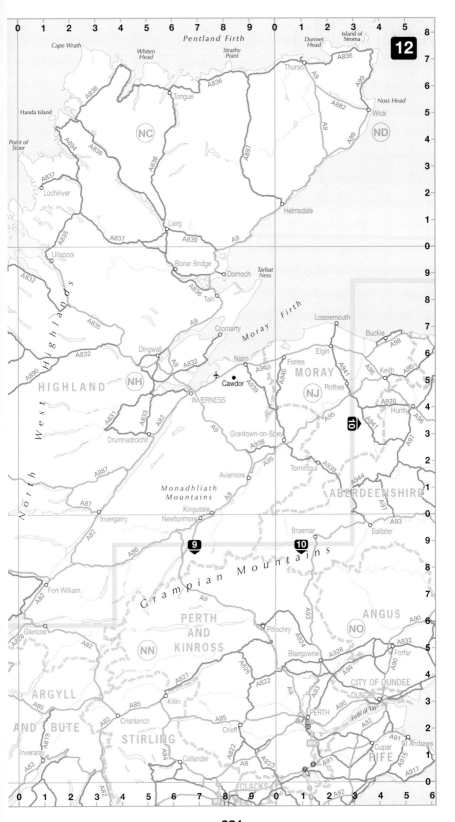

County Map

England

1	Bedfordshire
2	Berkshire
3	Bristol
4	Buckinghamshire
5	Cambridgeshire
6	Greater Manchester
7	Herefordshire
8	Hertfordshire
9	Leicestershire
10	Northamptonshire
11	Nottinghamshire
12	Rutland
13	Staffordshire
14	Warwickshire
15	West Midlands
16	Worcestershire

Scotland

17	City of Glasgow
18	Clackmannanshire
19	East Ayrshire
20	East Dunbartonshire
21	East Renfrewshire
22	Perth & Kinross
23	Renfrewshire
24	South Lanarkshire
25	West Dunbartonshire

Wales

26	Blaenau Gwent
27	Bridgend
28	Caerphilly
29	Denbighshire
30	Flintshire
31	Merthyr Tydfil
32	Monmouthshire
33	Neath Port Talbot
34	Newport
35	Rhondda Cynon Taff
36	Torfaen
37	Vale of Glamorgan
38	Wrexham

Location Index

Location Index

Location Index

Location Index

Location Index

Location Index

Location Index

Pub Index

Pub Index

Pub Index

Pub Index

333

Pub Index

Pub Index

Credits

The Automobile Association would like to thank the following photographers, companies and picture libraries for their assistance in the preparation of this book.

Abbreviations for the picture credits are as follows: (t) top; (b) bottom; (l) left; (r) right; (c) centre; (AA) AA World Travel Library.

4 AA/S Montgomery; 6 Royalty Free Photodisc; 8 Royalty Free Photodisc; 10 AA/S Montgomery; 11 Photodisc; 12 Photodisc; 14/15 AA/G Edwardes; 16 AA/M Birkitt; 17t AA/M Birkitt; 18 AA/J Tims; 25 AA/J Tims; 33 AA/M Birkitt; 35t AA/M Birkitt; 38 AA/V Bates; 42 AA/J Wood; 49t AA/R Moss; 51t AA/C Jones; 53 AA/E A Bowness; 56t AA/D Tarn; 63t AA/P Sharpe; 64 AA/G Edwardes; 70t AA/R Moss; 81 AA/A Burton; 84t AA/A Burton; 86t AA/J Tims; 88 AA/N Setchfield; 92t AA/N Setchfield; 94 AA/D Hall; 97t AA/S Day; 104t AA/F Stephenson; 110 AA/S Day; 113 AA/M Moody; 117t AA/R Fletcher; 120t AA/A Burton; 125 AA/H Palmer; 128t AA/C Jones; 130 AA/S&O Mathews; 133t AA/M Birkitt; 135 AA/A Burton; 137 AA/N Setchfield; 139t AA/P Baker; 142 AA/J Beazley; 149t AA/C Jones; 150 AA/M Birkitt; 151t AA/P Baker; 153 AA/L Whitwam; 154t AA/M Birkitt; 155 AA/W Voysey; 159 AA/W Voysey; 160 AA/;T Mackie 161t AA/A Baker; 164t AA/T Mackie; 167t AA/T Mackie; 170 AA/M Birkitt; 175 AA/J Beazley; 177t AA/R Coulam; 180 AA/M Birkitt; 183 AA/C Jones; 186 AA/C Jones; 194 AA/M Birkitt; 196 AA/A Tryner; 199 AA/R Newton; 201t AA/M Birkitt; 203t AA/C Jones; 209t AA/J Tims; 210 AA/M Birkitt; 214 AA/T Mackie; 219 AA/J Tims; 222t AA; 225 AA/J Miller; 226t AA/J Miller; 228t AA/P Baker; 234 AA/P Brown; 238t AA/J Miller; 240 AA/V Greaves; 241t AA/F Stephenson; 243t AA/P Baker; 247 AA/J Welsh; 248t AA/J Welsh; 249 AA/J Tims; 250t AA/C Jones; 253t AA/J Tims; 257t AA/D Hall; 259 AA/D Hall; 260t AA/C Jones; 261 AA/M Kipling; 269t AA/T Mackie; 271 AA/M Kipling; 276 AA/M Kipling; 277t AA/T Woodcock; 278t AA/M Kipling; 279 AA/G Rowlett; 280 AA/J Tims; 283 AA/L Whitwam; 284/285 AA/D Corrance; 286t AA/S Day; 290t AA/J Carnie; 292 AA/D W Robertson; 294/295 AA/J Gravell; 300 AA/C Warren; 304t AA/D Croucher; 305 AA/C Molyneux; 307t AA/C Jones; 308 AA/D Santillo

Every effort has been made to trace the copyright holders, and we apologise in advance for any accidental errors. We would be happy to apply any corrections in the following edition of this publication.